D1556908

Big Ecology

Big Ecology

The Emergence of Ecosystem Science

David C. Coleman

UNIVERSITY OF CALIFORNIA PRESS

Berkeley   Los Angeles   London

University of California Press, one of the most distinguished
university presses in the United States, enriches lives around
the world by advancing scholarship in the humanities, social
sciences, and natural sciences. Its activities are supported by
the UC Press Foundation and by philanthropic
contributions from individuals and institutions. For
more information, visit www.ucpress.edu.

University of California Press
Berkeley and Los Angeles, California

University of California Press, Ltd.
London, England

Library of Congress Cataloging-in-Publication Data

Coleman, David C., 1938-
    Big ecology : the emergence of ecosystem science / David
C. Coleman.
        p.   cm.
    Includes bibliographical references and index.

    ISBN 978-0-520-26475-5 (cloth : alk. paper)

    1. Biotic communities--Research. 2. Ecosystem manage-
ment--Research.   3. Ecology--Research. 4.
Interdisciplinary research. I. Title.

QH541.2.C63 2010
577.072—dc22   2009039093

Manufactured in [country name]
19   18   17   16   15   14   13   12   11   10
10   9   8   7   6   5   4   3   2   1

The paper used in this publication meets the minimum
requirements of ANSI/NISO Z39.48-1992 (R 1997)
(*Permanence of Paper*). ∞

Cover illustration: Sierra Nevada near Mineral King,
California. Photo by Nola Burger.

CONTENTS

PREFACE

Where is the wisdom we have lost in knowledge? Where is the knowledge we have lost in information?

T. S. Eliot

This historical account presents the personal side of how a major discipline like ecosystem science developed, and how individual scientists hagtve been able to grow with and, in turn, influence and shape whole-system studies over more than forty years. There are several dozen survivors who were literally "present at the Creation," in the sense used by Dean Acheson in his memoirs about his experience as Secretary of State during the tumultuous post–World War II years. Drawing, in part, on accounts from several of my colleagues, I present this account as "our story" of an incredibly active and fortunate generation who participated in what were, and what have continued to be, exciting times.

This book is a logical outgrowth of "A History of the Ecosystem Concept in Ecology" by Frank B. Golley (1993). Much of the early history of the ecosystem concept, and how ecosystems have been viewed from the time of Sir Arthur G. Tansley (1935) onward, is reviewed by Golley. The time since the mid-twentieth century led to the development of what became known as ecosystem science, funded principally by the Ecosystem Studies office of the U.S. National Science Foundation. Golley delineated these early developments, up to and including the International Biological Program. This book attempts to pick up the discussion where Golley left off. It recounts the seminal influence of the IBP and its successor programs up to the present time.

As has been noted often, "history is the record of the victorious." What is offered here is an account of a group of colleagues who were beneficiaries of peer-reviewed research funding across more than four decades. The review process, although stringent, is stimulating in generating insights and influencing individual scientists. Sometimes reviewers' comments energize individuals to demonstrate their ideas as correct, if not perhaps clearly communicated to reviewers initially. It may surprise members of the general public, and nonscientists in general, that science, although it relies on objective, verifiable phenomena (capable of being independently tested), has engendered vehement arguments and discussion along every step of the way. As is true in many other creative endeavors, scientists care deeply about their particular viewpoints, and defend them quite vigorously. Wherever possible, I try to demonstrate the roles of key personalities in ecosystem science, and the ways in which they influenced the field.

Ecosystem science involves the study of the assemblage of plants, animals, and microbes and their abiotic environment within a given area of study, and their conjoint effects, which are at times "greater than the sums of their parts," sensu E. P. Odum (1953, 1969). Because of the utility of measuring inputs and outputs of inorganic and organic compounds in an ecosystem, the favored unit of study has been the watershed, which is bounded geographically, and more readily studied (Likens et al., 1977). Questions about widespread human-driven alteration of biogeochemical cycles (e.g., of carbon, nitrogen, phosphorus), biological complexity and biodiversity, and ecological responses to climate change often focus on ecosystems (Pace and Groffman, 1998).

Ecosystems can be considered at many levels of resolution. Holistic studies of plant, animal, microbial, and faunal interactions and the abiotic factors affecting them can exist in a range of size dimensions from microaggregates in soil or in the ocean, to field sites, watersheds, regions, and the entire geosphere–biosphere that constitutes the planet Earth (O'Neill and King, 1998). In order to study ecosystems on larger scales, experience over the last forty years has shown that it is most effective to assemble teams of researchers from a variety of disciplines, working on common experimental questions. This approach was initiated in the early 1960s by the International Biological Program, and then pursued subsequently by the Long-Term Ecological Research Network, which encompasses research projects being carried out in more than fifty countries worldwide, and which is entering its fourth decade.

Ecology received a major boost in funding after World War II in the United States with the strong support of the Atomic Energy Commission and the formation of the National Science Foundation in 1950. Much of this growth, which reached its most rapid rate of increase in the "decade of the environment," the 1960s, has been documented in major reviews, including those of Bocking (1995, 1997), Hagen (1992), and McIntosh (1985).

Scientists who have participated in research projects, of whatever dimension in space and time, have been influenced by, and have in turn influenced, others. They hope their work left a mark on the history of their field. My goal is to convey to the reader that a several-decade history, as viewed from the inside by a participant, will enhance appreciation of the developments in "big ecology," sensu the "Big Biology" of Blair (1977). These early developments continue to influence the science of ecology as it increases its scope. This history of "big ecology" reflects both the interdisciplinary nature of the effort and the surprisingly international scope with which it has been, and is still being, carried out.

What is "big ecology," and what sort of a case can be made for doing it? The principal reason for doing a large study is that all ecosystems are inherently complex, and are the resultant of numerous physical, chemical, and biological phenomena. Drawing together an interdisciplinary team of scientists enables the group to tackle a wide range of studies that would otherwise be scarcely feasible. An example is the assemblage of a team of investigators to measure the changes that occur in a forested ecosystem after the outbreak of a defoliating insect in the tree canopy. There is the immediate effect of insects feeding on leaves, and the changes in primary production occurring in the tree canopy. In addition, one should measure the effects of the increased amount of falling frass (insect feces) on the forest floor, and its subsequent biochemical transformations in the soil, with the ensuing movement of mineral nutrients into the soil and groundwater, moving on into the stream flowing out of the watershed. All these processes are most effectively studied in a coordinated fashion by a team of scientists at a given site, allowing measurements of the ecosystem responses to a given perturbation. One person working alone on such a study would be able to document part of the story, but some of the more interesting interactions occurring during the process would be inevitably missed or overlooked.

As we shall see in later chapters, the interdisciplinary/multidisciplinary approach is being followed in an increasing number of research programs that are investigating the causative factors in Global Change. The research methods and ways that the research is administered have changed markedly over the decades. As new programs, such as the National Ecological Observatory Network (NEON) and others, begin their operations, it behooves us to remember the paths blazed by our intellectual forebears, and the battles they fought in getting their ideas accepted and their programs implemented, in order to benefit from the lessons learned in these large-scale programs.

This book is the result of scores of interviews with colleagues from all of the major U.S. IBP Biomes, as well as from numerous others from around the world. Their insights, their findings, and their enthusiasm enliven these pages. However, responsibility for any errors yet remaining in the book rests firmly with me.

ACKNOWLEDGMENTS

This book has benefited from the input of many friends and colleagues in the ecological community. The following list provides the names of these people.

University of Georgia colleagues Dac Crossley, Alan Covich, John Drake, and Ted Gragson read over several chapters, and the book has benefited greatly from their insights. Thelma Richardson, Samantha Connors, and Terry Camp provided invaluable assistance by formatting and tracking down references and providing top-quality figures. John Chamblee helped create the cover art. My wife, Fran, provided much needed moral support and advice.

The following colleagues from the Biome, LTER, and NEON programs provided comments and observations about the historical background:

Coastal Merryl Alber, Bruce Hayden, Wade Sheldon

Coniferous Forest Dale Cole, Kermit Cromack, Bob Edmonds, David Ford, Jerry Franklin, Henry Gholz, Mark Harmon, Dale Johnson, Jack Lattin, Art McKee, Andy Moldenke, Phil Sollins, Fred Swanson, Dick Waring

Deciduous Forest John Blair, Liz Blood, Dac Crossley, Frank Harris, Mark Hunter, Jerry Melillo, Knute Nadelhoffer, Dave Reichle, Bob O'Neill, Jerry Olson, Jim Kitchell, Orie Loucks, John Magnuson, Wayne Swank, Jim Vose, Bruce Wallace

Desert Scott Collins, Jim Gosz, Jim MacMahon, Larry Slobodkin, Fred Wagner, Diana Wall, Walt Whitford, Roman Zlotin

Grassland Sam Bledsoe, Alicja Breymeyer, Bill Hunt, George Innis, Dick Marzolf, Bill Parton, Eldor Paul, Paul Risser, Dave Schimel, Jai Singh, Dave Swift, Bob Woodmansee

Tropical Alan Covich, Jean Lodge, Ariel Lugo, Bob Waide, Xiaoming Zou

Tundra and Alpine Val Behan-Pelletier, Terry Chapin, Bill Heal, John Hobbie, Steve MacLean, Thomas Rosswall, Tim Seastedt, Gus Shaver, Pat Webber

Origin and Structure of Ecosystems Hal Mooney

NSF and Analysis of Ecosystems Joann Roskoski, Fred Smith

International programs in IBP Folke Andersson, Amyan Macfadyen, Dennis Parkinson, Henning Petersen

CHAPTER ONE

Intellectual Antecedents to Large-Scale Ecosystem Studies

Not everything that counts can be counted, and not everything that can be counted counts.

Albert Einstein

THE INFLUENCE OF THE INTERNATIONAL GEOPHYSICAL YEAR (IGY) ON INTERNATIONAL RESEARCH NETWORKS AND ECOSYSTEM STUDIES

International scientific collaborations have a long and illustrious history that extends back into the nineteenth century. Biological programs lagged the programs in physics and astronomy until the advent of the International Biological Program (IBP) in the middle of the twentieth century. As a result of the IBP and the recognition of biology as the basis of ecological science, all the later efforts to build a "big ecology" begin

1

with this program. Prior to IBP, a nearly ideal example for biologists was that of the International Geophysical Year (IGY), which had a beneficial impact far in excess of the immediate research carried out over a relatively short time period. IGY helped to make the case that many environmental processes are global in scale and interconnected across disciplines. This program's success and public support helped set the stage for "big ecology" and the use of advanced technology in studies of ecosystem change.

A paradigm of collaborative interdisciplinary research, the International Geophysical Year (IGY) began on July 1, 1957, continuing through the end of 1958. Although billed at the time in the popular press as a virtually unprecedented global initiative, the IGY had two important predecessors: the International Polar Years of 1882–1883 and 1932–1933 (Belanger, 2006). The second Polar Year was noteworthy in providing an increased knowledge of the ionosphere. This information significantly advanced the science of radio communications (Kaplan, 1956). Unlike its two predecessors, the IGY became a global endeavor, with considerable time and effort focused on the storied high-latitude South Polar region (Fraser, 1957; Belanger, 2006).

Support for IGY was impressive from its very inception. Thus, special symposia on meteorology and geophysics were convened before the program began officially. For example, a special symposium on geophysics was held on June 28–29, 1957, foreshadowing a number of projects to be carried out during IGY (Odishaw and Ruttenberg, 1958).

Initial work coincided with the launch of Sputnik, the first earth-orbiting satellite, by the Soviet Union in October 1957, which added scientific and political impetus to carry out new geophysical research. The IGY program was a pioneer in initiating and fostering extensive international collaboration, even in the midst of the Cold War years (Sullivan, 1961). The U.S. and Canadian governments were very active in launching IGY, with significant contributions from additional governments, including those of Argentina, Australia, Britain, France, Japan, Norway, the Soviet Union, and, a little later, Belgium (Fraser, 1957). The national academies of science of the countries listed above, as well as those of several others, coordinated their efforts through the International Council of Scientific Unions (ICSU) to make the IGY happen. Beginning in 1950, Drs. Sydney Chapman (a Briton) and Lloyd Berkner (an American) introduced the idea of the IGY to the ICSU at the headquarters in Brussels. In 1951, the Executive Board of ICSU appointed a special committee, the Comité Special de l'Année Geophysique Internationale, to coordinate the scientific planning of a worldwide cooperative program of geophysical observations (Kaplan, 1956). Numerous planning meetings occurred in the mid-1950s in Rome (1954) and in Brussels (1955), with the intention of carrying out a coordinated series of geophysical measurements in 1957–1958, designated the International Geophysical Year (IGY), when the solar flare activity was forecast to be at a maximum (Fraser, 1957). In sum, a total of fifty-four nations collaborated in this pioneering global study (Kaplan, 1956).

The scientific legacy of the IGY is impressive. As with all well-conceived and supported programs, it provided a channel for future collaborative activity that far transcended the immediate eighteen months of the study. Because the ICSU invited the world's scientists to participate in the research program directly, and was not encumbered by governmental bureaucracies, the management overhead was very low. Thus, the international secretariat in Brussels never exceeded eight people, with the annual cost not exceeding $50,000 (Belanger, 2006). The US Congress appropriated $43.5 million for the U.S. IGY, over half of which went to the orbiting satellite effort. The technical programs received an outlay of $18.2 million, with other agencies contributing logistical support of about $400 million, making the overall investment about $500 million for the eighteen months (Belanger, 2006). More important, the U.S. Navy, as the principal logistical support for Antarctic programs, continued this role, including by the provision of aircraft and crews to fly in hundreds of scientists per year from Christchurch, New Zealand. Over the remaining years of the twentieth century, the U.S. Navy provided logistical support to first the International Biological Program (IBP) and, more extensively, during the current, long-lived

(>30 years) Long-Term Ecological Research (LTER) Antarctic programs. LTER now has two large groups: terrestrial ecology at McMurdo station, and marine ecology at Palmer station. The latter studies are supported by the Division of Biological Sciences and the Office of Polar Programs of the U.S. National Science Foundation. The historical role of the U.S. Navy dates from the Antarctic exploration days of Rear Admiral Richard E. Byrd, who had considerable support during the 1930s to carry out exploration and climatological research on the continent.

The role of national pride and desire to be present "at the table" of ongoing research has certainly played a significant role in fostering continued support of scientific research in the Antarctic. For more extensive background on this complex interface between politics and science, see the later chapters in Belanger (2006).

THE EMERGENCE OF ECOSYSTEM SCIENCE

Ecosystem science per se arose contemporaneously with Eugene Odum's textbook (1953). Arising as the fruits of collaboration of E. P. Odum with his younger brother Howard Tom Odum (Craige, 2001), this textbook took a holistic ecosystem-oriented approach that was a marked departure from earlier ecology textbooks. It was issued in several editions, the latest revised in 2005 (Odum and Barrett, 2005). This book was the principal text in ecology for several decades from the 1950s to the 1980s (Golley, 1993). An interesting and seldom-read precedent for ecosystem scientists was set by Alfred J. Lotka, whose book (1925, 1956) on physical aspects of biology, including energetics and energy transformations, inspired early ecosystem ecologists.

The Atomic Energy Commission and Ecosystem Science

For the first thirty years after Arthur Tansley's promulgation of an initial ecosystem concept (1935) onward, ecosystem science was very much a "cottage industry" of a major professor and associated apprenticing graduate student(s) writing papers for a small number of ecology journals.

Ecology and ecosystem studies' progression arose out of a series of synergistic events that propelled the field along at a very rapid pace in the 1950s and 1960s. The development of "big science" really took off in the World War II years, between 1942 and 1945. In that short span of time, the Manhattan Project, as the atomic bomb project was called, was developed, with major research groups active at the University of Chicago, Los Alamos National Laboratory (New Mexico), and the large production facilities of Oak Ridge (Tennessee) and Hanford (Washington). The ultrasecret project involved many thousands of scientists and technicians in a colossally large (for the time) expenditure of $2 billion.

From 1945 to 1950, new federal funding sources for research, including the National Science Foundation (NSF), were established (Appel, 2000). This significantly increased funding in all aspects of basic scientific research, including ecology. A continuing growth of atomic energy and "peaceful uses of the atom" occurred from 1955 onward. The U.S. Atomic Energy Commission (AEC) seemed to be rather casual initially about the rapid spread of radioisotopes and radiation contaminants in the environment at its production facilities. One of the leading community ecologists of the time, Professor Orlando Park of Northwestern University, was asked by Dr. Edward Struxness, a mid-level administrator at Oak Ridge National Laboratories, to advise on the possible spread of radionuclides in the environment. Park came to Oak Ridge, talked to scientists in the Health Physics Division, and observed the accumulation of radionuclides, e.g. ^{137}Cesium, in a large drainage area, the White Oak Lake bed just a couple of miles from the main reactor areas.

Professor Park, when asked how to rectify the problem, urged Oak Ridge to hire fifty Ph.D.-level scientists immediately, to tackle such a large problem. Upon being informed that no more than two could be hired, he quickly recommended one of his recent Ph.D. students, Stanley Auerbach, an animal ecologist who specialized in invertebrate ecology, to set up a research program in radiation ecology (D. A. Crossley Jr., pers. comm.). Auerbach proceeded to develop a research team of young aspiring researchers to monitor the spread of radionuclides in the environment, and also to conduct studies on ecosystem dynamics of the grassland, forest, and aquatic ecosystems on the Oak Ridge reservation (Bocking, 1997). The first new hires were Charles Rohde, an acarologist, followed by D. A. "Dac" Crossley Jr., a newly minted Ph.D. from Kansas University Entomology Department, followed by Paul Dunaway, a mammalogist (D. A. Crossley Jr., pers. comm.). Thus a major impetus to ecosystem research came from a demonstrated need identified by the scientific community, and acted upon by a funding agency, to better understand the dynamics of ecosystem processes and to track rates of uptake by environmental processes. In so doing, "radio-ecological" tracers became a new tool for conducting ecosystem research at multiple scales. Radiation effects on organisms were reported in early studies of Auerbach (1958) on the survival of mites and Collembola after exposure to radiation from [60]Cobalt. The AEC provided both the concern (nuclear) and the tools (radiotracers) to study the fates and effects on ecosystems. The AEC was in the business of ecosystem studies before the NSF, as a result of the leadership of John Wolfe, who came from Ohio State University, where he had studied the microclimate of the Neotoma woods (David E. Reichle, pers. comm.). This included long-term studies at Rock Valley, Nevada, and the eruption of the Surtsey volcano in Iceland, and primary succession occurring on it (James MacMahon, pers. comm.). Stan Auerbach's group's unique contributions included use of radiotracers at ecosystem scales (Drs. Olson, Crossley, Reichle, and Witkamp), emphasis on systems ecology (Drs. Olson, Van Dyne, Patten, and O'Neill) and emphasis on bioinformatics to support the models. Two biome directors are in the above names, and are considered in detail in Chapter 2.

Nearly contemporaneously with this development, Eugene Odum was approached by AEC officials in 1951 to study ecosystems on the Savannah River reservation, a large 315 mi^2 (504 km^2) area set aside in western South Carolina along the Savannah River to produce plutonium and tritium for use in hydrogen bombs. Odum offered to conduct a wide-ranging study of the structure and functioning of ecosystems, asking for close to $100,000 per year. The AEC started with an initial grant of $7,000 per year for the research of one lead PI (Odum) and one graduate student. The program grew rapidly to include several senior staff members and technicians at the Laboratory for Radiation Ecology, soon renamed the Savannah River Ecology Laboratory (SREL). They made use of the ready availability of radioisotopes to study metabolism of animals, and also effects of radiation on organisms and entire forest stands (Golley, 2001). Odum hired Frank Golley, a newly minted Ph.D. from Michigan State University in 1958, and put him to work as the first director of SREL two years later (Smith et al., 2001).

Other environmental research groups were established at the Pacific Northwest laboratories at Hanford (Washington), Brookhaven (on Long Island), New York, and Los Alamos (New Mexico) laboratories. These programs transformed funding and how ecological science was conducted in the 1960s onward. The research groups tended to emphasize team research aimed at interdisciplinary studies of the movement of radionuclides in ecosystems and the effects of radiation on organisms in their habitats as well. A series of volumes on Radioecology were produced in the 1960s and early 1970s (e.g., Schultz and Klement, 1961; Nelson, 1971). By 1971, total funding for environmental, biological and technical studies in the AEC was $72 million, with about $34 million in the Division of Biology and Medicine (Larson, 1971). The total funding for ecology and ecosystem studies in the National Science Foundation totaled somewhat less than $20 million that year, making an interesting comparison of very different levels of resource allocation at that time for ecosystem research. Arriving at the Savannah River Ecology Laboratory as a Postdoctoral Fellow in 1965, I began using radionuclides to tag food items in the field, to further study microbial and faunal food webs. To gain the information and expertise necessary to carry out this work, Dick Wiegert, an invertebrate ecologist, and Frank Golley, two major researchers at the SREL encouraged me to go to "the source of knowledge," D. A. ("Dac") Crossley Jr., in the Environmental Sciences Division at Oak Ridge National Laboratory, Oak Ridge, Tennessee. Having read several of his papers (Crossley 1963; Reichle and Crossley, 1965),

I inquired if he would be willing to tutor me in a one-on-one short course in radioecology. Dac invited me to visit him in October 1965, and we spent a few days on a short tutorial concerning the mathematical calculations of biological half-lives, isotope counting methods, and so forth. He provided an overview of what he covered in a two-week short course in four days. I was very impressed at how much could be done by such a talented and focused person, all of this presented with a wonderfully dry sense of humor. I also met Jerry Olson, Dave Reichle, Stan Auerbach (head of the Division), Martin Witkamp, and several other colleagues. At this point, additional publications such as Witkamp and Crossley (1966) were in press, and I discussed their findings with them.

When I joined the staff of SREL in September 1965, the annual budget was nearly $200,000 per year. Later SREL grew to be one of the more well-funded (>$10 M/yr.) and highly influential ecological research laboratories nationwide under Mike Smith's direction (Smith et al., 2001). It is now operating on a much smaller budget as a result of drastic budget cuts made late in President George W. Bush's second term and is in the process of rebuilding its research program under new funding from the current administration.

U.S. Atomic Energy Commission support for research studies of radionuclides in the environment extended from Brookhaven National Laboratory on Long Island, New York, into the tropics, with a large study carried out by H. T. Odum and his colleagues at El Verde in eastern Puerto Rico throughout the latter half of the 1960s (Odum and Pigeon, 1970). H. T. Odum, Gene's younger brother, played a role in forming my early career. Shortly before Dick Wiegert moved from SREL to the UGA campus in Athens in the summer of 1966, he invited me to accompany him in April to work at the AEC-funded Irradiation and Ecology study site at El Verde, Puerto Rico. This project was funded for more than $5 million for five years through the Luquillo Experimental Forest, administered by the U.S. Forest Service.

Wiegert had begun work with H. T. Odum two years earlier, on the energetics and population ecology of termites (*Nasutitermes costalis*) at the radiation and control sites of the Luquillo rain forest. Dick suggested that

I conduct a short-term study project with him in Puerto Rico. This research led to a paper in the Tropical Rain Forest volume (Wiegert, 1970), discussed below. Wiegert was one of the pioneers in ecological energetics (Wiegert, 1965; Wiegert and Fraleigh, 1972), and co-developed a manufacturing company in Aiken, S.C., to produce the microbomb calorimeter that had been invented by John Phillipson (1964). The "microbomb" was widely used to determine calorific values of plant and animal tissues in the ecosystem science community in the late 1960s and 1970s.

H. T. Odum, E. P. Odum, and Other Ecosystem Pioneers

H. T. Odum was a "larger-than-life" character—six feet, four inches tall, full of ideas and enthusiasm (Fig. 1.1). He picked up Wiegert and me at the airport in San Juan in April 1966 and roared off to the east of the

Figure 1.1.   Eugene P. Odum and Howard T. Odum discussing ecosystem function at the Institute of Ecology, University of Georgia, ca. 1995 (used with permission of the Odum Library, University of Georgia).

island in his large government-gray Plymouth sedan. We stopped at a roadside cantina to sample the liquid refreshments offered. H. T. talked about the logistical problems operating the large canopy experiment. This project employed a large plastic cylinder sixty-seven feet tall by sixty feet wide. The turnover time of air in the chamber was five to twelve minutes, it being drawn through by a large fan built into the base of the chamber (Odum and Jordan, 1970). This work was verified by further studies of forest floor metabolism in microcosms (Odum and Lugo, 1970) and whole plant transpiration and photosynthesis (Odum et al., 1970). Ariel E. Lugo, Director of the International Institute of Tropical Forestry of the U.S. Forest Service, got his start with H. T. Odum on this impressive whole-system project. Dick Wiegert and I listened as we drank our ten-ounce beers, then Odum hurriedly caught up by draining his can in one enormous draught. I sampled the biomass of nematodes in the litter and soil of the study sites, which resulted in a two-page paper in the Tropical Rain Forest volume (Coleman, 1970).

Wiegert and I agreed that even if only one out of ten of Odum's ideas were proven to be true, he was way ahead of us in interesting and useful ideas generated per day. My impression of H. T. Odum was that he was the more brilliant of the two Odum brothers, and probably one of only three geniuses I have ever met in my life (the other two being Ramón Margalef and Jerry Olson). Margalef published widely, with two pioneering books being most noteworthy: *Perspectives in Ecological Theory* (1968) and *Our Biosphere* (1997). His ideas on cybernetic (self-governing, or self-organizing) principles have influenced generations of ecosystem scientists with their clear insights into ecosystem function. In fact, the characterization of nature in the metaphor of a "cybernetic machine" is the principal way in which funding for the U.S./International Biological Program (IBP) was granted by the U.S. Congress (Kwa, 1987), and is presented in detail in Chapter 2. I discuss more of Olson's scientific contributions in the next chapter.

Anyone who met H. T. Odum never forgot him. H. T. Odum exerted a major influence on the ecosystem science scene, not only because of his pioneering work in whole-system energetics, such as the energy pathways of Silver Spring, Florida, but also by his outreach to the larger community of scientists and interested laypeople with his book *Environment, Power and Society* (Odum, 1971, 2007), which addressed all aspects of societal activities from an energetics perspective. His doctoral dissertation at Yale University focused on the then internationally important aspects of atmospheric testing and the cycling of ^{90}Strontium in the atmosphere. Working under the direction of Professor G. Evelyn Hutchinson, a pioneer in ecosystems and biogeochemistry, H. T. Odum was able to conceptualize and model the "big-picture" dynamics that most ecologists were just beginning to understand. He used a pictorial engineering-based modeling scheme that included visual symbols for capacitance, resistance, flows, and so forth, that was not readily adopted by the ecosystem science community. Using this modeling scheme, he addressed numerous controversial topics. One such topic was the issue of fossil fuel subsidies of non–fossil fuel sources of energy, such as nuclear power. His concern was that the amount of fossil fuel subsidy required to build and then dispose of the nuclear waste produced by a power reactor would lead inevitably to excess fossil fuel inputs over the thirty- to forty-year lifetime of the reactor. Such a contention was not popular in the early 1970s, and still seems overlooked now. He also asserted that the value of the work done by petroleum products was such that the net worth of gasoline in automobiles was actually $6 per gallon. This was in 1970 dollars, when the cost of gasoline was well below 50 cents per gallon. H. T. Odum's *Systems Ecology* textbook (Odum, 1983) is a must read for someone looking for insights into his marvelous world of ecosystems.

Because of the force of his personality and strong networking abilities, Gene Odum (Fig. 1.1) was the more successful and influential of the two brothers in terms of his impact on the field of ecology, and on support for it nationwide. This arose not only from his seminal contributions to ecosystem science in the *Fundamentals of Ecology* textbook, but also with his activities as president of the Ecological Society of America in 1964–1965 and his greater prominence on the national scientific stage when he was elected to the National Academy of Science in 1971. Gene Odum was also featured in *Time Magazine* (in April 1970) to celebrate Earth Day, along with G. Evelyn Hutchinson. Hutchinson had a pronounced impact on both Odum brothers that dated from the time when H. T. attended Yale during the late 1940s and wrote his dissertation in 1950 (Craige, 2001). Hutchinson's erudition was demonstrated most strongly in his studies of biogeochemistry (e.g., 1944; 1950) and treatise on limnology (1957). One of Gene Odum's most influential and controversial papers was "The Strategy of Ecosystem Development" (1969), in which he analogized the successional stages of ecosystems (ecosystem maturation) with the ontogeny of organisms.

Both Odum brothers were strongly influenced by the example of their father, Howard Washington Odum, who was for many years chair of the Department of Sociology at the University of North Carolina, Chapel Hill. Odum Senior's studies of the deleterious effects of segregation on the economy of the Deep South of the 1920s drew considerable fire from the business community at large. This example of courage may have influenced the forthright and occasionally combative nature of both sons as they put forth their ideas (Craige, 2001).

Frank Golley and E. P. Odum teamed up with H. T. Odum to establish the basis of big science in the tropics (Puerto Rico and the Pacific) during the early 1960s, a bit ahead of the IBP studies in the United States (A. E. Lugo, pers. comm.). Lugo further notes: "E.P. Odum and H.T. together published a whole ecosystem study of a coral reef in the Eniwetok Atoll in the Pacific (Odum and Odum, 1955), a study twice followed up by large expeditions specifically oriented to verify the findings of the Odums. The first expedition was in 1972, and in ca. 2007 there was another one (Hall, 1995). Clearly the study by the Odums provided a foundation for whole ecosystem studies and big follow-up science up to the present" (Ariel E. Lugo, pers. comm.).

HISTORICAL ROOTS OF IBP IN NORTH AMERICA (1967–1974)

The IBP Biome sites got themselves established in the midst of a time of generally apathetic and weak support for ecosystem studies in North America.

Comments in Geier (2007) are illuminating. He notes observations by Sir Rudolph Peters (published in Worthington, 1975) that relate to something of a disarray among scientists in the United States. Peters cites comments of the developmental biologist, Dr. James Ebert, who asserted at the American Institute of Biological Sciences (AIBS) meeting in August 1962 that "[m]ost . . . of the proposals were for warmed-over ecology of the thirties and forties on a world-wide scale." His statement had "excellent shock value. I believe strongly in a well-planned international program . . . which is truly international in character, and which attempts to use the international aspect of the endeavor as a powerful tool, rather than just a gimmick to keep up with the physicists."

The actions and reactions to Dr. Ebert's comments possibly reflect the characterization of ecology as then carried out in the early 1960s as a sort of cottage industry as a "normative science," sensu Kuhn (1996). In this view, normative science is firmly based upon one or more past scientific achievements, ones that some particular scientific community acknowledges for a time as supplying the foundation for its further practice. The achievements were sufficiently unprecedented to attract an enduring group of adherents away from competing modes of scientific activities. These achievements are "paradigms," a term relating closely to normative science. In contrast to Ebert's criticisms, I think that the results of the collaborative, interdisciplinary approaches pursued below were the entering wedge to pursuing ecological studies in a hitherto unprecedented manner. The results of the IBP led to a "paradigm shift" in how ecosystem science was carried out.

One of the objectives of this book is to attempt to delineate the factors that gave the various IBP Biome research groups the necessary impetus that made them effective. As we shall see, the overriding influence of strong personalities and previous history of their interactions led to some intriguingly different management styles and operational modes. What scientific outlooks were changed in the course of the IBP program, and if they occurred, how extensive were they?

The beginnings of large-scale ecosystem studies are inextricably linked with the inception of the IBP in the United States, but that development might not have been predicted by Ebert or other biologists at the time. It is significant that the early history of the IBP in the United States had a rather tortuous beginning. In the early 1960s, ecologists and environmental scientists in Europe proposed an international program on the environment that they called the International Biological Programme, or IBP (Worthington, 1975). The program addressed all aspects of biological productivity in relation to human welfare. This broad approach to the biological basis of productivity included scientists from theoretical and applied disciplines in biology, including forestry, soil science, and freshwater and marine biology. Numerous governmental agencies in Europe provided funding for studies that began from 1963 onward, with Canada and other Commonwealth countries following soon after. Although there was considerable interest in the United States for the IBP concept, no funding mechanism existed for such a program. The history of the establishment and operation of the IBP Research Programs is presented in the next chapter and provides an example of how global issues are often identified and organized by many outside the United States. The recent slowness in the United States to sign international agreements regarding needs for research and policies on biodiversity and climate change is a similar example.

CHAPTER TWO

How the International Biological Program Swept the Scientific World

From the point of view of the constituent organisms in a community, the relative importance of different species can be compared more simply on the basis of their contribution to the energy flow of the community than in terms of biomass. The population which exploits the greatest quantity of stored energy is contributing most to the rapid liberation of nutrient substances. These will ultimately find their way back to the plants and thus contribute to raise the energy intake of the community as a whole.

Macfadyen, *Animal Ecology: Aims and Methods* (1963a)

The International Biological Program (IBP) was the largest, most successful scientific program of its kind in the 1970s. This success is measured by the number of graduate students and postdoctorals who went on to lead numerous large research groups around the world. Its legacy is still felt literally four decades later. The IBP had its early beginnings in Great Britain and Europe, with the United States lagging far behind (Worthington, 1975). As noted in Chapter 1, this lack of interest was in marked contrast to previous experience with the International Geophysical Year during 1957–1958, in which the United States and Canada were leading participants from its very inception. Reasons for this disparity between the IGY, which was a focused, short-term operation, and the IBP, which was very wide-ranging and open-ended in terms of projected funding, reflect the lack of strong support by many leading ecologists in the scientific community, who were not yet thinking of "big ecology" as relevant to their own research (Blair, 1977). Traditional ecologists also feared that IBP would bring on systems ecology and eliminate funding for conventional small-scale ecological research. In the end, what modeling did was create the focus and justification for decades of process-level research.

One of the objectives of this book is to identify and delineate the factors that gave the various IBP Biome research groups in North America the necessary impetus to succeed and to interact with the already ongoing efforts of IBP researchers around the world. As we shall see, the overriding influence of strong personalities and previous history of their interactions led to some intriguingly different management styles and operational modes.

The early history of the IBP in the United States had a rather tortuous beginning. In the late 1950s and early 1960s, ecologists and environmental scientists in Europe had proposed an international program on the environment, which they called the International Biological Programme (Worthington, 1975). The program addressed all aspects of biological productivity in relation to human welfare. The wide area of subject matter coverage is what enticed the leading British developmental biologist C. H. Waddington to throw his support behind this nascent program (Worthington, 1975). This broad approach to the biological basis of productivity included scientists from theoretical and applied disciplines in biology, including forestry, soil science, and freshwater and marine biology. Numerous governmental agencies in Europe provided funding for studies that began from 1963 onward, with Canada and other Commonwealth countries following soon after. The IBP left a lasting imprint on ecosystem ecology, as evidenced by the extensive involvement of IBP alumni in many of the Long-Term Ecological Research (LTER) studies that have been underway for the past 30 years, 36 years after the formal ending of IBP. Research results from numerous IBP programs and sites are still being referred to today (e.g., Johnson and Cole, 2005). After first considering the Canadian IBP and presenting an overview of programs in other countries, I then examine the U.S. IBP programs in more detail.

THE CANADIAN IBP PROGRAM

The Matador Project

The IBP program in Canada focused on a few key areas. Some freshwater (David Schindler and others at the University of Manitoba) and marine studies (William F. Ricker et al.) at the University of British Columbia) were quite successful. I will focus on the Productivity Terrestrial (PT) portion, which concentrated on two major sites: the

Matador site in southwestern Saskatchewan, and the Truelove Low-lands, on Devon Island, in the Canadian Arctic. As was the case in the United States, strong personalities came to the fore and guided (some might even say drove) the programs forward.

The Matador site was chosen because it was considered initially to be located in a relatively virgin (unbroken sod) prairie that had been used by a large Texas cattle ranching firm for the first few decades of the twentieth century. A long three-hour drive had to be made from Saskatoon out to the site by the investigators. Extensive kitchen, dining room, and bunkhouse facilities were built on site but were not heavily used, because many studies required the rapid transport of samples back to the university campus (E. A. Paul, pers. comm.). Another drawback was the very heavy (>70%) clay soil, which became impassable to motor vehicles for a day or two after any significant rainfall. Nevertheless, the Matador site project proved productive for graduate students and research papers. All of the senior faculty who had projects there were well supported with equipment, supplies, and travel (E. A. Paul, pers. comm.). The research group, led by Robert Coupland and Eldor Paul as co-PIs, included Eeltje De Jong on abiotic processes and John Stewart on phosphorus and sulfur cycling. Frank Warembourg and others carried out some pioneering studies of microbial turnover and soil respiration and measured the impressive amount of total productivity going belowground. These colleagues were an inspiration to the researchers at the Pawnee intensive site in northeastern Colorado, who began their studies two to three years after the inception of the Matador field research.

The Truelove Lowland Tundra Site

The Truelove Lowland site (on the northeastern coast of Devon Island (75° 33' N, 84° 40' W) was chosen, principally because it was representative of the high Arctic, the fifth largest island within the Canadian Arctic Archipelago (1,424,000 km²). It was reasonably accessible by air (315 km) from Resolute Bay, Cornwallis Island; had an existing research camp dating from 1960, had a background of scientific data, and contained herds of musk ox, which are representative of the eastern High Arctic (Bliss, 1977). The major objectives, as with all IBP studies, were to determine population numbers and standing crop, as well as the productivity (energy flow) of all trophic levels of organisms in the site. This research included an explicit consideration of the role of Inuit (Eskimo) as harvesters within these ecosystems. The hydrologic role of rivers, streams, and lakes, and the biological components of lakes, were investigated (Bliss, 1977). The study was one of the more extensive whole-system research projects carried out in a network of fourteen Tundra research sites in a circumpolar region, including Russia and the Fenno-Scandian countries. Ten countries were involved in the IBP tundra research (Austria, Canada, Finland, Greenland, Ireland, Norway, Sweden, UK, the United States, and the USSR) (Bliss et al., 1981). What were the interesting, even counterintuitive, aspects of this research? I asked this question of Dr. O. W. Heal, from the UK, who was the coordinator for decomposition studies across the Tundra sites. The results from these studies were integrated into systems models which formed a framework for the program.

Key features of the IBP Tundra experience were the value of a comparative study across a range of environments and comparisons of results across a wide range of conditions. The following comments are quoted verbatim from Dr. Heal's notes on the IBP Tundra Biome network to illustrate the active collaboration and communication among international investigators:

> The experience was encapsulated in a meeting of a small group of researchers discussing their research on rates of organic matter decomposition. The American (microbiologist) took litter samples back to the laboratory and measured the rate of respiration but the Brit (field ecologist) measured the weight loss from litter bags in the field. The modeller (mathematician) saw that respiration rate could be used to calculate weight loss for comparative purposes—but, given data on climatic conditions, it could also be used to predict

decomposition in other sites. The Swedish representative (microbi-
ologist) agreed to test this idea—and it worked! Thus we developed
new ideas through exchange of information—is summarised by the
equation:

$$2 + 2 = 5$$

[I].e., the whole is greater than the sum of the parts or put the pieces
together! This exchange of ideas, from different nationalities, different environments and different research backgrounds gave us
insights into the fundamental processes of decomposition and the
value of "synthesis". It has had a large influence on my career development. It was also the approach advocated by John Jeffers (Director
of the ITE, the Natural Research Council's Institute for Terrestrial
Ecology) and George Van Dyne who worked together and influenced the programmes under their control. Modelling was a key
element in their planning, implementation and synthesis and it was
an important element in the Tundra Biome."

Jeffers (1972) provides an extensive overview of modeling efforts
in several IBP programs worldwide. Dr. Heal's account encapsulates
the interactive, exciting nature of this productive international
collaboration. Certainly members of the Tundra Biome group were
among the most interactive of any of the Biomes in the IBP program.
Representative examples of these syntheses involving the international
Tundra Biome network include Rosswall and Heal (1974) and Bliss
et al. (1981).

OTHER NATIONAL PROGRAMS IN THE IBP

IBP programs were developed in many European and Asian countries as
well. Foremost among these were the Solling Project in Germany
(Ellenberg, 1971a, 1971b) and several study sites in Japan (Kitazawa,
1971; Tsutsumi, 1971), with considerable information on seasonal
ranges of forest floor respiration and nutrient cycling.

The IBP program developed quite early in India. The following comments are from one of the early researchers in the Indian IBP, Professor J. S. Singh, Banaras Hindu University, Varanasi:

It was largely through the efforts of late Prof. R. Misra that the message of IBP spread in India, as he was associated with the PT Section of IBP. From January 16–21, 1967, the International Society for Tropical Ecology organized an International Symposium at Varanasi in which IBP figured prominently, largely through the efforts of the then President of the Society, F. R. Fosberg, and in the Proceedings of the Symposium [Misra and Gopal, 1968] the first few papers originating from IBP research were published. Several papers were published in the proceedings of a symposium held in 1971 at Delhi and published as "Tropical Ecology with emphasis on organic productivity" [Golley and Golley, 1972]. These symposia had strongly promoted IBP-related studies. During the early 1960s, the Varanasi School began studying grasslands and forests in ecosystem perspective emphasizing primary production. The work on production ecology coincided with the launching of the International Biological Programme in 1964. The first two doctoral theses (on grasslands by J.S. Singh and on forests by K.P. Singh) related to the production ecology based on the ecosystem concept were completed in 1967. These studies provided a turning point in ecological researches in India, and created a tremendous wave of research in this direction throughout the country. It was in this period that hypotheses were proposed to account for the opposite trophic biomass structure in large aquatic systems [Misra and Gopal, 1968], diversity-productivity relationships in grasslands [J. S. Singh and Misra, 1969] and promoter effect of moderate grazing on grassland productivity [J. S. Singh, 1968]. Also, in dry tropical forests, rapid nutrient cycling was emphasized [K. P. Singh, 1968] and controlling effect of seasonality and litter chemical quality on litter decomposition was shown. The "Ecology Summer School" organized by the Varanasi School in 1966, and the "Ecology Work-Book" produced for the School, had a tremendous impact on the spread of ecology in other parts of the country. Many teachers and would-be researchers received first-hand training in hitherto unavailable ecological techniques and concepts.

There were many contacts made between researchers in other countries and IBP Biome studies throughout the IBP era. Some examples include:

1. The IBP Grassland Biome study in Iceland. Dr. Ingvi Thorsteinsson visited the NREL and worked with George Van Dyne, ca. 1973, for three months.

2. The research at Hardangervidda, a large, windswept tundra/grassland, was reviewed capably by Dr. Frans Wielgolaski. Frans visited Ft. Collins several times through the early 1970s.

3. The Danish IBP effort was focused on the Hestehave Beech Forest study, with much of its activity summarized in the publication by Petersen and Luxton (1982), as well as the Danish fungal experts.

4. The Dutch IBP grassland studies focused on one of the offshore islands, Terschelling, with a group led by Dr. Peter Kettner. J. Van der Drift (1971) summarized the Dutch forest IBP studies.

5. The French IBP had many forest and savanna studies at Lamto, on the Ivory Coast (e.g., Bernhard-Reversat et al., 1972). The field work there was an important beginning point for the research on earthworms and other soil fauna by Dr. Patrick Lavelle, who is now a professor at University of Paris V in Orsay, France. Dr. Albert Sasson, of the University of Rabat, in Morocco, was a collaborator with several French colleagues in the IBP.

6. The Belgian IBP focused on forest ecosystems, and was led by Duvigneaud and Denayer-DeSmet (1971). The Belgian acarologist Paul Berthet was active in additional syntheses (Berthet and Gerard, 1970; Berthet, 1972).

7. The Italian IBP focused on aquatic ecology, on Lago Maggiore. Professors Vittorio and Livia Tonolli were very active on IBP international committees.

8. The central European countries really came into their own during the IBP era. I refer elsewhere to the extensive Polish Grassland

and forest studies, under the aegis of Professor Kazimierz Petrusewicz (1967; Petrusewicz and Macfadyen, 1970). The Czechoslovakian IBP had numerous studies, such as in alluvial and montane grasslands (Ulehlova, 1973) and forests carried out by groups from Charles University, Prague, and the Czech Academy of Sciences (CAS), Brno. Our contacts were extensive with Dr. Blanka Ulehlova and her CAS research group in Brno (summarized in Coleman and Sasson, 1980). The Hungarian IBP focused on aquatic and forestry studies.

9. The Russian (Soviet Union) studies were comprehensive, with research extending into the southern steppes of Russia and into Siberia as well (e.g., Bazilevich, Drozdov, and Rodin, 1971; Rodin and Bazilevich, 1967; Rodin and Smirnov, 1975; Zlotin and Khodashova, 1980).

Other Asian studies included Thailand, with a few forest productivity studies, and the extensive Japanese grassland and forest studies. Japanese activities included those of Professor M. Numata working on *Miscanthus* grasslands, and those of T. Satoo (1971) and Y. Kitazawa (1971). China had very little IBP-related activities, possibly due to the aftermath of the "great leap forward" during the late 1960s.

The Australian government had an extensive involvement in IBP studies. The International Rangeland Congress of 1970 was held in Surfer's Paradise, Queensland. George Van Dyne gave several seminars and talks there, and managed to persuade several Australian grassland researchers to come visit him in the newly constructed NREL grassland lab on Lake Street on the southern edge of the Colorado State University campus. Several of the scientists stayed for up to six months, and were very interactive with Van Dyne, George Innis, and the simulation modeling group. New Zealand concentrated more on forest productivity and oceanic productivity studies in the IBP era.

The participation of African countries in the IBP lagged the rest of the world quite a bit. The only other group in addition to the French-supported Ivory Coast studies above was in the Union of South Africa.

The IBP Grasslands Biome played host to several visits from Dr. J. J. P. "Jak" Van Wyk of the University of Potchefstroom. Jak was quite a gadgeteer and devised various sorts of sampling equipment for insects and plant biomass. Van Dyne loved to have him around, in part because of Van Wyk's rather acerbic and self-deprecating comments.

THE U.S. IBP PROGRAM

The Establishment of IBP in North America

Although there was considerable interest by ecosystem scientists in the United States in the IBP concept, no funding mechanism existed for such a program. To assist in launching the U.S. IBP, senior scientists in the U.S. biological community, including W. Frank Blair, a population and community ecologist but strong ecosystem sciences supporter from the University of Texas, George M. Woodwell from Brookhaven National Laboratory, and Arthur D. Hasler of the University of Wisconsin, convened a series of planning meetings during 1966, including a pivotal one in August, held in Williamstown, Massachusetts, chaired by Eugene Odum. Frederick E. Smith, a leading American ecologist, referred to the IBP as "lifting a minor subject to a position of major status," and said, "Within the last year, the sudden support of IBP by a large number of ecologists, after strong initial resistance, has been surprising. The ferment that took place at Williamstown last October had all the excitement of a 'happening'" (Worthington, 1975). These ecologists developed an action plan to establish a series of IBP sites in each of the major Biomes of North America, beginning with the Grasslands Biome, followed by several others in later years (Blair, 1977). This gathering was foundational for numerous participants in it. Gene Odum, interested in having significant representation for deserts, invited Frederic Wagner of Utah State University to attend the meeting. Ultimately this led to the collaboration of David Goodall and Wagner as co-PIs on the Desert Biome a few years later (F. E. Wagner, pers. comm.).

Ironically, a tropical IBP failed to get underway in the Neotropics, probably because H.T. Odum was rebuffed by the U.S. establishment and H. Lieth took over but was unable to get any science done (Ariel E. Lugo, pers. comm.). Odum had strong reservations about the U.S. Biome programs, noting, "If the European IBP effort is producing this kind of focus by concentrating on basic productivity as a theme, perhaps the broader, ill-defined, and do-nothing program of the U.S. should be narrowed to conform to the European pattern" (Lugo, 1995).

One unique outgrowth of the Williamstown meeting was a proposal for the study of drainage basins and landscapes as a joint concept of the terrestrial (PT) and freshwater (PF) subcommittees of IBP that met at the Williamstown meeting. Several advantages were anticipated from the simultaneous study of terrestrial and aquatic systems within a given drainage basin, studies that would include effects of one on the other. This joint effort became known as the Analysis of Ecosystems program, with Fred Smith as PI, which began organizing the Biome studies (Loucks et al., 1974).

For both regional activities and on the national stage, it required a real mover and shaker to get things to happen. Several initial persons, while scientifically capable, did not have enough sway nationally to make things happen. "Later the Americans put in charge someone with the reputation of a real thruster, Roger Revelle" (Worthington, 1975). Funding support had been generally lacking, and Revelle, an oceanographer who was a successful administrator, as director of the Scripps Institution of Oceanography from 1950–1964 and a professor at Harvard University in the late 1960s interested in global population growth and impacts of climate change, really shone when it came to getting the process started. Through his personal friendship with California congressman George Miller, he encouraged Miller to introduce the first of several bills in the House of Representatives calling for federal recognition of and support for the IBP (Hagen, 1992). Subsequently, Congressman Daddario's Subcommittee on Science, Research and Development held five hearings in the spring and summer of 1967. At the first session, on May 9, Revelle led off with a very eloquent and supportive statement:

> Our goal should be not to conquer the natural world but to live in harmony with it. To attain this goal, we must learn how to control both the external environment and ourselves. Especially, we need to learn how to avoid irreversible change. If we do not, we shall deny to future generations the opportunity to choose the kind of world in which they want to live. Greater understanding will make it possible for man to respond to opportunity as well as to react to need. To gain such understanding is the underlying purpose of the International Biological Program. (Blair, 1977)

Congressman George Brown of California picked up on some of these comments and noted,

> The IBP effort of the United States can serve as an effective umbrella for many of the proposed activities related to environmental quality and baseline environmental studies with which the Congress is currently concerned. Virtually all of the bills before the Congress that are directed toward problems that are encompassed by the U.S. plan for participation in the IBP. (Blair, 1977)

To kick off the U.S. IBP program, after extensive testimony in the House of Representatives by leading ecologists and Dr. Revelle, several million dollars were authorized and appropriated by Congress in the summer of 1967 to establish an Ecosystems Studies program office in the Biological Studies Directorate led by Assistant Director Harve Carlson in the National Science Foundation (NSF) (Blair, 1977).

Programs in the U.S. IBP fell within two major subgroups: Environmental Management and Human Adaptability. There were sixteen programs: ten in the area of Ecosystem Analysis studies and six in the Human Adaptability program (Box 2.1) (NAS Rept. No. 6, 1974).

For the most part, this chapter focuses on the Ecosystem Analysis studies, primarily Productivity Terrestrial (PT) and also the convergent evolution of ecosystems program—i.e., the Chile and California

BOX 2.1. *Programs within the U.S. IBP (from U.S. National Committee for the IBP, 1974)*

ENVIRONMENTAL MANAGEMENT
  Ecosystem Analysis Studies
  Grasslands Biome
  Eastern Deciduous Forest Biome
  Coniferous Forest Biome
  Desert Biome
  Tundra Biome
  Origin and Structure of Ecosystems
    Structure of Ecosystems subprogram
      Desert Scrub subproject
      Mediterranean Scrub subproject
    Island Ecosystem Stability and Evolution subprogram
  Biological Productivity in Upwelling Ecosystems
Marine Mammals
Aerobiology
Biological Control of Insect Pests
  (later Integrated Plant Pest Control)
Conservation of Plant Genetic Materials
Conservation of Ecosystems

HUMAN ADAPTABILITY
Population Genetics of South American Indians
International Study of Circumpolar Peoples
  International Study of Eskimos Subprogram
  International Study of Aleuts Subprogram
Biology of Human Populations at High Altitudes
Biosocial Adaptation of Migrant and Urban Populations
Nutritional Adaptation to the Environment

(Mooney, 1977), and Argentina and Arizona (Orians and Solbrig, 1977) comparisons.

Biome research programs were established sequentially, with the Grasslands Biome being first, with headquarters at Colorado State University (CSU), Fort Collins. With the exception of the Grassland Biome study, most Biome programs used a somewhat decentralized model of organization, with satellite sites operating nearly autonomously from headquarters. Thus, the Eastern Deciduous Forest Biome, head-quartered at the Environmental Sciences Division of Oak Ridge National Laboratory had satellite sites at Coweeta (University of Georgia, Athens), Lake Wingra in Wisconsin (University of Wisconsin), Duke Forest (Duke University) and other sites around the eastern United States. Other Biomes operated similarly, including deserts, alpine and tundra, and coniferous forest (Figure 2.1). It is important to note that the U.S. Forest Service served as a key collaborator and participant in several Biome studies in Alaska (first Washington Creek, then Bonanza Creek, near Fairbanks), at Coweeta Hydrologic Laboratory in North Carolina, in the H. J. Andrews Experimental Forest in western Oregon, and at the Luquillo Experimental Site in the Caribbean National Forest, Puerto

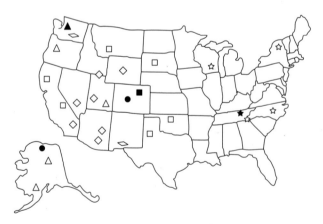

Figure 2.1.   IBP Biome field sites, USA (modified from U.S. National Committee, 1971). Solid symbols show headquarters sites.

Rico. Hubbard Brook, in New Hampshire, joined later, in the middle of the LTER development. Short histories of the Biome studies are covered in Blair (1977). Next I consider the ontogeny and function of the Biome programs in more detail. Because of my personal involvement in the Grassland Biome, its account is somewhat more detailed.

THE U.S. IBP GRASSLANDS BIOME PROGRAM

Brief History of George M. Van Dyne

This was truly an example of preparation meeting opportunity, because the principal investigator, Dr. George M. Van Dyne, was primed and ready for this large program. Van Dyne's life encompassed the transition from the old frontier to the current era of concerns about global biology and global change.

George Van Dyne grew up on a ranch south of Trinidad, Colorado, almost on the New Mexican border. George, an accomplished horseman who worked on the ranch as a hand, was enamored about all aspects of the West. George earned his B.S. degree in animal science at CSU and his master's in range science at South Dakota State University under James K. (Tex) Lewis, undertaking a total system study of rangeland ecology. Van Dyne then received his Ph.D. degree from the University of California at Davis, working with Dr. Harold Heady developing mathematical models of rangeland systems.

Looking carefully for somewhere to launch his career, George settled on Oak Ridge National Laboratory (ORNL), Tennessee, where Stan Auerbach led the Environmental Sciences Division. Jerry Olson and Bernard Patten had already formed a systems ecology group there. George joined them in 1963, and the three of them taught the first systems ecology course in the United States at the University of Tennessee in Knoxville. At that time, Oak Ridge was one of the few places in the world that had computers capable of solving the complex differential equation and matrix models being formulated by George and his two colleagues. They were the first to use both analog and digital computers to model natural systems (Bocking, 1997).

Because the three scientists worked full-time at Oak Ridge, they drove to Knoxville in a van on Saturdays, taking turns offering one-hour lectures presenting diverse ideas and methods for studying ecological systems. Van Dyne, being junior and serving in a "clean-up" role, would follow Drs. Patten and Olson during the noon hour, writing on the chalkboard with his right hand, eating a sandwich with the left, and talking in his soft, intense baritone voice about many exciting developments in ecosystem modeling (D. A. Crossley Jr., pers. comm.). Students who took the course were unanimous in their praise of the creativity and the dedication of these young instructors.

Suggesting to a delighted Stan Auerbach that the output of two scientific papers per person per month be considered the norm for full-time scientists in a research group, George proceeded to write up to four papers per month in the eighteen months he spent at Oak Ridge, drawing upon many data sets he had accumulated throughout his master's and Ph.D. research. Many of his more than 120 refereed scientific publications were written during his Oak Ridge days. George worked on a research project on a grassland area at Oak Ridge National Laboratory with Dac Crossley. George urged that, as they started the project, they should list the publications they anticipated from it. Auerbach commented to Crossley: "I like the way this man thinks!"

George Van Dyne's grasp of ecosystem science led him to edit a book entitled *The Ecosystem Concept in Natural Resource Management* (Van Dyne, 1969). The book contained chapters by various authors, all colleagues of George—namely, Herb Bormann, Chuck Cooper, Gene Likens, Jack Major, Stephen Spurr, and Fred Wagner—who led advances in ecosystem ecology.

Drs. Olson, Patten, and Van Dyne were instrumental in developing the concept of systems ecology, a quantitative approach for studying and integrating entire ecosystems together with their biotic and abiotic components. Patten went on to a distinguished career at the University of Georgia, where he developed new theories on modeling ecosystem self-organization, nutrient cycling, and energy transformation (Patten, 1971–1976). Olson remained at Oak Ridge and became widely recognized for his pioneering work on global carbon dynamics. His paper on the energy balance of producers and decomposers in ecosystems (Olson, 1963) had over 200 literature citations by 1985 (Kwa, 1989) and by May 2009 had more than 1,020 citations in the Science Citation Index (SCI).

Chronology of the U.S. IBP Grassland Biome Program

Van Dyne moved to Colorado State University in fall 1967, establishing the Natural Resource Ecology Laboratory (NREL) as his vehicle to pursue the Grassland Biome studies. He began with a secretary and two graduate students (L. J. "Sam" Bledsoe and R. Gerald Wright), along with an initial seed grant from the Ford Foundation until funds from the NSF Ecosystem Studies office began arriving. Van Dyne followed the initial plans agreed to in the 1966 action plan on how to set up a Biome program, although other Biomes were more decentralized. He established a central headquarters at the NREL and an intensive study site (the Pawnee Site) near Nunn, Colorado, located on the shortgrass steppe northeast of Fort Collins on the Central Plains Experimental Range, a USDA research station administered by the Agricultural Research Service.

Here are a couple of instances of Van Dyne's fabled chutzpah. At one point, he proposed to a CSU vice president that he needed to acquire a building off campus to provide several thousand more square feet of floor space. When the vice president insisted that only a dean could make such a decision, George immediately shot back, "So, make me a dean!" George was eager to promote social interactions in the Biome group whenever possible. This included having picnics out at his ranch west of town north of Horsetooth Reservoir. Nearly 100 people, including families, with small children in tow (we were a young group, as were most of the Biome participants) would show up with picnic lunches, with George and senior staff providing kegs of beer. There was usually a baseball game in the afternoon—and yes, George invariably played the role of pitcher.

Within two years, George had a burgeoning program in place. He brought Don Jameson into the program as assistant director over research at the Pawnee Site and hired a Pawnee site manager. Numerous graduate students worked on a diverse and extensive series of studies designed to understand and parameterize various grassland ecosystem processes. These included such subjects as feeding and assimilation studies of animals ranging in size from arthropods to bison, effects of grazing on both aboveground and belowground productivity, and plant–water–nutrient relationships of species, communities, and ecosystems.

A series of extensive or satellite study sites were established from the Osage tall-grass prairie in Oklahoma in the east (led by Paul Risser of the University of Oklahoma, who would become a noted ecosystem scientist), to the annual grassland in California in the Sierra foothills east of Fresno (Figure 2.1). In all, over one dozen network sites, supervised by Dr. Norman French, were in operation, and generating data, by 1969.

All data, including those from the outlying network sites, were sent to the NREL for archiving and analysis. The Biome's statistical design was to collect field data sufficient to estimate population means within 20 percent, and with 80 percent reliability. Another protocol required all sites to use the same plot size for estimating plant biomass. The NREL provided each site with screening statistics of submitted data, including the sample size necessary to achieve the abovementioned sampling adequacy. Dictating Biome-wide procedures was a feature of all the Biome programs.

Dr. George Innis, a mathematical modeler, joined the Grassland Biome in 1970 and assembled a cadre of postdoctoral fellows from a variety of disciplines. These scientists included Jerry Anway, Chuck Rodell, William Parton, William Hunt, and Robert Woodmansee.

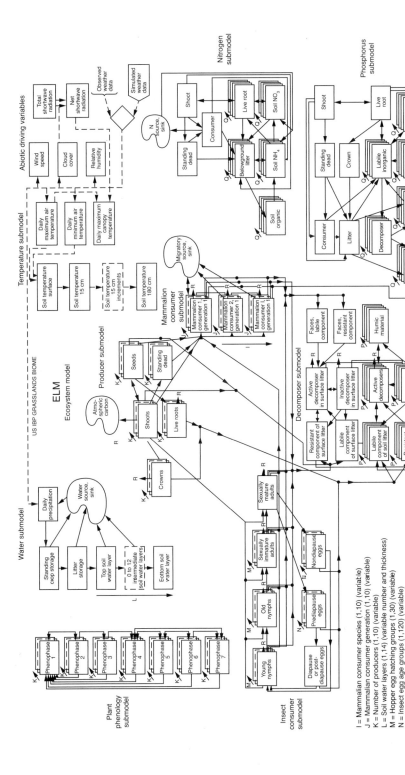

Figure 2.2. Schematic diagram of the ELM 1973 model, US/IBP Grassland Biome (redrawn from Innis et al., 1980; used with permission from Cambridge University Press).

I = Mammalian consumer species (1,10) (variable)
J = Mammalian consumer generation (1,10) (variable)
K = Number of producers (1,10) (variable)
L = Soil water layers (1,14) (variable number and thickness)
M = Hopper egg hatching groups (1,30) (variable)
N = Insect egg age groups (1,120) (variable)
P = Decomposer belowground layers
Q = Nutrient (N and P) belowground layers
R = Respiration flows

The Grassland Biome's "crown jewel" was the development of a total system model, called ELM (Figure 2.2), an abbreviation for "Intermediate Level Model" (Innis, 1978; Innis et al., 1980). It received this appellation to differentiate it from other models that were higher-resolution (L. J. "Sam" Bledsoe's) or linear (B. C. Patten's) (G. S. Innis, pers. comm.).

The questions addressed by ELM included

1. What is the effect on net or gross primary production as the result of the following perturbations:
   (a) Variations in the level and type of herbivory?
   (b) Variations in temperature and precipitation or applied water?
   (c) The addition of nitrogen or phosphorus?
2. How is the carrying capacity of a grassland affected by these perturbations?
3. Are the results of an appropriately driven model run consistent with field data taken in the Grassland Biome Program, and if not, why?
4. What are the changes in the composition of the producers as a result of these perturbations? (G. S. Innis, cited in Kwa, 1989)

This approach focused on the impact of abiotic factors, which were considered paramount in controlling the model, which had a series of "state variables" (or variables internal to the system, such as herbivorous insects or stable organic phosphorus) vs. "driving variables" (such as rainfall or incident photosynthetically-active radiation) (Innis, 1978).

It took George Innis and many postdoctoral fellows and research associates working long hours to produce a very detailed model that had 4,400 lines of code, 180 state variables, and 500 parameters. It required roughly seven minutes to compile and run a two-year simulation with a two-day time step on a CDC 6400 mainframe computer. Roughly twenty man-years of effort went directly into its development and reporting. Today all of this could run easily on a laptop computer.

Viewed from the more process-oriented perspective of three decades later, structure of the ELM model was probably overly elaborate, including ecosystem components that might have been omitted. Further, its stated objectives were somewhat vague; perhaps its real objective was to prove that it could be built. In other words, Van Dyne and Innis wanted to demonstrate that ecologists knew enough about grassland processes, mathematics, and systems analysis that a mathematical construct that acted like a grassland system could be developed. In their view, such a construct could be used to examine grassland dynamics in place of, or as a complement to, field experimentation. Indeed, "[the] goals of the modeling effort were to create a model that would serve as a communications device and organizer of information, be useful as a research tool, and yield results that could help in elucidating biological phenomena in grassland ecosystems" (Woodmansee, 1978a). The issue of the feasibility of developing such a model was very much an open question at that time (Golley, 1993). The model was not terribly robust in predicting multi-year changes in organic matter, but reached a level of being within 20 percent of the mean 80 percent of the time for trends in aboveground biomass and soil respiration rates, and so was a success for its time.

Although it was an excellent conceptual tool, the ELM model itself was never much of a success in terms of being used to answer questions about grasslands, but it was a necessary precondition for the development of simulation modeling in ecology—hence in the wider view of the history of ecosystem ecology, it was quite successful. Much more useful simulation models quickly followed the development of ELM, and modeling was no longer considered to be aberrant behavior among ecologists. Most of the large-scale, long-term, multivariable questions now being addressed by those interested in the ecology of our planet would be largely unapproachable in the absence of the modeling capabilities developed and proven in the IBP.

My Introduction to, and Involvement in, the Grassland Biome Program

I first met IBP Grassland Biome researchers in September 1969, when Van Dyne and a group of his co-investigators and the Canadian IBP group at the University of Saskatchewan met at Saskatoon and at the

Grassland research site on the old Matador ranch in southwest Saskatchewan (details in Coupland et al., 1975). A few weeks earlier, I had invited myself to the meeting by inquiring of Van Dyne whether I could participate. I had met George once before at SREL a few years earlier. I had some new data on compartmental analysis of soil respiration at my old field site, and so proceeded to promote it as a way of publicizing our research at SREL in what I rather grandiosely termed an "Eastern Tallgrass Prairie."

Robert Coupland and several colleagues at the University of Saskatchewan hosted the synthesis meeting. Van Dyne chartered a DC-3 airplane to fly two dozen scientists from around the Grassland Biome network from Denver to Saskatoon to participate in the symposium. The ride up there was very rough, and the ashen-faced participants were uncharacteristically quiet the first day of the meeting. By the time we moved out to the Matador site, interests and volume of discussions had intensified, as had our collective thirst, which was slaked by many cases of good Canadian lager over the course of the three days of presentations and discussions. During these sessions, I met Francis E. Clark of the USDA Agricultural Research Laboratory in Fort Collins. I was to have fruitful interactions with him over the next several years.

The Matador site meeting of September 1969 led to a lifelong collaboration and interactions with Eldor Paul and Francis Clark. The latter proved his mettle in supporting my rather tentative early studies at SREL of the compartmentalization of total soil respiration into litter, soil, and root contributions, which I presented as a short paper to the assembled group at the Matador meeting. During question time, Eldor and George Van Dyne attacked some of my methods and inferences drawn from such a simple approach. Feeling quite nonplussed, I saw a large, shiny-headed man at the back of the room waving his hand to be recognized. This was Francis Clark, whom Eldor Paul termed "the dean of North American soil microbiologists." Francis suggested that there might be some merit in my approach, and urged the others not to be hasty in condemning the method. Judging from the deference shown him by both Eldor and George, I realized I had a strong ally in my corner. Later on, toward the end of that memorable meeting out on the black clay soils of the Matador site, I watched Eldor and Francis go out to a low hill on the site in the early morning, where they sat and discussed matters for a long time. I found out they were discussing what would become a landmark among synthesis papers, "The Microflora of Grassland" (Clark and Paul, 1970). This paper covered the principal ecosystem processes associated with grasslands, and was very influential on our future research in the Natural Resource Ecology Laboratory, particularly the modeling component.

In September 1970, Francis invited Victor Bartholomew, from North Carolina State University, and me to serve as his advisers on his studies out at the Pawnee site and to listen to the results of the annual meeting of the IBP Grassland Biome in November. Bartholomew was one of the pioneers in the use of stable isotopes of nitrogen to follow key nitrogen cycling processes. Another invitee at the meeting was Dr. Lech Ryszkowski, from the Polish Academy of Sciences, Poznan. This involvement of international participants was central to the IBP concept.

Francis invited me to work with him on measurements of soil respiration at the Pawnee site for six months in the spring and summer of 1971. I drove out to the Pawnee site with Francis, or rode in the big red Chevy suburban that made daily trips to the site. We set up a series of field experiments, with and without irrigation or rainfall, and determined the respiration rates of various strata in the nearly rock-hard soils out there. Francis thought big and purchased two-foot lengths of eight-inch diameter steel well casing to be pounded into the soil in numerous field plots. After he and I tried to drive the casing in with short lengths of steel rail, he observed that "we need someone with a weak mind and a strong back." I told Francis that I failed on both counts, and he hired a strong young undergraduate and got the job done in record time. This study on soil respiration in various layers was quite an education for me. I worked up a fancy analysis of variance of the hundreds of soil respiration measurements I had taken, with the help of our statistician, Marilyn

Campion. Francis said that was fine, but he wanted to see the raw data as well. I took over a stack of large thirty-column data forms, suitably labeled, but almost impossible to read through. He spent nearly twenty minutes scanning them all, made a few comments, and seemed relieved that all data were present and accounted for. The marked increases in soil respiration ($13 \times$ within 24 hr after a 2-cm rainfall at the end of four rain-free weeks) were impressive. Clark and I coauthored a Grasslands Biome Technical Report (number 169) that served us well in later synthesis activities in my years as a decomposer integrator, and proved useful in validating models of decomposition later on (Hunt, 1977).

Francis Clark was an inspiration to work with, because he had interests other than the immediate science that he pursued along with the ongoing research. After working for several hours in the hot sun, he would declare it was time to take a break and look for arrowheads. We charged across the Pawnee site on the winding dirt roads in his big government-gray USDA/ARS Rambler Ambassador, looking for suitable sites on nearby hilltops. He invited me to imagine the Pawnee braves making arrowheads using flints, and speculated on the large herds of bison that must have been there. We saw old buffalo wallows, and the thought experiment was most enjoyable.

The Role of "Integrators" in the Grassland Biome Program

By late 1971, it was apparent to both Van Dyne and the NSF that the program's rapid growth had reached a point at which no one person could provide all of the scientific direction and leadership required to make the Biome study a success. To coordinate the numerous ongoing data gathering and modeling activities, four more persons were hired to serve as "integrators" of the project. The initial persons hired were Freeman Smith (a new Ph.D. from Colorado State University, abiotic factors); John Marshall from the Division of Plant Industry, CSIRO, Australia (followed soon after by Jai Singh from Banaras Hindu University, Varanasi, India), primary producers; Jim Ellis, a new Ph.D. from

U.C. Davis, consumers; and myself on decomposers. I came from the Savannah River Ecology Laboratory, and was the last one hired, beginning in January 1972. The integrators' principal job was to advise researchers at network sites and encourage synthesis in the form of internal "gray literature" publications, called Technical Reports, and refereed journal and book articles. While several of the modeling postdocs stayed on with the NREL, only Jim Ellis of the original four integrators remained to lead the lab into major international research projects in the 1990s and beyond. Dr. Ellis's tragic death in an avalanche in March 2002 caused his many colleagues around the world to reflect upon his preeminent work on understanding interactions between natural processes and human societies (e.g., Coughenour et al., 1985; Ellis and Swift, 1988; Little et al. 1990). Jim's ability to conceptualize and synthesize large, complex systems was second to that of none, with the possible exception of George Van Dyne.

The roles that the four "integrators" in the Grassland Biome had were largely carved out by us in our efforts to synthesize the vast amounts of raw data that were being collected by researchers at the network of eight extensive field sites (Figure 2.1) The four integrators traveled to all of the sites at least once per year, and sometimes twice, usually by light plane. Much of our travel was during spring and summer, and we frequently had to dodge large thunderstorms over the Great Plains. On one trip with George Van Dyne and some of the data managers, we flew in two four-seater planes down to the Jornada site in Las Cruces, New Mexico. Upon our return two days later, we ran into a large thunderstorm and had to land at Las Vegas, New Mexico, and spend the night in an old railroad hotel, the Hotel El Fidel. Rooms were $4.95 for a double, and we got a good steak dinner for under $5.00. George Van Dyne found a pool hall next door and took on all comers, playing yet another competitive role as visiting "pool shark," defeating most of the local talent.

Looking back on those few and hectic years, I often wonder if I really earned my keep as an "Integrator." Much of the data were being gathered by researchers and graduate students under the watchful eyes of

Dr. Norm French, manager of the extensive site network. About all we could do was to insist on (encourage) standard methods for measuring state variables—e.g., peak standing crop biomass—and process variables, such as leaf litter decomposition, soil respiration, and hope for the best in terms of data quality and quantity. It was an early foray into the field now known as Quality Assurance/Quality Control (QA/QC). The site visits and the annual science review meeting held in mid-autumn in Fort Collins were the major ways we had of trying to track what was being done at the extensive sites.

The role of the integrators was never widely heralded by fellow scientists, and the duration of our role in the Grassland Biome program was very short, only three years or so, so our ultimate impact is not particularly noteworthy when viewed through the prism of thirty years' reflection on our activities.

The Grassland Biome years were short and intense, lasting from late 1967 until 1974, one year after George Van Dyne stepped down as NREL director. They were characterized by many planning meetings and extensive travel; in essence, an experiment in "top-down" Big Ecology. The travel included numerous site visits by those in leadership positions, and trips to Fort Collins and other central locations for synthesis activities by participating scientists. This interaction and synthesis were, perhaps, the Biome program's strongest contribution to science. Under the leadership of George Van Dyne and other pioneers in systems ecology, the IBP provided the first broad forum in history to integrate the various disciplines in ecology, soil science, climatology, and so forth into a comprehensive representation of grassland ecosystems. Synthesis and collaboration extended to numerous international meetings and symposia.

International Travel Experience in the IBP Grassland Biome

One of the more memorable international trips I ever made for the Grassland Biome was to an International Tropical Grassland ecology conference in mid-January 1974 at Banaras Hindu University, Varanasi,

India. As with most international IBP meetings, airfares of U.S. IBP Biome participants were paid by State Department "counterpart funding" from Public Law 480, established at the end of World War II. Our tickets were purchased by the Indian government and issued by Pan American Airlines for travel along any route we could justify scientifically. In early January 1974, I flew westward from Denver via San Francisco, Tokyo, and onward with stops in Hong Kong and Bangkok, arriving in New Delhi at four in the morning. I had seen crowding and masses of people on dusty streets in northern Mexico, but nothing like the scenes of northern India. We flew from New Delhi to Lucknow, and then rode a train for most of the afternoon to the eastward, arriving in Varanasi in early evening. The meetings ran for five days, with time for cultural interactions, including classic Indian dancing and a field trip out onto the Deccan plateau. In one of the dance exhibitions, a group of beautiful sari-clad women danced a line dance to the music of sitars and wind instruments. George Van Dyne got up from the audience and began dancing with the women. The Indian men, after looking scandalized, proceeded to join the dance so as not to lose face. George once again was testing the limits of social interactions, and thoroughly enjoyed the episode.

After the meetings, Jai Singh, Freeman Smith and I rode a train from Tundla Junction to Agra. After seeing the famous Taj Mahal, we chartered a cab from Agra and rode 200 miles, over more than six hours, from Agra to New Delhi.

The remainder of the trip was a study in contrasts, as I flew via Air India from Bombay, with a fueling stop at Kuwait City (gas flares eerie in the night sky), and onward via Rome to a two days' stopover in Paris, where I met with several coauthors of the decomposition synthesis article discussed below, under the heading "International Syntheses and Experiences" (Coleman and Sasson, 1980). From there, I flew to Stockholm, where Thomas Rosswall, a good friend from earlier Grassland–Tundra synthesis meetings in Fort Collins, met and drove me to Uppsala, where I presented a seminar on our recent work at Fort Collins. The marked contrast between the heat and vegetarian cuisine of India and the steak tartare served up by the inimitable microbial ecologist Marianne Clarholm was one of the major memories of that whirlwind three-week trip. Many colleagues from other U.S. IBP Biomes traveled extensively in the early 1970s, including David Reichle and Jerry Olson from the Eastern Deciduous Forest Biome, Jerry Franklin, and Dick Waring, especially to Japan (J. F. Franklin, pers. comm.). The Desert Biome had numerous contacts with colleagues in North African Countries and Israel (Frederic Wagner, pers. comm.). Perhaps the greatest international travelling personnel were researchers in the Tundra Biome, with numerous trips made to Scandinavian countries and Russia by several senior investigators (Steven MacLean, pers. comm.).

The "Winding Down" Process of the IBP Grasslands Biome Program

By spring of 1974, there was "no joy in Mudville"; the IBP Grasslands Biome renewal proposal had been declined by the National Science Foundation. We were instructed to go into a wind-down phase, with continuing funding for two more years at the most. George Van Dyne responded to this by calling a meeting of all the Grassland Biome personnel in the Pacific Northwest Forest and Range Experiment Station. He presented a pessimistic talk entitled "Save Six for Pall-Bearers." This got our attention in a hurry. With a staff of nearly fifty, that would be a Herculean cut, indeed. George's approach was to press onward at all costs, and if the NSF wanted streamlining, he would, by God, give them streamlining. He proceeded to outline what he called a "mini-Biome" that would include representatives of the major processes plus one or two data managers.

How did the Grassland Biome program come to such a sorry pass, and was this reaction justified, or even necessary? We of the junior scientific staff had been working on a renewal proposal during George's absence on sabbatical in the fall of 1972 and spring of 1973 at the Grasslands Research Institute at Hurley and the University of Reading in England. His sabbatical ended with a whirlwind tour of nearly a dozen research institutes in Central Europe in early to midsummer. Upon his return, George took exception to several new initiatives we had come up with in the renewal proposal. After meeting with a couple of key senior scientists, he offered a co-PI role to one of them, Mel Dyer (who turned the offer down). Over the next several weeks Van Dyne substantially rewrote the proposal, working long days and nights to get it submitted by the early January 1974 deadline. The NSF Ecosystem Office rejected it, thus triggering the meeting of scientists and staff noted above.

This was the real moment of truth for the dedicated group of Ph.D. scientists in the NREL Grasslands Biome group. Our understanding had been that it was within our job description to facilitate the evolution of the Grasslands Biome program along the lines that we had seen developing in the few short years of its existence. This included a greater emphasis on belowground processes, due to results of studies such as those of Singh and Coleman (1974), Coleman (1976), Clark (1977), and Marshall (1977), which demonstrated a preponderance of carbon being shunted belowground, and much of the energetics and nutrient cycling occurring there as well, carried out by microbes and the fauna grazing upon them (Coleman et al., 1976).

Perhaps we would have benefited from the assistance of a group facilitation counselor in resolving scientific differences at the critical juncture. That process was suggested in the early phases of the LTER program in the early 1980s, and was used by several NREL scientists in post-Grassland Biome research projects, most notably the SO_2 effects on grasslands project of Jerry Dodd and Bill Lauenroth (Dodd et al., 1982; Lavenroth and Preston, 1984; Leetham et al., 1982), the Nitrogen Cycling in grazing lands study of Robert Woodmansee and others, plant-animal interactions study (Dyer and Bokhari, 1976), the Great Plains Project of Vernon Cole and others, and the Belowground Project of Coleman and others (Elliot et al., 1979, 1980). All these projects were active in the late 1970s and early 1980s. The facilitator was Dr. Jack Hautaluoma, an industrial psychologist in the psychology department at Colorado State University. I use the qualifier "perhaps" for this consultation, because the primary requirement for the facilitation process to be carried out successfully is that all of the participants must sign on to the process and be willing to work through any problems encountered. For more insights into some of the problems encountered by interdisciplinary research groups, see Hautaluoma and Woodmansee (1994).

Working with George Van Dyne was always a challenge, because he would encourage people in a meeting to offer conflicting ideas and judgments, usually offered up with considerable heat (which often amused him). The follow-up was solely in George's hands, so that aspect of the conflict resolution was not often to the liking of the junior scientific staff. This "strong-leader approach" is another example of what seemed to us an inordinate emphasis on top-down control of the program. This decision making process is all the more surprising in retrospect, because George was very generous with his time, and would make time available to talk with us, one on one, about any scientific problems, including statistical analysis of data. Some of George Van Dyne's top-down approach was also observed and commented upon by senior scientists who interacted with him in the early 1970s (e.g., Mooney, 1999).

The bottom line was that none of the junior scientists were willing to sign on to the "mini-Biome" idea of Van Dyne, so we proceeded to work on a series of research projects that were logical offshoots of the IBP Grassland Biome program.

The Grassland Biome Program contained the germs of its renaissance in the postdoctoral researchers who were brought in by Dr. George Innis to work on the ELM model. Several of these postdocs, including William Parton, William Hunt, and Robert Woodmansee, remained at CSU and established distinguished careers as senior scientists in the NREL. They continued to participate in large international programs in East Africa, Asia, South America, and Antarctica. Dr. Woodmansee served as the third Director of NREL between 1984 and 1992. The NREL continues as a very productive research laboratory with as many as sixteen senior staff, including four to six postdoctoral fellows at any particular time.

THE U.S. IBP CONIFEROUS FOREST BIOME PROGRAM

Early History of the CFB

The Coniferous Forest Biome (CFB) was funded initially in 1970 by the NSF and grew out of two strong groups of researchers in the School of Forestry at the University of Washington, Seattle, and in the Forest Sciences Laboratory of the U.S. Forest Service and Forest Sciences Department at Oregon State University, Corvallis. The CFB operated with Professor Stan Gessel as principal investigator, and Jerry Franklin as co-PI. Dale Cole served as site manager for the A. E. Thompson and Findley Lake sites southeast of Seattle, and Richard Waring as site lead PI at the H. J. Andrews site at Blue River, east of Corvallis (Edmonds, 1982).

The major overall goals of the CFB program were "development of ecosystem theory and definition of the structure, function, and behavior of natural and manipulated coniferous forest and associated aquatic (stream and lake) ecosystems" (Edmonds, 1974). After initial studies on structure and function, the group focused later on ecosystem behaviors when stressed or manipulated (Edmonds, 1974).

The two groups in Oregon and Washington had a friendly and spirited rivalry, and held quarterly and annual research review meetings. The Seattle group concentrated on senior scientists and graduate students conducting research at the forest and lake sites. Dale Cole had some very productive research students, including Dale Johnson and Helga van Miegroet. Bob Edmonds' students included Daniel Vogt, Ph.D.; Gregory Antos, M.S.; Stephen Piper, M.S.; Willis Littke, Ph.D.; Heather Erickson, M.S.; and Kristina Vogt, postdoctoral.

The Operational Setup at Corvallis

In contrast, Drs. Franklin and Waring began with a few senior professors and graduate students, and found that the amount and quality of research being done was not up to their expectations. By late 1972, they allowed contracts with several senior investigators to lapse, and proceeded to hire several postdoctoral fellows, with consequent increased research productivity. The decision to use a group of postdoctorals is interesting, and somewhat different from how several of the other Biomes operated. The postdocs included Kermit Cromack, Phil Sollins, Fred Swanson, and, later on, some of the freshwater scientists, including Jim Sedell and Stan Gregory. In the mid-1970s Andy Moldenke signed on to work with John Lattin on soil arthropods as well. Fred Swanson got his Ph.D. in geomorphology at U. of Oregon, and met Franklin and Waring and was captivated by the prospect of working with an interdisciplinary team that included close coordination with the USDA Forest Service.

The development and evolution of working groups and studies is exemplary with this group, perhaps one of the better known ones being the development of the tree canopy processes group with Bill Dennison (OSU) and George Carroll (UO) and colleagues working on the abundance and activities of cyanobacteria and lichens in the canopies of old-growth Douglas Fir. This carried on into the 1990s with the establishment of the Wind River Crane Facility in southern Washington by Jerry Franklin and others. This facility is now the focal point for efforts in the coniferous ecosystem studies within the NEON network.

Some of the graduate students produced by the Coniferous Forest Biome researchers have gone on to considerable fame in productive scientific careers. Several students of Waring's may be noted: Henry Gholz worked on a transect of sites from the lowland Cascades up to the summit and on to the east side, in the Ponderosa pine ecosystems. Gholz, now at NSF, directs the LTER Program and works with the current Ecosystem Studies Program. Steve Running got his master's in process modeling and is now in the forefront of large-scale climate change modeling studies, leading a large group at the University of Montana. He was in the group of scientists in the Intergovernmental Panel on Climate Change (IPCC) that received a Nobel Prize in 2006. Pamela Matson worked on tree physiology with Waring, and went on to a successful career in ecosystem studies and administration at Stanford

University. Barbara Bond, current lead PI on the Andrews LTER, worked on ecosystem gas fluxes, and has an extensive program at the Andrews now.

Art McKee, the Andrews site coordinator, mentioned having very positive interactions with the NSF permanent staff and temporary science officers (rotators). Virtually all of them were able and willing to discuss ways to facilitate getting research done at the Andrews. He singled Mary Clutter out as someone who always liked to discuss what he was up to, and to get some of his ideas about developing trends in the LTER area. John Brooks was always ready to assist—as, of course, was Tom Callahan also. It was apparent that John Brooks functioned as Tom's mentor and protector, a protection lost later, after John's retirement. Perhaps some of Tom's past actions and attitudes caught up with him on into the early 1990s. Bruce Hayden, who was his supervisor in the late 1990s, observed Tom cutting across lines of command quite frequently. This enabled Tom to make many fruitful contacts with personnel in other directorates, but led to some friction with Assistant Director Mary Clutter (B. P. Hayden, pers. comm.).

Scientific Review Meetings in the CFB

Meetings in the CFB were frequent, usually quarterly, to discuss various ideas and hot topics going on. Several scientists at Corvallis mentioned the excitement and sheer hard work engendered during several group efforts in the field ("pulses") that Jerry Franklin had organized over the years. One of the most arduous was a trip into the Hoh River area of the Olympic National Park, camping out in the continuously pouring rain. The main organizational meetings were held yearly, and much of the conflict over who would be allocated funding or apply for new funding came out then. It would be interesting to know how the main decision making was done, between the two active groups in Seattle and Corvallis. By all accounts of alumni of these meetings, the scientific give-and-take was quite exhilarating.

Without exception, the IBP participants from the Conifer Biome days viewed their experiences as transformative. Jerry Franklin commented on the succession of "epiphanies" that the group had as they began to appreciate the multifaceted nature of their large and complex ecosystem. This transformation became more pronounced as they pressed forward with studies of old growth forest that had been ignored as "overmature and decadent" in previous decades of forest service research. Dick Waring noted that they had science review meetings at least monthly, and at times weekly. He deliberately held back about 5 percent of the total funding allocation for the year and used it to help encourage researchers who went above and beyond their immediate research responsibilities. One example was the group that came to be known as the "stream team" (e.g., Jim Sedell, Ken Cummins, Robin Vannote, and Stan Gregory). They gave impressive presentations and frequently qualified for supplemental funding to carry out some of their trailblazing work on the stream continuum and other process-based studies. The results of this several years of research were summarized in Triska et al. (1982), noting the transformative nature of heterotrophic interactions in streams, with microbes, collectors, predators, shredders, and grazers playing key roles in immobilizing and releasing organic substrates along the river network, the "river continuum concept," ranging from first- to eighth-order streams.

Scientific Contributions of the CFB

The level of synthesis of existing knowledge in this group was impressively high, as shown by several review papers in the book edited by Edmonds (1982). In a major synthesis paper, Johnson et al. (1982) noted the differences in cation leaching processes in forests, with tropical and lowland temperate ecosystems being dominated by carbonic acid and bicarbonates and organic acids dominating in subalpine and more northerly sites, primarily as a function of soil solution pH levels of <4.5 in the latter. They then commented on the large gaps in knowledge of

nitrogen cycling; in the areas of nitrogen fixation, nitrification and denitrification deserve further study. They noted further that much work is
needed in the area of weathering release of cations, and relations
between acid rain, soil sulfur status, and stand sulfur deficiencies. All of
these areas have been important in follow-up studies sponsored by the
U.S. EPA, NOAA, and other agencies. Some of these concerns were
foreshadowed in a classic synthesis paper by Sollins et al. (1980), who
noted that anionic balances in entire watersheds were of great concern,
and only beginning to be studied at the time of the IBP. Cationic balances of key mineral elements, e.g., calcium, were studied vigorously in
the IBP forest Biomes. One of the early cross-Biome synthesis papers
noted the significant accumulations of Ca oxalate in ectomycorrhizal
fungal mats at both the Andrews and Coweeta IBP sites (Cromack et al.,
1979). This work continued into the LTER period, with enhanced
populations of collembolans, mites, nematodes, amoebae, and ciliates
measured in the fungal mats as compared to fungal-free areas of soils
nearby (Cromack et al., 1988).

As noted earlier, the pioneering studies of Bill Dennison (OSU) and
George Carroll (UO) and colleagues on the abundance and activities of
cyanobacteria and lichens in the canopies of old growth Douglas fir
totally changed our views of the contributions of canopy biota to overall
ecosystem nitrogen fluxes. Additional concerns about nitrogen saturation of forested landscapes have arisen during the LTER program, and
will be commented on later on in this book.

Physical transfer of organic and inorganic components in an ecosystem is a key factor in studying nutrient cycling in ecosystems. By focusing on key processes, such as solution transfer, litterfall, surface erosion,
debris avalanche, creep, root throw, slumping, and earthflow within
watersheds and entire river basins, Swanson et al. (1982) helped to bring
a longer-term landscape level of analysis to the CFB and ultimately
influenced several research sites within the LTER network in later years.
For many of the western forests, clearcutting and road construction
have replaced wildfire as major disturbances of these landscapes. Insights

from the studies of Swanson and others have also been key components of successful postperturbation studies of infrequent perturbations such as volcanic eruptions—e.g., at Mount St. Helens in 1980. The follow-up studies at Mt. St. Helens were ably led by Fred Swanson, who was essentially "preadapted" to leading an interdisciplinary team from his experiences with the Andrews IBP study in the 1970s (J. F. Franklin, pers. comm.).

THE U.S. IBP EASTERN DECIDUOUS FOREST BIOME PROGRAM

Early History of the EDFB

The Eastern Deciduous Forest Biome (EDFB) Program began soon after the establishment of the Grassland Biome Program, and operated from 1969 to 1975. Stanley I. Auerbach was director, and Robert L. Burgess deputy director. Management and modeling of other sites' data was at Oak Ridge National Laboratory, with additional sites at Coweeta Hydrologic Laboratory in North Carolina; Duke Forest at Durham, North Carolina; Lake Wingra in Wisconsin; and Lake George in New York (see Figure 2.1). The mix of sites encouraged extensive studies of both aquatic and terrestrial ecology. The history of how the Cesium forest and Walker Branch watershed got added after the other sites in the EDFB network is fascinating. David Reichle (pers. comm.) notes:

> I wanted to take our Oak Ridge research team (including technicians) to Coweeta to learn what they were doing on watershed research. Stanley (Auerbach) wouldn't pay for that much travel—so we went on our own and camped at a nearby campground with Auerbach paying the gas for vehicles only. I believe that it was that visit where DAC "grunted" earthworms up (from the soil) for me and I lost that bet. ORNL became the principal site in the Biome for ecosystem nutrient cycle and carbon balance (energetics), but Coweeta was the lead for watershed scale hydrologic and nutrient processes.

By June 1976, a total of 262 research papers had appeared in the open literature, with one synthesis volume also completed (Blair, 1977).

Principal Scientific Contributions of the EDFB

The major contributions of the EDFB were energetics and nutrient-cycling studies focusing on a watershed level of resolution. There were several findings that were new to science. In addition to book-length syntheses of EDFB results (Reichle, 1981), numerous international meetings and colloquia brought together research results on productivity of forest ecosystems worldwide (e.g., Duvigneaud, 1971; Franklin et al., 1975). These studies compared results of primary and secondary production and decomposition processes and employed numerous process-level models to address the key limiting factors (e.g., Witkamp, 1961; Witkamp, 1971a,b). Thus Witkamp measured changes in dry matter losses from litter in the presence and absence of macroarthropods such as millipedes, and noted that transient losses of mineral nutrients, such as cesium and potassium, are readily absorbed by growing microbial populations. The system buffers well even with transient inputs of carbon and nutrients from simulated insect defoliation events. Following up on this, Reichle (1971) stated that energy is seldom a limiting factor in the food chain dynamics of terrestrial ecosystems. He noted the strong predilection of forest floor invertebrates for substrates with higher-quality (i.e., greater N content), which then cascades through the food chain. Reichle listed pioneering attempts to measure key measures of ecological efficiency, including the trophic level assimilation efficiency (assimilation at level n/ingestion at n), which ranges from 0.10 to 0.20 for saprovores, from 0.36 to 0.78 for herbivores, and from 0.47 to 0.92 for predators. He also noted a marked lack of knowledge concerning ecological efficiency (ingestion at n/ingestion at $n - 1$), which is important in whole-system energetics studies. This gap in knowledge was addressed in later publications from the IBP, notably the papers presented in Petersen and Luxton (1982). For a cross-Biome comparison of ecosystem energetics, see the heading below, "Inter-Biome Synthesis Results in the United States."

Early studies at the Coweeta site focused on cation budgets on four experimental watersheds with contrasting vegetations and land-use histories: a weed-to-forest succession, a hardwood coppice stand, an eastern white pine watershed, and an undisturbed hardwood forest control stand. Total cation outputs from the coppice were somewhat larger than those from the pine, but were considerably less for the hardwood stand. These results must be viewed in the context of the forests' being in an aggrading (net growth) phase that continued from the virtual cutover nature of the stands when they were turned over to the U.S. Forest Service in the early 1920s some fifty years earlier (Johnson and Swank, 1973) and that continues today (Coleman et al., 2002). Some interesting comparisons were made with two other watershed studies in the eastern United States: Hubbard Brook Experimental Forest in New Hampshire, and the Walker Branch watershed at Oak Ridge, Tennessee. All three sites are on similar igneous substrate, but precipitation quantities and types (snow comprising over half of the total precipitation at the more northern Hubbard Brook site) and the nature of the Oak Ridge substrate, dominated by karst topography, underlain by dolomitic limestone, led to much greater outputs of Calcium ions at that site (Ca^{++} outputs being 6.9, 10.6, and 100.0 kg ha^{-1} for Coweeta, Hubbard Brook, and Oak Ridge, respectively). All of this presaged the long-term studies of clearcutting and its effects on inorganic and organic nutrient losses to streams that were carried out subsequently in watersheds at both Coweeta and Hubbard Brook (Likens et al., 1977; Swank and Crossley, 1988; Swank et al., 2001; Wallace, 1988).

As a laboratory experimental variant on the above noted watershed studies, Van Voris et al. (1980) measured the outputs of calcium ions in leachates of replicate intact old field microcosms 15 cm dia. × 10 cm deep. They applied 1,350 μequivalents of cadmium chloride as a perturbation agent and followed a suite of biological variables (microbial, faunal, and plant species measurements) as well as system-level responses (carbon dioxide output, calcium outputs in leachates, extractable ATP as a measure of live microbial biomass). Within the ten-week posttreatment period, calcium concentration in the leachate returned toward the pre-treatment level in all microcosms. The response was biologically medi-ated, because the posttreatment CO_2 efflux was altered significantly. Van Voris et al. (1980) calculated power spectra for all microcosms showing differences in frequency richness (Figure 2.3). The perturbation integral (O'Neill, 1976) was used to measure the total area under the recovery curve for each of the ten replicates. By measuring the total area under the recovery curve, Van Voris et al. (1980) measured both the resistance and resilience (time necessary to return to a reference state) of these ecosystems. Assuming that these variables and their variations are indica-tors of ecosystem function, the authors argued that the results indicate that the complexity–stability hypothesis may hold for an intact system, even though the relationship has been difficult to demonstrate at the community level of organization. This study admittedly took a "black box" approach to study the system behavior, and definitive mechanisms cannot be specified. It does seem, however, that more extensive studies over wider ranges of environmental perturbations could provide some more definitive answers to further questions regarding relationships between complexity–stability in communities and ecosystems.

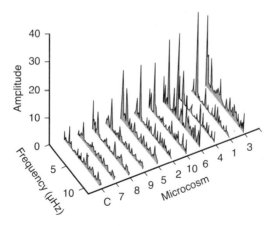

Figure 2.3. Power spectra for old-field microcosms, showing differences in frequency richness (Van Voris et al., 1980; used with permission of the Ecological Society of America).

Additional findings by the EDFB program included the very prominent role of roots in the total input and turnover of organic matter in the forest floor. Thus roots in a *Liriodendron* forest contain 60 percent of the belowground pools of N and K, and 50 percent of root contribution to annual element return to the soil occurred through root death and decay, with the remaining 50 percent returned by exudation, leaching, and root surface microbial activity (Cox et al., 1978). This contribution of roots, while large, is exceeded by root carbon and allocation patterns in a shortgrass prairie, in which over 70 percent of the total net primary production (NPP) goes belowground, and the turnover rates of roots are similarly large, with significant losses to herbivory by nematodes (Coleman et al., 1976; Smolik and Lewis, 1982).

Historical Perspective on the EDFB and the IBP

Dr. Orie Loucks, who was program coordinator for the Lake Wingra program and, later, in 1973, environmental management coordinator for the national program staff in Austin, Texas, provided a "birds' eye view" of developments in the IBP years. He noted that the U.S. IBP effort resulted in a paradigm shift from descriptive studies to analysis of ecosystem regulation and function. Adoption of this paradigm within the U.S. LTER, and also by programs in Sweden and South Africa, were noteworthy. Also, the Electric Power Research Institute (EPRI) used an ecosystem modeling approach toward its studies of impacts of acid rain on ecosystems.

Some comments by John Magnuson, one of the IBP investigators on the Lake Wingra project and a former program director at NSF, offer some important historical perspective. When comparing IBP with its successor LTER program, IBP seemed a very top-down organization. IBP was more disciplined, and narrower in scope. The overall goal of the Lake Wingra group with the EDFB was to develop the entire structure of lake bioenergetics and biogeochemistry of food webs. Scientists were not so much peer-reviewed in the fashion of the individual grants process of NSF as they were selected to help build the entire picture and fill in the boxes in a whole-system model (reminiscent of aspects of the U.S. IBP Grasslands

Biome). As with numerous other Biomes, interactions with scientists elsewhere in the program to build a lake model were not very informative. In contrast, Bob O'Neill from Oak Ridge headquarters office was an itinerant process and subsystem modeler, and was very constructive in developing these models. Both Magnuson and Jim Kitchell commented that these sorts of activities were "career-changing," when viewed in retrospect. A newly hired John Magnuson (in 1970) signed on to teach limnology and conduct research at Lake Wingra. John made an offer of a postdoctoral fellowship to a recently graduated Dr. Jim Kitchell and told him to "work on fishes." Kitchell proceeded to study aquatic food webs and recalls interacting with the modelers out of Oak Ridge, led by Dr. Bob O'Neill, who dropped in occasionally on the group at Madison. They worked intensively on modeling every possible flow in the lake food web (in a heavy cloud of O'Neill's cigarette smoke), and then went off to other sites for similar exercises. Jim wrote up coauthored model and experiment interaction studies in refereed journals within weeks of these intense meetings.

Role of the EDFB in Major Synthesis Efforts

The Deciduous Forest Biome programs built on a strong base of literature synthesis, encompassing the results of many research groups nationwide, as exemplified in Reichle (1970). This work had cross-fertilization effects from ongoing studies supported by the U.S. Atomic Energy Commission on global carbon cycles (Woodwell and Pecan, 1973). A case in point is the synthesis paper by Reichle et al. (1973), which noted the large amounts of carbon stored in standing crop biomass and soil organic matter that would be subject to marked changes due to changes in global climatic regimes. An interesting comparison was made between the net ecosystem production (NEP) (the summed autotrophic and heterotrophic production) rates of tulip poplar in Tennessee vs. pine forest stands at Brookhaven, Long Island, New York. Harris et al. (1975) noted a much greater turnover rate of aboveground and belowground net primary production (NPP) in the tulip poplar (particularly due to pulsed production of fine roots (<0.5 cm dia.) in winter and autumn months (Edwards and Harris, 1977). This difference was attributed largely to greater rates of root turnover, leading to a doubled heterotrophic respiration rate in the hardwood vs. the pine forest. They also commented on the inherently greater carbon uptake by young-growth vs. old-growth forests, suggesting that that would be a useful way to sequester additional amounts of atmospheric carbon dioxide. Interestingly, that controversy continues on into present times. The long-term effects of whole-tree vs. conventional harvesting on ecosystem nutrient budgets is a source of current concern as well (Rosenberg and Jacobson, 2004; McLaughlin and Phillips, 2006).

On the aquatic side, there were active research groups at Rensselaer Polytechnic Institute at Troy, New York, and the lake Wingra group operating at Madison, Wisconsin, as well as the nascent "stream team" at the Coweeta site in the LTER years, comprised of Judy Meyer and Bruce Wallace from Univ. GA and Fred Benfield and Jack Webster from Virginia Tech. Young staff members from universities (University of Georgia and Virginia Tech) and the USDA Forest Service were a hallmark of this effort as well. The group at Rensselaer was primarily engineers, and they proceeded to pursue research after the IBP in non-ecosystem studies aspects with other federal agencies.

THE U.S. IBP DESERT BIOME PROGRAM

Early History, Rationale, and Personnel Involved in the Study

The Desert Biome IBP was organized in 1968 and early 1969, with modeling efforts beginning in 1969 and field studies at validation sites starting in 1970. The Desert Biome program was originally established by Frederic Wagner and David Goodall, of Utah State University. Fred Wagner was responsible for bringing David Goodall to Utah State to organize the simulation modeling. The program was billed as a model based on energy flow, and that model would provide answers to the many pressing questions about arid ecosystems (overgrazing, desertification, expansion of undesirable shrubs, etc.). Supporting that work was a cadre of scientists who operated the validation sites where data were collected with which to validate the system model. Process studies examined what were thought to be key processes, such as photosynthesis, decomposition, and herbivory. The validation sites were various. At the Mojave Desert–Nevada Test Site, Dr. Fred Turner, from UCLA, was the site coordinator–PI. Other scientists at the test site included Drs. Robert Chew, Jim McBrayer, and Sam Bamberg, plus a large cohort of grad students and technicians. The Great Basin Validation Site was Curlew Valley in northern Utah with Dave Balph as coordinator, and Randy Shinn, R. D. Anderson, and Clayton Gist as PIs. The Sonoran Desert Site was the Tucson Basin, with John Thames as coordinator. The Chihuahuan Desert Site was the Jornada, with W. G. Whitford as coordinator and John Ludwig and Gary Cunningham as PIs (see Figure 2.1). Another rangeland validation site was established at Pine Valley in southern Utah, with Clive Jorgensen as coordinator, and staffed by professors and students from Brigham Young University. The Desert Biome program also had an aquatic component driven by an aquatic model. There were two validation sites: Deep Creek, with Wayne Minshall of Idaho State as coordinator, and Locomotive Springs in Curlew Valley, with J. Anne Holman of Utah State as coordinator.

Wagner hired Jim MacMahon to be the site research coordinator in 1971. Jim learned to fly and traveled in a light plane so that he could visit each research site at least once per month (James MacMahon, pers. comm.). In essence, Jim was the "integrator" of research at all four major research sites.

The Desert Biome's Role in Developing New Talent

Some of the successes of the program were the products of talented graduate students and visiting scientists. The "pulse–reserve" model for the responses of arid ecosystems to pulses of rainfall was developed by the collaborative efforts of grad student Mark Westoby (now at

Macquarie University in Sydney, Australia) and Emanuel Noy-Meir of Israel. The mega-ecosystem model never did come to fruition, perhaps because the investigators were more comfortable with process-level models (James MacMahon, pers. comm.).

As was true with the other Biome programs, the Desert Biome was an excellent place for scientists to get a start in long-term ecological research. Thus, Diana Freckman (now Wall) began her postdoctoral studies with Ron Mankau at UC Riverside in 1971. Diana Wall later served as director of NREL and helped with coordination of multiple LTER sites while working at the Antarctic Dry Valley site. Other young scientists getting their research underway included Phil Rundel, Art Volmer, and Sam Bamberg at Mojave. Cliff Crawford worked at Las Cruces, along with Whitford. In Whitford's words,

> The most valuable result of the IBP program was the support and education of graduate students who are now leading ecologists. Example from the Jornada IBP: Dr. James Reynolds, systems modeler Duke University[;] Dr. Stuart Pimm, conservation ecologist and fellow at Duke University[;] Dr. Stan Smith, Univ. of Nevada Las Vegas[,] most recently a PI on the desert FACE project[;] Dr. Thomas Bellows, Professor of Entomology, U Cal Riverside[;] Dr. Norman Dronen, parasite ecology, Texas A&M. These scientists are one legacy of the IBP program of immeasurable value.

An interesting example of the more vertical than horizontal administration of the later Biome programs is demonstrated by the following anecdote regarding a young Diana Freckman (later Wall). In 1974, working on a postdoctoral fellowship, Diana sampled nematodes in the Rock Valley, Nevada site, measuring nematode community energetics, including respiration. Unfortunately, further salary funding for Diana was in doubt, because this ecosystem energetic information on nematodes was not provided to the network office by Diana's supervisor, Dr. Mankau. Mankau apparently was more interested in providing species lists than nematode energetics. Diana phoned Fred Wagner to ask what was required to reinstate her salary. Once she gave the energetics data directly to him, he continued her funding. The energetics results were summarized in Desert Biome Technical Reports, and later in Freckman (1982b) and Freckman and Mankau (1986). This research pioneered the measurement of anhydrobiosis (an inactive, coiled, dehydrated nonmetabolic state) of nematodes in field studies, which enabled nematodes to continue under conditions of extreme dryness (<2.7% of dry mass), which occurs at numerous times in desert sites worldwide (Freckman and Mankau, 1986). By means of this complex physiological mechanism, nematodes in extreme environments are considered "K strategists" (Wallwork, 1982), avoiding the boom-and-bust strategies of "r strategists," and hence are able to participate in detrital food webs throughout most of the year.

Diana also worked with Philip Rundel and Arthur Gibson, who summarized deep root studies in Rock Valley (Rundel and Gibson, 1996). These studies demonstrated very deep penetration of nematodes and microarthropods, following roots growing into phreatic groundwater zones to ten- to twelve-meter depths in desert soils (Freckman and Virginia, 1989). For a wide-ranging summary of desert ecology, see Whitford (2002).

Scientific Contributions of the Desert Biome

Perhaps the principal contribution from the Desert Biome was the discovery of surprisingly large amounts of net primary production going to roots in several of the study sites. For example, in the cool semidesert of northern Utah, prominent shrub species—namely, *Atriplex confertifolia*, *Ceratoides lanata*, and *Artemisia tridentata* (sagebrush)—root productivity was three times greater than shoot production. For *Ceratoides*, the root and shoot productivities were 186 and 64 grams dry mass m^{-2}, respectively, and for *Atriplex*, the corresponding productivities were 443 and 154 grams dry mass m^{-2}, respectively (Caldwell and Camp, 1974). The turnover rates of the two pools of belowground and aboveground biomass were in a correspondingly similar ratio of approximately 3:1. Additional studies in warm deserts by Whitford et al. in the Chihuahuan desert and Freckman et al. in the Mojave desert showed considerable numbers of organisms and concomitant activities of root-associated insects and microarthropods. This research entailed use of well-drilling equipment to reach depths exceeding ten meters, especially when working with phreatophytic (deep water–seeking) shrubs (Diana H. Wall, pers. comm.; Freckman and Virginia, 1989).

On a landscape scale, several researchers followed the effects of water limitations on shrub distributions and abundance. When viewing a plant's position on a soil–plant–atmosphere continuum, rationales for the distributions of shallow and deep-rooted perennials and annuals in the landscape became more apparent (see review in MacMahon and Schimpf, 1981).

Some of the findings in nitrogen cycling were impressively prescient as well. Thus blue-green algae (now termed cyanobacteria) were found to be key contributors to nitrogen fixation in a wide range of deserts (Rychert et al., 1978). The major role of algal crusts in increasing soil fertility and reducing erosion and enhancing water filtration were also noted by Rychert et al. (1978), foreshadowing the more recent extensive research efforts led by Jayne Belnap and others (e.g., Belnap and Phillips, 2001) in similar high deserts in Utah and elsewhere in the region.

Some pioneering work was also carried out by researchers on fauna in cool and warm deserts and their interactions with plants (Whitford, 1988; summary in Whitford, 2000). Similar groundbreaking studies of soil nematodes and their effects on decomposition and detrital food webs in deserts were presented by Whitford et al. (1982) and Freckman (1982a).

Long-term Benefits of Collaboration

Walt Whitford made the following observations based on his experience as coordinator of the Chihuahuan Desert efforts:

> Personally, I benefited from a steep learning curve by interactions with established ecologists who had a great influence on my career. Dr. Robert Chew got me to focus on what animals "do" in ecosystems rather than how much energy passes through the consumer box. Chew described "ecosystem engineers" in the mid 70's without using

the engineer term. Dr. William Nutting, Univ. of Arizona, at an IBP meeting, convinced me that I should focus research on subterranean termites and that conviction has been validated by 20+ years of research and a number of papers. Dr. Floyd Werner, U. of Arizona, helped me develop studies of insects in order to fill in a gap in the expertise available at New Mexico State U. His mentoring has provided an interesting and valuable effort in my research career.

Whitford comments further:

> Another benefit of the IBP program was learning to work together toward a common goal. Our very small group of PI's got involved in every aspect of desert ecology and learned to work with organisms for which we had never had any formal training. We also learned that the heuristic value of models is in the generation of questions and identification of important gaps in our knowledge and not in the predictive power of the models.

As discussed below, this observation on the value of models is shared by many others who worked in various IBP programs.

THE U.S. IBP ARCTIC AND ALPINE BIOME

Organization and International Scope

The Arctic and Alpine IBP program included ten countries with twenty-four sites in a farflung network stretching from the USSR to Finland, Norway, Sweden, the UK, Ireland, Greenland, Canada, and the United States (Bliss et al., 1981). In the United States, the research focused on Point Barrow in Alaska, and at Niwot Ridge in the high Alpine of Colorado (see Figure 2.1). Dr. Jerry Brown was the principal investigator; funds went to fifteen different universities, but each investigator had his own grant.

Scientific Findings and Synthesis

The Tundra Biome had annual science review meetings, in which many ideas and results were exchanged. The U.S. Tundra Biome was more foresighted than some others, devoting a full summer of work in 1974 at Boulder, Colorado, to a synthesis of studies at the Barrow, Alaska, site (Brown et al., 1980). Internationally, synthesis efforts occurred even earlier, with a group of microbiology, decomposition, and invertebrate researchers meeting at Fairbanks, Alaska, in August 1973, producing an overview of decomposition and nutrient cycling in tundra (Holding et al., 1974). Some of the findings are particularly noteworthy. In a comparison of fungal hyphal density and mite density across eight circumpolar sites, a negative correlation was found between the two in seven out of eight sites. The causative effect was the heavy rate of feeding, particularly of Oribatid mites, on fungal hyphae in studies of Valerie Behan (Whittaker, 1974; Behan-Pelletier and Hill, 1983). Enchytraeids, which constitute from 35 to 92 percent of litter-comminuting invertebrates in bogs and Alaskan tundra soils (MacLean, 1974) accounted for several percent of the total heterotrophic respiration in these ecosystems. In one of the more eloquent cases for whole-system thinking, MacLean (1974) urged IBP scientists to go beyond the direct effects model of who contributes how much to total carbon dioxide efflux from decomposition, and instead to focus on the rate-limiting or rate-regulating factors in the ecosystem, such as indirect effects on nutrient mineralization by fungi and bacteria, and their possible effects on plant growth, the synthesis results of Whittaker (1974), noted above. These efforts were elicited, in part, by a foresighted synthesis by Amyan Macfadyen (1963b) of microbivorous faunal effects on soil decomposition processes, using pre-IBP soil micro- and mesofauna data across several Biomes. Macfadyen raised the question, and MacLean and Whittaker addressed it effectively in their papers. Other groups addressed the effects of soil micro- and mesofauna on decomposition and nutrient cycling in post-IBP studies (e.g., Vossbrinck et al., 1979; Clarholm, 1985).

One of the high points, scientifically and administratively in the program, as recalled by one of its senior investigators, was that money was often left over for further small studies (John Hobbie, pers. comm.).

Hobbie could hire postdoctorals such as Park Rublee to work on protist ecology (also Ralph Daley, as a graduate student). Tom Fenchel came to Hobbie's lab in 1975 and used Hobbie's acridine orange method to follow protozoa-ingesting bacteria (Fenchel, 1975). This research, in which the grazing impacts of protozoans on bacteria were demonstrated to have an impact far in excess of the biomass of the protozoan grazers, was summarized in Hobbie (1975) and Hobbie et al. (1980). Hobbie suggests that this was the first field demonstration of the "microbial loop" (Pomeroy, 1970, 1974; Azam et al., 1983). Interestingly, these ideas were foreshadowed nearly two decades earlier in terrestrial ecosystems by John Stout (1963), who suggested that the pool of soluble nutrients ensuing from microfauna grazing on microbes constitutes the main substrate of microbial proliferation, supports the "terrestrial plankton," and either directly or indirectly provides the principal source of nutrients for the vast majority of the soil biota (Coleman, 1994). These microbially mediated processes were foreseen as well by Amyan Macfadyen (1963a), whose comments on effects of nutrient turnover on ecosystems are presented at the beginning of this chapter.

At one point the tundra aquatic group had twenty-seven people working on more than twenty-four ponds in the Arctic. All investigators, many from different scientific backgrounds, worked on at least two ponds in common, as noted so beneficially in the example cited above, and then they could study other ones in addition, as time permitted.

One of the most important accomplishments of the terrestrial tundra Biome group was to show that N and P limitation and cycles were important in what had previously been talked about as a strongly "cold-dominated" system where soil-available nutrients had been largely ignored before 1970. Ideas about ecosystem function in extreme environments were undergoing considerable revision during the IBP and afterward. Thus Valentine et al. (2006) make it unquestionably clear that the N and P cycles limited the C cycle, not the reverse (Gus Shaver, pers. comm.).

Generation of New Talent in the Tundra Biome

F. Stuart "Terry" Chapin III and Gaius "Gus" Shaver were among the more noteworthy graduate students working on the IBP. Terry had separate funding to work on phosphorus relations of tundra and alpine plants on altitudinal gradients, with Hal Mooney; Shaver worked on primary production processes, including pioneering studies on root production of arctic plants with Dwight Billings (Shaver and Billings, 1975). Shaver and Billings showed that root production and turnover was a significant proportion of the total allocation of photosynthate, which had been unanticipated in this cold climatic region with much permafrost present. In essence, the dominant species at Barrow actually partition the soil environment and have distinctly different rooting strategies, reflecting a strong competition for soil resources that were limiting (e.g., N and P). By the end of the IBP, a number of scientists, including Drs. Chapin, Shaver, Walt Oechel, and their students had a much different idea of how nutrient limitations operated in tundras (Gus Shaver, pers. comm.).

The U.S. Alpine Site in the Colorado Rockies

The only U.S. alpine tundra site in the IBP program was at Niwot Ridge, Colorado, which had been established by Dr. John Marr in the Front Range Ecology project in 1950, with several environmental monitoring stations set up to quantify climatic and vegetational gradients associated with elevational change. The pioneering work of Marr (1961), and Niwot Ridge's inclusion as a participant in the IBP (e.g., Caldwell et al., 1974), led to further involvement in a DOE-funded snow modification study, and the National Oceanic and Atmospheric Administration's (NOAA) long-term air monitoring led to its inclusion as one of sixty-seven National Experimental Ecological Reserves (in 1977), putting it in line as an ideal site for the LTER program (Bowman, 2001). It was one of the original six founding members of the LTER, which began in 1980.

The alpine site was perhaps the most successful of the IBP sites in demonstrating the important role that alpine landscapes serve as "early warning detectors" of changes in air quality and as an indicator of global change.

POST-BIOME EVALUATIONS

An evaluation of the three senior Biome programs, the Eastern Deciduous Forest, Desert, and Grassland Biomes (Mitchell et al., 1976) was generally critical of the more centralized Biome approach, claiming that it was not cost-effective and that the scientific findings were not very significant. The patterns of net primary production and consumer and decomposition activity were deemed of little interest. With these reviewers having little sympathy for ecosystem science, perhaps that response should have been anticipated. As noted by replies from Biome administrators (Gibson & Blair, 1977; Auerbach et al., 1977), it was premature in its conclusions. Thus, a series of papers published on Grassland Biome studies one to two years after the aforementioned critique were widely cited by other researchers in ecosystem science (Cole et al., 1977; Hunt, 1977; Reuss and Innis, 1977; Woodmansee, 1978b). The lattermost paper has been cited more than 100 times (ISI Web of Science), more than any other in this series. Four synthesis volumes were produced in the late 1970s as well, with a volume on the ELM model (Innis, 1978) and the major findings of the U.S. IBP Grassland Biome study (French, 1979). International compendia on grassland ecology provided a worldwide synthesis of standing crop measurements (Coupland, 1979) and process measurements of production and decomposition (Breymeyer and Van Dyne, 1980). A similar flood of publications came out of the other Biome programs in the late 1970s onward (e.g., Edmonds, 1982; Evans and Thames, 1981; Reichle, 1981; Waring, 1980; West and Skujins, 1978).

The efficiency of the use of funds by the Biome programs must be considered in perspective. The summed U.S. IBP budgets (the

Grassland Biome's budget in 1972 and 1973 was about $2.1 million), easily doubled NSF's support of ecological science. When compared with budgets for large research groups in physics and astronomy, however, the total expenditures were quite small. Examples abound in industry, government, and the military that show the extreme difficulty of wisely expending funds under a rapidly expanding budget. This allocation process was complicated by the fact that in any really new undertaking, such as the IBP, there is a certain amount of experimentation with approaches, not all of which work. When viewed in retrospect, failed approaches seem wasteful, but they are an unavoidable outcome of searching for the successful ones. Indeed, Loucks (1986) observed that nearly one generation later, it was too soon to draw a definitive conclusion about the IBP. He noted that the dominant paradigm by which ecology was pursued in the 1980s, the era of growth of the LTER program, was much changed from that in the early 1960s, which had been characterized by one professor and one or two graduate students.

LEGACIES OF INTERNATIONAL PROGRAMS IN THE IBP

The Swedish IBP effort was very extensive in both the Tundra and Coniferous Forest Biomes. Interestingly, there was early expansion into post-IBP studies in Sweden, with the advent of SWECON. Andersson (2010) notes:

> In Sweden an integrated forest ecosystem project was started
> after the IBP programme in 1972 and continued until 1981—
> the SWECON project [Persson 1980] with focus on the
> Boreal coniferous forests. The project was built upon the
> experiences gained in national and international IBP-projects
> as well as the research tradition in the country. The results of
> the project have been discussed in a similar way as other Biome
> projects. Besides analyses of forest ecosystem structure and
> processes it had also an experimental approach and a modelling
> component.

SYNTHESIS EFFORTS IN THE IBP

International Syntheses and Experiences

Dr. John Phillipson, a soil ecologist at Durham University, UK, organized a major synthesis in soil ecology. In November 1967 Phillipson convened a five-day meeting at the United Nations Educational Scientific and Cultural Organization (UNESCO) building in Paris, France (Phillipson, 1970). It was an ideal chance to meet some of the "greats" in the field, including Eldor Paul, Dennis Parkinson, and Clive Edwards as they summarized their recent studies. Numerous scientists attended from Asia and Africa as well. Dr. Ian Healey, whose productive life was cut short by cancer only a few years later, presented a fascinating paper on production and impacts of collembolans on soil systems, particularly emphasizing rates of grazing on litter and soil fungi (Healey, 1970). One of the really memorable papers presented results studying tree root growth in situ in rhizotrons, which was a very advanced concept in the late 1960s (Head, 1970). The amount of root growth and turnover during cool winter months was an unexpected revelation.

Gene Odum, Frank Golley, and Dick Wiegert were all interested in our having some representation from Georgia in the Paris meeting (UNESCO paid for my airfare to present Odum's invited talk, ultimately published as Wiegert, et al., 1970). The concept of soil as an "external rumen", a popular concept in the soil ecology community, was first presented in this paper. I gave a paper based on my research using [65]Zinc-labelled fungi to trace its movement through fungal-feeding microarthropods in the principal old field (field 3-412) at the Savannah River Ecology Laboratory (SREL). The results provided information on who eats whom in the soil fungal food web (Coleman and McGinnis, 1970).

The working meeting on Secondary Productivity in Terrestrial Ecosystems held in Jabłonna, Poland, in September 1966 was an earlier international synthesis. The site was next to the Białowieza National Park, home of the wisent, or European Bison. The hosts were Professor Kazimierz Petrusewicz and his colleagues of the Institute of Ecology, Dziekanow,

Figure 2.4. Participants at the Working Meeting on Secondary Productivity of Terrestrial Ecosystems, Jabłonna, Poland, September 1966. From the left, Drs. Frank B. Golley and Richard G. Wiegert, University of Georgia; D. A. Crossley Jr., Oak Ridge National Laboratory; Prof. Kazimierz Petrusewicz and Dr. Alicja Breymeyer, Polish Academy of Sciences, Warsaw; Prof. Francis C. Evans, University of Michigan. The gentleman in the background is Dr. Tadeusz Prus, Polish Academy of Sciences (used with permission from the Odum Library, University of Georgia).

near Warsaw, Poland. Petrusewicz was legendary in eastern European circles, having built up an ecology group in little more than one decade with nearly 100 Ph.D.-level scientists and over 200 support staff. Both Frank Golley and Dick Wiegert attended from UGA, and Dac Crossley, soon to join the faculty of the Institute of Ecology in Athens, also participated (Figure 2.4). A star-studded cast of colleagues from Europe, Asia, and North America participated (Petrusewicz, 1967). These included David E. Reichle, later director of the Environmental Sciences Division of Oak Ridge National

Laboratory, 1986–1990), and Frank Pitelka of U.C. Berkeley, one of the senior participants in the U.S. IBP Tundra Biome Program. The distinguished looking scientist at the far right of the picture was Professor Francis Evans of the University of Michigan, one of the foremost scientists in North America promoting usage of the ecosystem concept (Evans, 1956). One of the interesting findings of this meeting was the notion, presented by Drs. Wiegert and Evans (1967), that it was much more efficient energetically to consume insect herbivores, such as grasshoppers (locusts) in Africa than to employ the more wasteful mammalian herbivores such as cattle—which, due to higher maintenance energy costs, passed along much less of the ingested primary production as new body tissues to the next trophic level.

Professor Amyan Macfadyen (pers. comm.) wrote an interesting vignette of interactions with the dynamic Professor Kazimierz Petrusewicz:

> I had Kasimir Petrusewicz to stay with me for a week in Northern Ireland while we worked on a book in the Blackwell series for the IBP called "Secondary Productivity". It was one of the most exciting and controversial weeks of my life! He loved an argument and we fought over every point, only after much argument coming to a consensus. At the Jabłonna IBP meeting we thrashed out equally vigorously the problems of measuring secondary productivity and he afterwards led excursions to the marsh country in the North where he had control of an island in the Baltic which was "covered" with live traps for small mammals, manned by numerous students. Practically all the small mammals were marked[,] so that was probably the most intensive population study ever. We also went to the vast Bialowicza forest which crosses the border into Russia and was the hide-out of irregular forces during the German occupation (he was one of them, which explains why he became the darling of the Communist administration afterwards). We stayed in a hunting lodge (quite primitive) in the forest and he showed us how to live off the wildlife resources. I remember a fantastic meal of parasol mushrooms (*Lepiota procera*). He could do no wrong under the Communists at that time but eventually someone unearthed his (wife's) Jewish ancestry and he fell from favour and shortly afterwards died (in 1982) [Ryszkowski, 1982].

Amyan Macfadyen was (and is) a fascinating person in his own right. He would talk much of the time in very soft tones and seem almost detached. However, once someone got him going on a pet topic, particularly ecological energetics, he would come alive and propose grand ideas and sweeping concepts in a very animated fashion. I experienced this with him several times during my postdoctoral year (1964–1965) at the University College of Swansea, Wales. Amyan went out to sample with me the first time I was setting up my field study on Cefn Bryn (Ridge Hill in Welsh) just a few hundred meters above his house in Reynoldston, on the Gower Peninsula. As we were taking cores and trying to keep track of what came from where, Amyan suddenly exclaimed: "Doesn't the soil smell good!" Dr. Paul Berthet, of the University of Louvain in Belgium, worked with Amyan for three months in early 1965 during my postdoctoral ten months at University College Swansea. They would spend afternoons working on the electrolytic respirometer for measuring oxygen uptake by individual Oribatid mites that Macfadyen was perfecting. The session would begin rather quietly and then escalate to more sweeping comments, with very dry witty comments by both researchers; it was fun to see the creative sparks fly.

During my duties as "Decomposer Integrator," I attended numerous national and international synthesis meetings to compare notes and report on progress in this large group research effort. In 1972, I experienced two scientific meetings with diametrically opposed results. In July, I traveled to Louvain, Belgium, to participate in a soil fauna and decomposition workshop. There were several working group sessions on various taxonomic groups and process studies of decomposition in several Biomes, ranging from arctic to tropical. While there, I met Dr. J. van der Drift, one of my heroes from the Witkamp and van der Drift series of papers in Ecology in the late 1950s on microbial ecology and decomposition processes. Dr. van der Drift was very cordial, encouraging me to pursue quantitative studies of the effects of protozoans and nematodes in our grassland ecological studies. He agreed readily that these faunal groups might be more active than the larger fauna in feeding on microorganisms in litter and soil and thus have a more significant regulating influence on nutrient cycling phenomena. Armed with this verbal encouragement, I proceeded to sound out colleagues at the NREL, including Ted Elliott, Bill Hunt, and Vern Cole about the prospects for developing collaborative studies using laboratory incubations, popularly known as "microcosms" to measure the effects of the micro- and mesofauna. This approach led to a successful post-IBP "Belowground Project," which was funded by the National Science Foundation at approximately $210,000 per year (1975 onward), increasing at 5 percent per year over the next eight years, big money for those times. We demonstrated that the protozoan and nematode activities mineralized significant amounts of microbial biomass (35–40% of total N mineralized), encouraging further plant growth and nutrient uptake under laboratory conditions (Elliott et al., 1979, Ingham et al., 1985).

In contrast, the AIBS/ESA annual meeting in Minneapolis in August 1972 was quite a disappointment. Convinced that our cadre of four integrators, after working for a total of six months, was fully capable of taking massive amounts of data from several field sites and reporting rapidly on significant trends in them without prior consultation with us, George Van Dyne had arranged (even before some of us had been hired!) for a half-day symposium at the Ecological Society meeting to present the Grassland IBP results to date. Unfortunately, a number of our data sets were not fully analyzed yet, but we had to make the best of an awkward situation. As luck would have it, a few members of the Science Advisory Board (SAB) to the National Science Foundation, including Nelson G. Hairston Sr., were in the audience, and the level of negative commentary was uncomfortably high. Nearly one decade later, Dr. Fred Smith, one of the SAB members, told a group of us at the NREL that numerous votes were taken across several years about continued funding of the IBP and the tally was usually eight for and seven against. Because Smith was an IBP participant, he had to recuse himself when votes were taken by the SAB on IBP matters (F. E. Smith, pers. comm.).

One year later, in July 1973, one of the more successful synthesis meetings in the history of the IBP Grassland Biome worldwide, held in Dziekanow, near Warsaw, Poland, showcased the large (200-person) research group led by Professor Kaszimierz Petrusewicz. This successful synthesis meeting was our first with several grassland ecologists from western, central, and eastern Europe. Drs. Roman Zlotin of the Institute of Geography, Academy of Sciences, USSR; Blanka Ulehlova of the Department of Biology, Academy of Sciences, Czech Academy of Sciences, Brno; and Yvon Dommergues from the Institute of Pedology, Nancy, France were among the colleagues there. We agreed to write a synthesis chapter on decomposition processes as part of a volume edited by Alicja Breymeyer and George Van Dyne (Coleman and Sasson, 1980). This more deliberate and thoughtful approach to synthesis was in marked contrast to the experience of the 1972 ESA meetings.

Additional cross-Biome syntheses were a high priority in the IBP internationally. Within Productivity Terrestrial (PT), only four became fully operational: decomposition and soil processes, small mammals, granivorous birds, and social insects (Brian and Pętal, 1972; Worthington, 1975). An international decomposition volume had been planned during the 1970s, to be edited by Michael Swift and Bill Heal, but was postponed indefinitely due to time involvements in writing the now well-known book authored by Swift, Heal, and Anderson (1979), *Decomposition in Terrestrial Ecosystems*. Henning Petersen, Malcolm Luxton, Annelise Kjøller, and Sten Struwe (1982) edited an offshoot of the proposed IBP volume as an issue of Oikos. This issue, with a wealth of information on soil fauna and soil microfungi and their roles in decomposition processes, was one of the more impressive and useful syntheses to come out of the entire IBP. It was strongly supported by a group of senior scientists interested in decomposition biology, chief among these Professor Dennis Parkinson of the University of Calgary.

Viewed through a prism of experiences in many interdisciplinary research projects in the United States and worldwide, some important principles can be drawn and considered in the framework of "lessons learned." The inter-Biome syntheses which we had in the early 1970s invariably addressed the utility of conceptual and simulation models in relation to current or proposed experiments. One major thread running through all of these meetings and planning sessions was the importance of understanding that all models that we used were inherently simplified versions of the complex ecosystems we were studying. We invariably found out more from where the model behavior was "wrong"—i.e., not in accordance with observations. George Innis, the supervisor of the ELM modeling efforts in their heyday in 1972–1973 and a black-haired Irishman with a wicked sense of humor, insisted that we "ping the system," making it do unusual things in a simulation run, to see whether we could learn anything from it. This skeptical approach to modeling was encapsulated most fittingly in a little gem of an essay entitled "Theological Ecology; or, Models and the Real World" (Bunnell, 1973). I am convinced that the healthy skepticism of this approach is equally necessary in the current era of global circulation models and other new approaches to understanding complex dynamics.

Some of the loudest times we had in the NREL Grassland Laboratory were when George Innis was working with one of the senior investigators. I particularly recall his loud disagreements with Vern Cole and a visiting John Stewart, on sabbatical from the University of Saskatchewan, Saskatoon. The secretaries down the hall asked me on more than one occasion: "Is everything all right? It sounds pretty bad in there (Innis' office)." I assured them that it was their way of working things out, and a paper would be coming out subsequently, which it did (Cole et al., 1977).

INTER-BIOME SYNTHESIS RESULTS IN THE UNITED STATES

As the IBP matured over the years, a variety of synthesis activities were carried out. One of the more noteworthy ones from the U.S. Biomes examined a range of ecosystem phenomena, including comparative hydrology and energetics across all of the Biomes. There were marked differences in the dynamics of key nutrients, such as nitrogen. Thus, forests tend to have an "internalized" N cycle, by incorporating N in soil organic matter materials, available for subsequent plant uptake (Reichle, 1975). In contrast, much of the nitrogen in the dominant shortgrass prairie grass, *Bouteloua gracilis*, is recycled from shoots into roots and crowns, and remobilized for further use in subsequent years (Clark, 1977). At another extreme, in deserts, nitrogen is fixed in large amounts in cyanobacterial crusts, and then volatilized as ammonia in the high pH soils prevailing in those ecosystems (West and Skujins, 1978). Thus, approximately 70 percent of the N fixed annually is lost to this volatilization process, and is unavailable for plant growth (Reichle, 1975). As shown in Table 2.1, the production efficiency, R_A = Autotrophic respiration/Gross primary production (GPP), was very similar across widely different Biomes. The total amount of net primary production, NPP, varied considerably, from a low of 120 g m^{-2} y^{-1} for tundra to 680 grams m^{-2} y^{-1} for mesic forests. Net ecosystem production (NEP), or GPP – R_E = ecosystem respiration (R_H + R_A) was more similar, ranging from a high of 0.23 for a shortgrass prairie to a low of 0.10 for tundra (Reichle, 1975). This comparative study was a pioneering effort in cross-Biome synthesis, and pointed the way to further cross-Biome comparisons, many of them carried out in the LTER program. There are many opportunities to better refine the crude estimates of energetics of the belowground system. Measurement of consumption rates of soil and litter fauna *in situ* (Petersen, 1995), as well as more sophisticated ways to separate root from soil respiration (Gaudinski et al., 2000, 2001; Sistla et al., 2006), are in particular need of further study.

MAJOR SCIENTIFIC CONCEPTS AND FINDINGS OF THE IBP

Viewed through a prism of nearly four decades later, the scientific findings of the IBP were numerous, and had a significant impact on large-scale interdisciplinary studies that were the intellectual successors to it. These include the LTER, the International Geosphere and Biosphere Program (IGBP), and several others. Under the IBP, a more holistic approach to ecosystems research, including explicit measurement of microbial biomass and its turnover and the dynamics of belowground and tree canopy processes, flourished (Box 2.2). The watershed concept, made popular by Likens et al. (1977), extended onward to entire river basins in the river continuum concept (Triska et al., 1982). The utility of model–experiment interactions in subsequent environmental research studies has been demonstrated repeatedly (Box 2.2).

Table 2.1.   *Comparative Metabolic Parameters of Four Contrasting Ecosystems*

	Mesic Forest[a]	Xeric Forest[b]	Prairie[c]	Tundra[d]
Gross primary production (GPP)	1,620	1,320	635	240
Autotrophic respiration (R_A)	940	680	215	120
Net primary production (NPP)	680	600	420	120
Heterotrophic respiration (R_H)	520	370	271	108
Net ecosystem production (NEP)	160	270	149	12
Ecosystem respiration (RE)	1,460	1,050	486	228
Prod'n. Effic. (RA/GPP)	0.58	0.52	0.34	0.50
Effective Prod'n. (NPP/ GPP)	0.42	0.45	0.66	0.50
Maint. Effic. (R_A/NPP)	1.38	1.13	0.51	1.00
Resp. Allocation (R_H/R_A)	0.55	0.54	1.26	0.90
Ecosystem Productivity (NEP/GPP)	0.10	0.20	0.23	0.05

NOTE: All values in grams of carbon per square meter per year. Adapted from Reichle, 1975. Gross primary production (GPP) = Total photosynthetic fixation; Autotrophic respiration (R_A) = GPP – NPP; Net primary production (NPP) = GPP – R_A; Heterotrophic respiration (R_H) = Consumer and decomposer respiration; Net ecosystem production (NEP) = GPP – R_E; Ecosystem respiration (R_E) = R_A + R_H.

[a] Early successional deciduous forest on alluvial soil (Reichle et al., 1973).

[b] Quercus and Pinus forest on sandy soil (Woodwell and Botkin, 1970).

[c] U.S. IBP Grasslands Biome program, personal communication of raw data—calculations and interpretation by the author. Based in part on Andrews et al. (1974).

[d] Adapted from data of P. C. Miller et al. in Bowen (ed., 1972) Tundra Biome Symposium. Revisions of preliminary data after Tieszen and Coyne (pers. comm.).

BOX 2.2. *The Principal Scientific Contributions of the IBP to Ecosystem Science*

1. The importance of belowground processes in terrestrial ecosystems. This involved both carbon and nutrient flows, and in some sites, comprised up to 75 percent of the total production and turnover per year.
2. Roles of canopy processes in nutrient cycling, particularly N fixation.
3. The stream continuum concept developed out of several watershed-level studies, originating in collaborative studies in the Coniferous and Deciduous Forest Biomes (Triska et al., 1982; Wallace, 1988). Corollary of this: "nutrient spiraling," comparing paths of uptake and release of key nutrients, such as N and P in streams (Webster et al., 1992)
4. The emergence of microbial processes as being of paramount importance in ecosystem function. Some of the Biomes, e.g., Grassland and Desert, began with studies of "microbiology and decomposition," and these later morphed into "decomposition and nutrient cycling."
5. A corollary of No. 4 was the development of cross-Biome and international collaborative studies of detritus/decomposer food webs (examples from Tundra, Grassland, Forest Biomes with major syntheses and symposia, e.g., The International Colloquium on Soil Zoology in Uppsala, Sweden in June, 1976).
6. The pulsatile nature of ecosystem function—infrequent events in deserts and forests leading to major changes not only in biota, but also underlying geomorphology.
7. The absolute necessity to conduct whole-system experiments to better understand mechanisms occurring. Examples: changes in surface and vadose water regimes after clearcutting, pulses of nitrates and other ions after forest defoliation insect outbreaks.

8. The paramount importance of studying old-growth forests, and mature stages of other ecosystems, to fully understand ecosystem nutrient cycling and overall ecosystem resilience. Most notable case: the Coniferous Forest Biome.

9. Simulation models are tools, not ends in themselves. The growth and proliferation of subsystem process models has proven to be a key heuristic and research tool by generations of researcher post-IBP.

10. Ecosystems are active all year round. Phenomena such as root growth, microbial turnover, and so forth, are pulsatile and very dynamic outside of the commonly considered "growing season." For examples of this from the Tundra, Grassland, and Forest Biomes, see text.

THE LEGACIES OF IBP FOR INTERNATIONAL SCIENCE

The legacies of IBP for subsequent developments in international science are impressive and manyfold. Group after group in North America have attested to the strong impact that IBP had, with its many international synthesis meetings and books resulting from them (Table 2.2).

Perhaps the most international in scope was the IBP tundra program, which had impacts reverberating for several decades later. One of the key researchers from this program, Dr. O. W. Heal, commented,

> The synthesis of UK Moorland (Moor House) and Grassland (Snowdonia) results was published in 1976 [Heal & Perkins, 1976] and the final Tundra Biome Cambridge University Press synthesis in 1981 [Bliss et al., 1981]. The effort required to complete these national and international syntheses was considerable and highlighted for me the great importance in planning for the synthesis stage in research programmes—field studies are exciting and rewarding but the research is not completed until the results are synthesized and published. This type of synthesis takes a major effort and can produce unexpected results. This experience influenced the rest of my career and led me

Table 2.2. *IBP International Synthesis Book Sales*

Number	Title	Total Sales
25	Tundra Ecosystems	615
24	IBP Survey of Conservation Sites	447
23	Dynamic Properties of Forest Ecosystems	1600+
22	Functioning of Freshwater Ecosystems	1351
21	Human Biology of Circumpolar Regions	631
20	Marine Production Mechanisms	985
19	Grasslands, Systems Analysis and Man	933
18	Grassland Ecosystems of the World: Analysis of Grasslands and Their Uses	1399
17	Arid Land Ecosystems, Vol. 2: Structure, Functioning and Management	
16	Arid Land Ecosystems, Vol. 1	
15	Human Physiological Work Capacity	1631
14	The Biology of High Altitude Peoples	1030
13	Production Ecology of Ants and Termites	1200
12	Granivorous Birds in Ecosystems	
11	Population Structure and Human Variation	1139
10	Marine Mussels	1679
9	Studies in Biological Control	1455
8	Worldwide Variation in Human Growth	1556
7	Symbiotic Nitrogen Fixation in Plants	1853
6	Nitrogen Fixation by Free-Living Micro-Organisms	1689
5	Small Mammals	2070
4	Food Protein Sources	
3	Photosynthesis and Productivity in Different Environments	2132
2	Crop Genetic Resources for Today and Tomorrow	
1	The Evolution of IBP	873

NOTE: Blanks after some books indicate sales figures that were lacking.
Courtesy of Cambridge University Press.

to generate and participate in co-operative research programmes both nationally and internationally. One of the main things learned in the IBP and subsequent interdisciplinary ecological research efforts is that the synthesis stage in research takes more time than is usually planned. The work is not completed when the project results are published; there are always/often unexpected emerging insights (synthesis) that were not envisaged in the initial planning but can be expected to take time and effort.

Subsequent efforts arising as offshoots of the Tundra Biome were as follows:

The next steps involved the European Union which funded programmes that involved collaboration between European nations. In discussion with European officials Heal developed the idea of collaboration between Arctic nations as part of the EU Terrestrial Ecosystems Research Initiative (TERI). They established an Arctic Terrestrial Ecosystems Research Initiative (ARTERI) involving UK, Denmark–Greenland and Sweden as EU nations, with the addition of Norway and Iceland as non-EU nations. ARTERI was designed to develop comparative observations in terrestrial ecology, much like IBP. Moor House (UK), Kevo (Finland) and Abisko (Sweden) were focal points, with the addition of sites in Iceland, Norway and Greenland (Denmark). The theme of these programmes and projects was climate change. This program took us through the 1990s and included SCANTRAN—a Scandinavian transect of field sites extending up to Abisko in Northern Sweden—one of the original IBP sites. SCANTRAN is an ongoing programme led by Terry Callaghan (Director at Abisko in Sweden).

More recent Tundra Biome legacies are: These northern studies and programmes funded by European Union were driven by concerns over global change. Northern programmes extended around the Arctic through the influence of the Arctic Council of the 8 Arctic nations. Programmes included CAFF (Conservation of Flora and Fauna) and AMAP (Arctic Monitoring and Assessment Programme). These generated comprehensive reviews (which included information from earlier studies and evolved, in the late 1990s and 2000s, into the Arctic Climate Impact Assessment (ACIA), led by the

United States (U. of Alaska)—a very large international programme, led by Bob Corell [Symon et al., 2005].

The formation by the 8 Arctic Nations of the Arctic Council has been critical in maintaining and developing collaboration around the Arctic Circle. It has had its ups and downs, but has maintained a forum for communication and a mechanism for organisation of programmes around the Arctic. There are Observer Nations[,] e.g., U.K[.,] which have influence but no vote on the Council. Thus, there is a powerful international drive amongst the Arctic nations with particular focus on conservation and pollution through organized programmes on Conservation of Arctic Flora and Fauna (CAFF) and Arctic Monitoring and Assessment Programme (AMAP). Although it is only faintly recognized now, there is a residual influence of IBP, including use of some of the old sites such as Abisko in Sweden, Kevo in Finland, and Point Barrow in Alaska. Devon Island in Canada and Hardangervidda in Norway have virtually closed, but new field study sites have emerged in Iceland, Greenland and Russia.

Dr. Heal concludes with these comments about future legacies:

One variation on the theme of circum-arctic collaboration was the establishment of a University of the Arctic—a genuine circumpolar collaboration with international exchange of students, supported by the Arctic Council and the eight Arctic nations. It was initiated by a chance remark that I made to Swedish and Canadian colleagues over a beer at an AMAP meeting! (I was there as a UK observer). It was followed by a two page outline that I wrote at the invitation of the Canadian rep. and was submitted to the Arctic Council by Canada in March 1997. The time was ripe because the Council needed to have something to show for their efforts but could not find anything that was not political! U. Arctic is now a fully established, circum-arctic organisation. The first students graduated in 2006. *The concept was very strongly influenced by my IBP experience of exchange of ideas and information through common experience.* There is now a Secretariat in Finland, but it is a genuine circum-arctic organisation which provides the students with an international experience. (See the University of the Arctic Website: http://www.uarctic.org.)

This continued collaborative exchange will prove the importance of baseline and long-term studies as climate change alters many ecosystem processes that are already having an enormous impact in polar regions and elsewhere.

On another level, the IBP program as a whole was considered a mixed blessing by observers on the outside. For example, McIntosh (1985) noted the extensive administrative burdens shouldered by the Biome program administrators, as well as the short number of years allotted to complete these ambitious programs.

The initial assessment by Mitchell et al. (1976), together with pressure from the National Science Board, probably impelled ecologists in the NSF to consider a post-IBP model of medium-sized grants for ecosystems studies, currently in the Long-Term Ecological Research (LTER) network (Callahan, 1984, 1991). This model is being followed today, with the average annual grant to an LTER (including overhead, or indirect cost recovery for the university or sponsoring institution) equaling approximately $800,000, which would have equaled less than $250,000 in early 1970s dollars, roughly one-tenth of the Biome budgets at their peak. The total number of personnel supported by an LTER grant is no more than fifty to sixty (and usually far fewer), with many of the senior scientists drawing no salary or, at most, a month of summer funding. In contrast, some Biome programs had more than two dozen full-time scientists, programmers and support staff, and supported numerous graduate students as well. Most Biome programs encouraged the participation of colleagues from cooperating federal agencies, such as the USDA Forest Service and Agricultural Research Service and U.S. Geological Survey, a successful practice that continues today at many of the LTER sites.

One wonders what would be the impact of roughly ten times more funding at each LTER site, to bring it more into line with funding levels for the Biome Programs in terms of purchasing power. With the strong interest of other federal agencies and research groups, it is probably best that the current generation of scientists in successor programs such as

LTERs have a more diffuse network of funding sources than the Biome Programs had in the early 1970s.

SOME NONSCIENTIFIC ASPECTS OF THE IBP YEARS

The many programs and projects under way during the few years of the IBP program exacted a significant toll on human relationships. A number of the participants were away from home at meetings or working in the field for months at a time. With many informal social gatherings, liaisons inevitably occurred. It is fair to say that a significant percentage of every Biome program's senior scientists and graduate students underwent divorces or other breakups as the result of these absences and temptations. This social disruption is perhaps simply human nature; similar stresses occur in societal groups, whether in the armed forces or in other circumstances in which groups of researchers are far from home for many weeks at a time.

LESSONS LEARNED FROM THE IBP EXPERIENCE

Extensive syntheses within countries, and also internationally, were a hallmark of IBP-era studies. This "leveraged," in effect, the amount of work being carried out, and helped ensure a wider audience for the research that was conducted. The numbers and kinds of international synthesis meetings were impressive and had a significant impact on researchers and the theory and practice of subsequent studies. Noted scientists, including François Bourliére (France), James Cragg and Robert Coupland (Canada), Bill Heal, Amyan Macfadyen and John (UK), Kazimierz Petrusewicz (Poland), Thomas Rosswall (Sweden), and George Van Dyne (United States) led these syntheses.

One of the most significant contributions that the IBP Biome programs made to ecosystem thinking and modes of research activity was the conjoint consideration of all trophic levels, including an explicit measurement of microbial biomass and activity in these studies. As IBP synthesis papers accumulated, it became apparent that we really do live in a "microbial world," dominated by microbially mediated nutrient cycles (Coleman et al., 1983; Clarholm, 1985; Whitman et al., 1998; Coleman and Whitman, 2005). This emphasis has continued into the LTER era. A major legacy of this work is that it provided the basis of ecosystem level carbon budgets and fluxes for major ecosystem types that were, and still are, the data inputs for global carbon cycle models— so important to understanding CO_2 fluxes and climate change. A notable example of the IBP legacy being expressed in terms of model–experiment interactions is the Ecology of Arable Land study (Andrén et al., 1990). Experimental manipulations of large field sites in southern Sweden led to a series of international comparisons of trophic interactions and nutrient cycling in agroecology, particularly in the synthesis chapter of Paustian, et al. (1990).

As an outgrowth of the numerous IBP synthesis meetings, the participants developed a modus operandi of sharing research ideas and fostered an approach to collaborative research that frequently led to subsequent funding via NSF proposals or other mechanisms. This process began somewhat slowly at first, but accelerated as the LTER program began from 1980 onward.

Perhaps the greatest legacy that the IBP has produced in North America and elsewhere in the world is the development of the LTER network, and soon afterward, internationally, with the ILTER network. Several LTER sites are direct descendants of their Biome congeners, including the H. J. Andrews site in Oregon, the Bonanza Creek LTER site in Fairbanks, Alaska, the Niwot site on the Colorado Front Range, the Natural Resource Ecology Laboratory in Fort Collins, and its affiliated Shortgrass Steppe LTER site in eastern Colorado, and the Coweeta LTER site in western North Carolina, affiliated with the University of Georgia. In fact, the Coweeta site has generated up to 7 percent of the total personnel involved in the LTER network nationally, more than any of the others, although the Coniferous and Desert Biomes come in a close second (Ted Gragson, pers. comm.). A partial list of IBP "alumni" is given in Table 2.3. Ph. D. and post doctorals supported by IBP programs in North America are presented in Table 2.4.

Table 2.3. *North American "Alumni" of the International Biological Program and Current Affiliations*

Biome	Name and Affiliation
Grassland	Sam Bledsoe (Consultant, Davis, California)
	Con Campbell (Canada Agriculture, Ottawa)
	Dave Coleman (Consultant, University of Georgia)
	Jim Detling (Consultant, Colorado State University)
	Jerry L. Dodd (University of Wyoming)
	Mel Dyer (Consultant, Port Townsend, Washington)
	H. William Hunt (Colorado State University)
	William Lauenroth (University of Wyoming)
	William Parton (Colorado State University)
	Eldor A. Paul (Colorado State University)
	Paul G. Risser (University of Oklahoma)
	David M. Swift (Colorado State University)
	Gordon Swartzman (University of Washington)
	Kristina Vogt (Yale University)
	John A. Wiens (The Nature Conservancy)
	Bob Woodmansee (Consultant, Oak Creek, Colorado)
Coniferous Forest	Dale Cole (University of Washington)
	Kermit Cromack Jr. (Oregon State University)
	Robert Edmonds (University of Washington)
	Jerry F. Franklin (University of Washington)
	Stan Gregory (Oregon State University)
	Chuck Grier (Consultant, E. Wash. Univ.)
	Dale Johnson (University of Nevada)
	Jack Lattin (Oregon State University)
	Art McKee (University of Montana)
	Helga van Miegroet (Utah State University)
	Phil Sollins (Oregon State University)
	Fred Swanson (Oregon State University)
	Dick Waring (Oregon State University)

Table 2.3. (*continued*)

	Fred Benfield (Virginia Tech. and State Univ.)
	D. A. Crossley Jr. (Consultant, University of Georgia)
	Clayton Gist (Consultant, Oak Ridge, Tennessee)
	James Kitchell (University of Wisconsin)
	Orie Loucks (Consultant, Miami Univ. of Ohio)
	John Magnuson (University of Wisconsin)
Deciduous Forest	Jerry S. Olson (Consultant, Oak Ridge, Tennessee)
	Robert O'Neill (Consultant, Oak Ridge, Tennessee)
	David E. Reichle (Consultant, Kingston, Tennessee)
	Hank Shugart (University of Virginia)
	Wayne Swank (Consultant, Franklin, North Carolina)
	Jack Webster (Virginia Tech. and State Univ.)
	J. Bruce Wallace (Consultant, University of Georgia)
	Thomas Bellows (U. of Calif., Riverside)
	Martyn Caldwell (Consultant, Utah State Univ.)
	Norman Dronen (Texas A. & M.)
	Clayton Gist (Consultant, Oak Ridge, Tennessee)
	James MacMahon (NEON, Inc., and Utah State Univ.)
	Wayne Minshall (Idaho State University)
	Philip Rundel (University of Calif., Los Angeles)
	Duncan Patten (Arizona State University)
Desert	Stuart Pimm (Duke University)
	James Reynolds (Duke University)
	Stan Smith (U. of Nevada, Las Vegas)
	Frederic Wagner (Consultant, Utah State University)
	Diana H. Wall (Colorado State University)
	Neil West (Utah State University)
	Mark Westoby (Macquarie University, Australia)
	Walter G. Whitford (Consultant, New Mexico State Univ.)

Table 2.3. (*continued*)

Arctic and Alpine	George Batzli (Consultant, Champaign, Illinois)
	Kim Bridges (University of Hawai'i)
	Jerry Brown (Consultant, Falmouth, Massachusetts)
	Fred Bunnell (University of British Columbia)
	F. Stuart Chapin III (University of Alaska, Fairbanks)
	Stanley Dodson (University of Wisconsin)
	Patrick Flanagan (Consultant, Reston, Virginia)
	John Hobbie (Marine Biology Lab., Woods Hole, Massachusetts)
	Steven MacLean (Consultant, Fairbanks, Alaska)
	Walt Oechel (Calif. State Univ., San Diego
	Gus Shaver (Marine Biology Lab., Woods Hole, Massachusetts)
	Larry Tieszen (Consultant, Huron, South Dakota)
	Keith VanCleve (Consultant, Friday Harbor, Massachusetts)
	Les Viereck (Consultant, Fairbanks, Alaska)
	Patrick Webber (Consultant, Taos, New Mexico)
Origin and Structure of Ecosystems	Martin Cody (UCLA)
	Rob Colwell (U. Conn.)
	Rachel Hays (Consultant, Ft. Collins, Colorado)
	Tony Joern (Kansas State University)
	Jon Keeley (USGS and UCLA)
	Hal Mooney (Stanford University)
	Andy Moldenke (Oregon State University)
	Gordon Orians (University of Washington)
	Mike Rosenzweig (University of Arizona)
	Otto Solbrig (Harvard University)
Analysis of Ecosystems	Fred Smith (Consultant, Falmouth, Massachusetts)

NOTE: Many are active in the LTER; a few, in NEON.

Table 2.4. Training Resulting from Some Ecological Programs in the U.S. IBP Biome Programs

	Students Supported at Ph.D. Level	Ph.D.s in Systems or Environmental Science	Ph.D.s from Other Disciplines Trained at Postdoctoral Level	Foreign Students Supported	Foreign Senior Scientists Collaborating at U.S. IBP Sites
Grasslands Biome	55	14	3	2	11
Eastern Deciduous Forest Biome	43	43	4	4	5
Coniferous Forest Biome	11	5	3	3	4
Desert Biome	27	3	5	6	2
Tundra and Alpine Biome	11	0	0	1	2
Origin and Structure of Ecosystems	49	29	1	21	19
Upwelling Ecosystems	7	3	0	1	1
Aerobiology	4	4	2	0	0

NOTE: Modified from USNC/IBP 1974 (from Burgess, 1981).

In the next chapter, I present an overview of the origin and growth of the Long-Term Ecological Research (LTER) network, which has grown from an initial six sites in 1980 to twenty-eight, and continues growing internationally as well.

CHAPTER THREE

The Origin and Evolution of the Long-Term Ecological Research Program

We shall not cease from exploration. And the end of all our exploring will be to arrive where we started and know the place for the first time.

T. S. Eliot, *Little Gidding*

The IBP served to consolidate ecosystem ecology, resulting in a permanent increase in funding support for the field. By pioneering in the use of computer modeling in ecology, IBP led to the creation of numerous smaller-scale models of ecological systems, and trained a generation of ecological researchers. "If you now look at a lot of the leadership in American ecology today, these folks cut their teeth on IBP" (W. Frank Harris, pers. comm.).

The LTER arose from the IBP, but it was established as part of a gradually evolving network (Hobbie et al., 2003). Using an ecological metaphor, the IBP had a rapid, or "r" growth strategy, reaching its full complement of Biome programs within four years. In comparison, the LTER began slowly and continued its slow growth rate, or "K" strategy, across more than two decades until reaching its current extent of twenty-six sites.

With the exception of H. J. Andrews and Coweeta, the IBP Biome studies had only limited applicability to the practical problems of environmental management. Interestingly, a smaller-scale integrated project, the Hubbard Brook Ecosystem Study (Likens et al., 1977), which had been funded since 1963, before the inception of the IBP, became an example of a fruitful way to proceed in the post-IBP era. Such management oriented studies as how forests recover from clear-cutting and the impact of acid rain on North America, demonstrated the power of taking an ecosystem approach to understanding environmental responses, but proceeded over a longer time scale (decades) than was typical for the IBP projects (Bocking, 1997). The successor programs to the IBP are now integral to the Long-Term Ecological Research program, LTER, which is now in its thirtieth year (2010) and includes five former IBP sites and Hubbard Brook among the twenty-six research programs.

In this chapter, I present the development, or ontogeny if you will, of the LTER program. I then present an overview of some of the key players in the development of LTER, including NSF program staff and the Coordinating Committee chairs who have been active in this long-running program. Major scientific findings are also presented, and some comparisons are made with its predecessor, the IBP. Additional synthesis activities, such as the National Center for Ecological Analysis and Synthesis (NCEAS) are also discussed.

LTER ORIGINS

Of the first six LTER sites established in 1980, four of them originated from previous IBP projects. These include the H. J. Andrews site (coniferous forest, Oregon State University, Corvallis); the Coweeta site (deciduous forest, University of Georgia, Athens); North Temperate Lakes (University of Wisconsin, Madison); and Niwot Ridge (alpine tundra, University of Colorado, Boulder). The two new sites were Konza (tallgrass prairie, Kansas State University, Manhattan) and North Inlet (marshland, University of South Carolina, Columbia). An additional twenty-three sites were added across the years, enabling the inclusion of virtually every natural Biome and three largely human-dominated ones (Kellogg Biological Station (agroecosystem, Michigan State University); Baltimore Ecosystem Study (urban, the Institute for Ecosystem Studies, Millbrook, NY); and Central Arizona–Phoenix (urban, Arizona State University, Tempe) in the network. By working with other funding sources within the NSF, a total of four polar projects were funded in part through the Office of Polar Programs: Arctic (Ecosystem Center, Woods Hole, MA); Bonanza Creek (boreal, University of Alaska, Fairbanks); McMurdo Dry Valleys (University of Colorado, Boulder); and Palmer (Ecosystem Center, Woods Hole, MA), the latter two are in the Antarctic. Several other NSF directorates help to support some of the LTER research, including Biological Oceanography and Geosciences.

Some comments on LTER origins by Wayne Swank, a rotating scientist member of the NSF's Ecosystem Studies office in 1978, are enlightening. The major responsibility of the NSF staff personnel was to convince the National Science Board (NSB) of the need for the LTER program. Some earlier groundwork had already been done by Paul Risser, Bill Reiners, John Brooks, Tom Callahan (Division of Environmental Biology), and Bill Sievers (Research Facilities and Equipment program). Swank gave a presentation to the National Science Board, in which he emphasized that funding had remained relatively flat during the ten preceding years, with five large biome programs, plus Hubbard Brook and some smaller programs such as origin and structure of ecosystems, human adaptability, and integrated pest management, being funded in that time period. He noted a large number of holistic projects being funded at levels in excess of $150,000 per year. Swank et al. (with Callahan being integral to this effort) made a strong case for larger-scale, multi-year site-based investigations that evoked a sympathetic response from the science board. Also, and of perhaps paramount importance, permanent NSF staff within the Division of Environmental Biology (e.g., Drs. Brooks and Callahan) had managed to keep the funding that had supported the IBP within their program, and they desired to support a long-term study of ecosystems that was markedly different from the IBP program (B. Hayden, pers. comm.).

A proposed experimental ecological reserve network (NSF, 1977), comprised of several dozen possible sites, revealed extensive interest nationwide in a possible national network of ecological sites. It led directly to a Long-Term Ecological Research Network, the formative stages of which are considered next.

LTER PLANNING WORKSHOPS

To explore the prospects for long-term studies, the NSF sponsored a series of three workshops during 1977–1979 to consult with the scientific community. The first two were convened by Daniel Botkin, and the third one by Orie Loucks. Over 100 scientists, potential users, and cooperators from private and governmental entities participated in the planning process. The emphasis in the workshops changed over time from "monitoring" to "research," with intermediate pauses at "measurement" and "observation and study" as well (Callahan, 1984). The emphasis on research focused on ecological questions and hypotheses testing was viewed as central to solving problems of long-term environmental resource management. In the first workshop, on March 16–18, 1977, three working groups addressed major questions in terrestrial, freshwater, and marine environments. The four basic issues of broad ecological interest were (1) global effects on populations and ecosystems (concerning increasing CO_2 and climate changes across several decades), (2) ecosystem stability (with three generic hypotheses), (3) population regulation, with concerns about intrinsic and extrinsic factors, and (4) community structure, with a series of specific hypotheses—e.g., the size of herbivore fauna on an introduced plant increases at first, and then (decades later) becomes asymptotic. The desirable long-term measurements were considered in three main areas: climate, chemical, and biotic (Botkin, 1977). These concerns were expanded upon in the third and final workshop (Loucks, 1979) into five core research questions: (1) dynamic patterns and control of primary production, over time, and in relation to natural and induced stresses or disturbances, (2) dynamics of selected populations of seed plants, saprophytic organisms, invertebrates, fish, birds, and mammals in relation to time as well as natural and induced stresses or disturbances, (3) patterns and control of organic accumulation (biomass) in surface layers and substrate (or sediment) in relation to time or natural and induced stresses or disturbances, (4) patterns of inorganic contributions (atmospheric or hydrologic) and movement through soils, groundwater, streams, and lakes in relation to time and natural or induced stresses or disturbances, and (5) pattern and frequency of apparent site interventions (disturbances) over space and time (drought, fire, windthrow, insects, and other perturbations) that may be a product of, or induce, long-term trends. The five core areas of investigation in the LTERs are discussed further below, under the heading "Core Areas of Research."

There was concern in the non-ecosystem ecology community that they should have some representation in the proposed LTER. Daniel Simberloff, then of Florida State University, was among the more vocal proponents of the presence of a significant amount of research on population processes. This was reflected in the second of the five core areas presented below. Also, this series of interactions probably led to the establishment of the small-scale LTERs, known as Long-Term Research in Environmental Biology (LTREBs) (J. J. Magnuson, pers. comm.).

In 1979, NSF announced a call for proposals for pilot projects in long-term ecological research with goals of (1) initiating the collection of comparative data at a network of sites representing major biotic regions of North America and (2) evaluating the scientific, technical and managerial problems associated with such long-term comparative research.

CORE AREAS OF RESEARCH

Five core areas of research in the LTER Network were defined to enable the scientific community to focus on common problems needing study in any ecosystem so chosen. These include (1) pattern and control of primary production, (2) spatial and temporal distribution of populations selected to represent trophic structure, (3) pattern and control of organic matter accumulation in surface layers and sediments, (4) patterns of inorganic input and movements through soils, groundwater, and surface waters, (5) patterns and frequency of disturbance to the research site. All of the above, relating to biological (including human) and physicochemical constraints on ecosystem function, have proven most useful to the LTER research community (Callahan, 1984; Hobbie et al., 2003). These core areas allowed studies to be structured around groups of structural and functional attributes common across a large suite of biomes with a range of climatic regimes ranging from polar to temperate and tropical (Luquillo, University of Puerto Rico, San Juan) (Fig. 3.1).

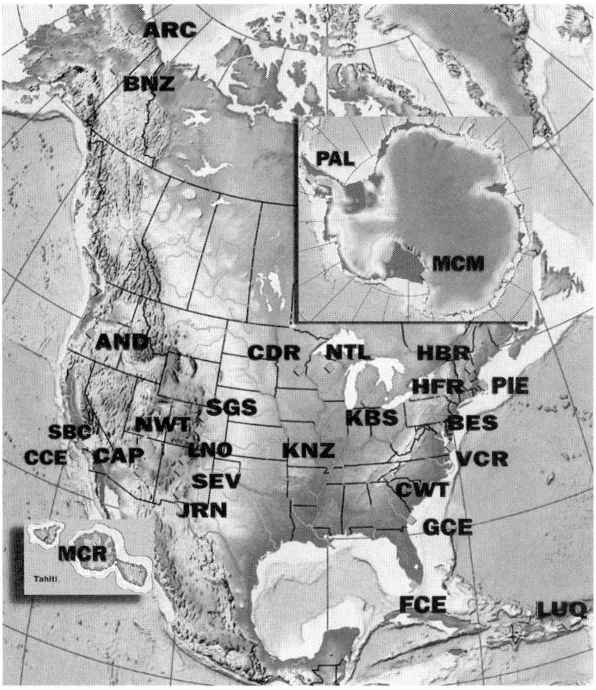

Figure 3.1   All twenty-seven LTER sites, ranging from tropical to polar. Note two Antarctic sites and two Arctic sites (used with permission of the LTER Network Office).

LTER CHRONOLOGY

The following is a chronological account of the formation and development of the LTER program. The first six sites were established in 1980 and include the H. J. Andrews site (coniferous forest, Oregon State University, Corvallis); the Coweeta site (deciduous forest, University of Georgia, Athens); North Temperate Lakes (University of Wisconsin, Madison); Niwot Ridge (alpine tundra, University of Colorado, Boulder); Konza (tallgrass prairie, Kansas State University, Manhattan), and North Inlet (marshland, University of South Carolina, Columbia).

In October 1980 the founding meeting for the network was convened in Washington, D.C., by Tom Callahan. Richard Marzolf from the Konza Prairie was chosen to chair the "LTER Network Directorate," with Dick Waring as vice chair. The first meeting was set up for December 1980 to support activities of the network, including possible studies in meteorology/atmospheric chemistry, analytical chemistry, hydrology, belowground biology, archiving, primary production, consumers, and data management (Magnuson et al., 2006c). NSF mandated annual reports from the network. All sites were requested to send a list of participants, including phone numbers (there was no e-mail yet) (Magnuson et al., 2006c). In 1981, the first All Scientists' meeting, in effect, was held in Las Cruces, New Mexico. The atmosphere was enthusiastic, with many papers offered, and several informal grant proposals for intersite research turned in. Not all of the participants were prepared for this, and cried "foul." Fortunately, the total budgets for the proposed studies were quite low, mostly consisting of anticipated travel costs to visit one or two sites to take samples, so many of the initial intersite proposals were approved (D. A. Crossley Jr., pers. comm.).

Evolution of the LTER Network from 1982 Onward

An NSF proposal competition resulted in five new sites' being added in 1982: Central Plains Experimental Range (now called Shortgrass Steppe) in Colorado (Colorado State University), Okefenokee in Georgia (University of Georgia), Illinois Rivers (Illinois Natural History Survey), Cedar Creek Natural History Area in Minnesota (University of Minnesota), and Jornada Basin in New Mexico (New Mexico State University).

In 1987 a proposal competition resulted in the addition of five new sites: Arctic Tundra at Toolik Lake on the Alaskan North Slope (the Ecosystem Center, MBL, Woods Hole, MA); Bonanza Creek Experimental Forest, University of Alaska, Fairbanks; Hubbard Brook Experimental Forest, New Hampshire; Kellogg Biological Station of Michigan State University; and Virginia Coastal Reserve, University of Virginia, Charlottesville, VA.

In 1988, another NSF proposal competition resulted in addition of three new sites: Luquillo Experimental Forest in Puerto Rico, University of Puerto Rico; Sevilleta National Wildlife Refuge in New Mexico, University of New Mexico; and Harvard Forest, Harvard University.

In 1990, NSF announced an Antarctic LTER site competition, supported by funds from Polar Programs and Environmental Biology divisions. In 1991, the NSF Antarctic research proposal competition resulted in addition of a new site: Palmer Station, Antarctica LTER (the Ecosystems Center, MBL, Woods Hole, MA). In 1992, NSF announced a second Antarctic LTER site competition with funds from Polar Programs and Environmental Biology divisions. In 1993, the NSF Antarctic research proposal competition resulted in the addition of another site: McMurdo Dry Valleys, Antarctica (Portland State University).

In 1997, after a special competition for urban LTER sites, two new sites were added: Central Arizona Phoenix (CAP) (Arizona State University), and Baltimore Urban LTER (BAL) (the Institute for Ecosystem Studies, Millbrook, NY).

In 1998, the NSF proposal competition resulted in the addition of a new Land Margin Ecological Research (LMER) site: Plum Island Ecosystem (PIE), The Ecosystems Center, Woods Hole, MA. A special LTER competition for additional land margin sites in 2000 resulted in three new coastal LTER Network sites: Georgia Coastal Ecosystem (University of Georgia), Florida Coastal Everglades (Florida International University), and Santa Barbara Coastal (University of California, Santa Barbara). In 2004, two new sites joined the LTER Network: California Current (CCE) (University of California, San Diego) and Moorea Coral Reef (MCR) (University of California, Santa Barbara).

History of Coordination of the LTER Network

In 1981, Dick Marzolf (Konza Prairie) was named as the first LTER Steering Committee Chair. NSF awarded a coordination grant to

Kansas State University (with Marzolf as PI). In 1982, representatives from five new sites formed a Steering Committee. The Steering Committee created a policy for workshops supported under the coordination grant. In 1982, Jerry Franklin replaced Marzolf as LTER Steering Committee (now Coordinating Committee) chair. A coordination grant was awarded to Oregon State University (Jerry Franklin, PI), and the LTER Network Office was established. A coordination grant was awarded to University of Washington–Seattle (Jerry Franklin, PI). Much of the growth of the LTER Network occurred during Franklin's leadership. The LTER Network Office was enlarged and established on the University of Washington campus, in the College of Forest Resources. In 1995, Coordinating Committee Chair Jerry F. Franklin announced his retirement as chair after more than twelve years of service. James R. Gosz was elected LTER Coordinating Committee Chair. In March, 1996, the Network Office officially began operation at the University of New Mexico, and Bob Waide was hired as executive director. During Gosz's tenure international outreach was substantially increased, Land-Margin Ecosystem Research (LMER) and coastal sites were added, and closer interactions between sites and the Network office were established. Much of this was due to the efforts of Bob Waide in his role as executive director, providing continuity of activities between sites and the network office in Albuquerque. In 2005, Jim Gosz resigned after ten years of service as chair of the LTER Executive Board. Phil Robertson was elected as chair of the LTER Executive Board and Science Council. He and lead PI s in the network have developed an extensive forward-looking plan for the future between 2010 and 2020 ("The Decade of Synthesis"), which is discussed below, under the heading "Looking Forward in LTER."

History of LTER Governance

The LTER Network assessed leadership and governance in response to the ten-year review and in preparation for the election of a new

Coordinating Committee chair. The LTER Publications and Synthesis committees were established, and the LTER Network World Wide Web site was established at the Network Office. The First International LTER (ILTER) Steering Committee meeting was held in Rothamsted, and UK NSF, and USDA Forest Service signed a Memorandum of Agreement to continue cooperation/collaboration in LTER Program research. NSF and the National Biological Service signed a Memorandum of Agreement to cooperate/collaborate in LTER Program research.

A section was set up separately for Schoolyard LTERs: In 1999, Schoolyard LTER Supplements were added to LTER grants ($15,000/year to each site) for the first time. This addition proved to be very popular with school districts in which LTER sites are located. Probably as a result of this impetus, several books for children or the general public have been produced by a few LTER sites. The amount of effort devoted to Schoolyard LTERs has been quite impressive, and without exception, LTER sites have reported allocating more than the $15,000 dollars received per year. In view of the positive benefits accruing with more local support and interest in LTERs, this seems to be one of the "underfunded mandates" that will continue on into the future. Research Experience for Undergraduates (REU) has been funded for many years during the LTER program. The availability of funds in some years when funding in the NSF is flat tend to make this program somewhat variable, and occasionally non-existent (Scott Collins, pers. comm.), despite the demonstrated beneficial effects on undergraduate education and familiarization of the wider public.

Ontogeny of Socioeconomic Studies in the LTER

One of the more intriguing developments to arise across the LTER network has been a steadily increasing interest in the incorporation of socioeconomic studies within the LTER network site research activities. In response to the expressed desire of LTER scientists to address research at more regional scales, and with a socioeconomic emphasis, the NSF held a special competition for augmentation of LTER projects with the wider scope in mind. North Temperate Lakes (NTL) and Coweeta (CWT) LTERs received nearly $500,000 as supplements to address aspects of regionalization, comprehensive site histories, and increased disciplinary breadth, especially in the social sciences.

From the vantage point of a former Coweeta lead PI (1996–2002), I can attest to the fact that the overall impact of the socioeconomic and greater emphasis on historical aspects in our LTER research was very beneficial. Getting our group of twenty-eight co-PIs to talk the same scientific language was somewhat difficult initially. The NSF advisory panel sensed this as well, and put us on two years' probationary funding between 1997 and 1998. Facing impending financial collapse focuses the mind wonderfully, as many research scientists know, and we redoubled our efforts on our overall research agenda in some special workshops. Several of our working groups developed improved conceptual and simulation models to predict the socioeconomic–biological future of the southern Appalachian region. Fortunately this resulted in a more cohesive approach to our new research (Wear and Bolstad, 1998), and we received longer-term funding shortly afterward. The enthusiastic participation of our colleague Dr. David Wear from the U.S. Forest Service Research Triangle Park lab was a helpful catalyst in this process. Dr. Wear was one of the key participants in the Southern Appalachian Assessment (part of the Man and the Biosphere (MAB) project). We added Dr. Ted Gragson as an anthropologist to join our team of social scientists on the Coweeta LTER grant. He took over as lead PI of CWT in 2002, and continues in that role to the present.

An extensive set of studies have been carried out to follow ecosystem responses to urbanization and pollution along a continent-wide scale. A group of investigators, largely from LTER sites (Grimm et al, 2008), posed an intriguing set of hypotheses: (1) Human sociodemographic changes are the primary drivers of land-use change, urbanization, and pollution at continental and subcontinental scales; in turn, these patterns are influenced by a continental template of climate and geography.

(2) Human activities, their legacies, and the environmental template interact with gradients of air pollution and nitrogen loading to produce substantial variation in ecosystem patterns and processes on the continent-wide gradient. (3) Within urbanizing regions, landscape alteration and management result in a relative homogenization of form and function of urban land cover across climate zones. (4) Urbanization will generally increase connectivity via wind and animal vectors, but will disrupt connectivity via water vectors, especially at local to regional scales. (5) Humans fundamentally change biogeochemical inputs, processing, flow paths, and exports in areas undergoing development. (6) (a) Urbanizing regions will be less vulnerable than wildland ecosystems to many broad-scale, directional changes in climate due to the capacity of humans to modify their environment, and cities' access to political power and resources. However, (b) urbanizing regions will be more vulnerable than rural and wildland systems to extreme events, because of the greater concentration of people and infrastructure that cannot be moved or modified over the short term. In addition, (c) efforts by urbanizing regions to adjust to change will place added stress on rural and wildland ecosystems that are connected to cities due to greater resource exploitation. For more information on socioeconomic studies in the LTER, see Gragson and Grove (2006).

Grimm et al. (2008) describe in detail a multi-year, multi-institutional approach, using LTER sites, the National Atmospheric Deposition Program, and the planned NEON network as being an ideally suited "pre-adapted" set of observation platforms to test these intriguing hypotheses.

LTER LEADERS

Tom Callahan

With a membership of several hundred scientists, the LTER network has benefited from the presence of a strong hand on the tiller by permanent staff in the NSF Long-Term Studies office. Dr. James T. (Tom) Callahan was the pioneer among the permanent staff. Tom played a pivotal role in enabling scientists to develop and flourish under the IBP program in the early to mid-1970s. He then worked in collaboration with senior scientists from the IBP to make the transition to the LTER. The planning meetings for the LTER that occurred between 1977 and 1979 were carefully nurtured by Dr. Callahan. I knew Tom from his days as an undergraduate and graduate student working with me in the late 1960s on his master's and Ph.D. degrees at the University of Georgia's Savannah River Ecology Laboratory in Aiken, South Carolina. Tom spent most of his time from 1970 to 1972 on campus at UGA, completing coursework and being active in the original Earth Day in Georgia in April 1970. Ecology had not become a byword in public until then, and Earth Day helped bring it about. Tom finished his degree work in zoology with Dac Crossley in June 1972, as I had gone to a new job in the IBP Grassland Biome program in Fort Collins, Colorado in January of that year. As an ecologist, Tom wanted to hit the ground running; he accepted the job of Ecosystem Studies Program Director at the NSF in August 1972 and never looked back. I was at Tom's first IBP coordinating committee meeting, held in Alta, Utah, in October 1972, where he was the bearer of sad tidings. Some budgets were to be cut back significantly in 1973, and Tom got a first-hand impression of how much senior scientists hate to be told they are getting cuts in funding. I often wonder if that first early experience is what made him so assiduous in garnering funds for Ecosystem Studies, especially in the early days of the Long-Term Ecological Research Program (LTER), which began formally in 1980. In that era of flat funding for NSF (through much of the '70s and '80s), Tom found funds to keep the Ecosystem Studies budget growing at 2–3 percent above inflation, which was a major accomplishment.

Tom's devotion to his "baby," the LTER—for which he, Frank Golley, John Brooks, Paul Risser, Jerry Franklin, and Wayne Swank were jointly responsible—is by now legendary. His seminal paper in BioScience (Callahan, 1984) setting forth the rationale and long-term goals for this kind of research is one of the classics of the early LTER era. Tom attended or supervised hundreds of site reviews, mostly of LTER projects. He let the external reviewers handle much of the hour by hour reviewing tasks, but was more than ready to administer what he termed a "whup along the side of the head" when the occasion demanded. Those of us who served on panels convened by him at NSF headquarters were always impressed by his erudition and grasp of the facts in the many proposals being covered, and more importantly, the science behind the proposals. Tom was not one to beat around the bush. His comments offered as a program officer were always direct, and for that reason they were welcome, even when they contained adverse criticism.

Tom was very widely read, a virtual polymath in terms of competence, and also quite assertive and confident of his opinions. This was leavened by his strong support for the LTER program when it was faced with several years of virtually flat funding by NSF. How can a program grow when new resources seem to be non-existent? One answer is to encourage other programs within the foundation to sign on as cosupporters of this innovative international program. Thus the Office of Polar Programs and others joined in support of the LTER to provide a more diverse base of support. That did not provide all of the additional funding. In a "now it can be told" anecdote, it is safe to say that something happened in NSF after Tom had pursued a successful, nearly fifteen-year career tending this program. Callahan was moved back into the Ecosystems Studies directorate, and returned to evaluating the more standard proposals. The only admission that Tom would ever make to his old friends and colleagues was an enigmatic: "I was a bad boy." This leaves one to wonder what specifically occurred. The personnel decisions in a federal agency of only a few thousand persons must have been intriguing. Joann Roskoski, Deputy Director of Biology, Behavior and Social Sciences at NSF, suggested to me that the move of Tom from LTER back into Ecosystems was not punitive, but rather was a conscious decision made by Dr. Mary Clutter, the Deputy Division Director. Clutter felt all permanent staff needed to be moved around to different responsibilities every decade or so. Tom continued as a permanent

Program Officer in Ecosystems for the last few years until his untimely death from liver cancer in September 1999.

Looking back across the years, it is worth noting that Tom was not above using some social suasion to gain his objectives. During the 1981 annual meeting of the Ecological Society of America (ESA) at the University of Indiana, Bloomington, Callahan got Dac Crossley, Frank Harris (also from NSF) and me together to entertain Dr. Eloise (Betsy) Clark, then Deputy Director for Biological, Behavioral and Social Sciences at NSF. Dr. Clark, who was from a cellular biology background, was something of a skeptic about the value of the LTER program, and was not in favor of an LTER Network (J. F. Franklin, pers. comm.). The entertainment consisted of our having cocktails before dinner, several glasses of wine during dinner, and then further discussion over drinks well past midnight. At virtually every turn, Tom steered the conversation around to what was being done by who at various LTER sites and the significant benefits from long-term studies. The final capstone on this effort was the sight of Dac Crossley and Tim Seastedt, two coauthors on a poster the next morning, providing free cans of beer from a cooler at the session, which began at 8:30 the next morning. Dr. Clark came by during the session, and when Dac said she could have a beer only if she read the entire poster, she duly read it, drank some beer, and had an enjoyable chat with the coauthors, as if that happened every day in her life. We never asked Tom Callahan if that social evening and morning helped with an extra "something" to raise the LTER in Dr. Clark's esteem, but it probably didn't hurt.

Other Permanent Staff Involved in the LTER

Tom Callahan supervised a number of short-term appointees, who were called "rotators," in the LTER and other long-term programs such as the Long-Term Research in Environmental Biology (LTREB) program. When it became obvious that Tom was to be reassigned to Ecosystem

Studies program in the early 1990s, he proceeded to work with a new hire, Dr. Scott Collins. Dr. Collins had gotten his Ph.D. degree in 1981 with Paul Risser at the University of Oklahoma. After a postdoctoral with Ralph Good at Rutgers University, he returned to the University of Oklahoma where he worked his way up from assistant to associate professor, focusing on studies of plant community ecology. In 1992 he moved to the NSF and served as program director in several programs including Ecology, LTER, Conservation and Restoration Ecology, and Integrated Research Challenges. During his time in the NSF, he had many interactions with Tom Callahan, who called Scott "my best student." This is high praise indeed, as Callahan supervised and influenced an entire generation of ecologists as they came through the foundation on either long- or short-term appointments. Scott was one of the pioneers in pushing for the adoption of the NEON program, and more comments on his role in this are given in Chapter 4. In 2003 Scott moved to the University of New Mexico, where he took over as lead PI of the Sevilleta LTER from Jim Gosz. He has also carried on long-term collaborations with the scientists of the Konza Prairie LTER program, helping to design the long-term burning and grazing experiments. The fire effects studies in particular have been demonstrated to have interesting feedbacks from global climate change phenomena.

From 2000 onward, the program director of LTER in NSF has been Dr. Henry Gholz, who came to the NSF from the University of Florida after a long and successful career in forest ecology, particularly focused on tree root production and turnover studies. Henry obtained his Ph.D. degree at Oregon State University in 1977 working with Dr. Richard Waring in the Forest Sciences Department. He had a variety of sabbaticals in the United States and abroad, and worked his way through the academic ranks from assistant professor to full professor at the University of Florida across two decades. Dr. Gholz retains his professorship at Florida, being on extended leave from that institution. He has been particularly effective in encouraging a more scientific approach to agroforestry in the United States and in a variety of developing countries. As an example of this, Henry served as International Forestry Advisor in the U.S. Agency for International Development (USAID). Dr. Gholz has played a key role in providing moral and logistical support for the venturesome "Decade of Synthesis" in the LTER program.

A partial list of other "rotators" in the Ecosystem Studies part of the Division of Environmental Biology includes Mike Allen, Todd Crowl, Cliff Dahm, Richard Dame, Jerry Melillo, and Gus Shaver.

Other NSF Staff Involved in LTER

One needs to keep in mind that the heart of the system in NSF is the Advisory Panel, who review all proposals submitted to a given program office and then make recommendations as to the suitability of each proposal in terms of scientific excellence and focus on programmatic or topical themes. This is one of the key jobs that the permanent staff and rotators carry out once or twice a week in their roles as supervising or observing the deliberations of the advisory panels.

The roles of permanent NSF staff personnel in many programs in the National Science Foundation have been noted in histories of the organization, namely Appel (2000), and McGraw (in preparation). To persons in the general public and students just entering the field, grants may seem to be processed automatically, to appear later in the recipients' hands. Nothing could be farther from the truth! The efforts of the permanent staff, as noted in the section above on Tom Callahan, and the many "rotators," who are our peer scientists who agree to serve for one or two years at a time in the Foundation, are indeed often unsung heroes, essential to the process of moving the field of ecological research forward. In every case, proposals that have been submitted are reviewed by several members of an advisory panel made up of peer scientists who evaluate them and make recommendations concerning funding, and if viewed positively, the priority in which they should be considered, given limited funding (usually). Several scientists have been influential in stewardship of the Long-Term Studies program in the NSF. From the mid-1970s and throughout the 1980s, John Brooks served as deputy program director and facilitated the transfer of former IBP funding lines to the burgeoning LTER program. He was followed by Bruce Hayden, and others. Additional staff personnel who have aided in reviews and panel deliberations include Dr. Penny Firth, who has provided expertise in several aquatic biology programs and new initiatives. For joint funding with the Office of Polar Programs, Dr. Polly Penhale has provided invaluable advice and counsel. Long-term continuity is provided by Dr. Joann Roskoski, a microbial ecologist who has served as deputy director for the Division of Biology, Behavioral and Social Sciences (BBS). Dr. Mary Clutter took over the leadership of BBS from Betsy Clark in the mid-1980s and continued until 2005. The current director, Jim Collins (through 2009), has been most supportive.

With only a few exceptions, the principal difficulty in this system of peer scientist staff and rotators is the general reluctance of the scientific community to "step up to the plate" to become direct participants in the evaluation and funding process. From personal experience, I have always found it scientifically rewarding to participate in proposal reviewing and serve on site review teams. I was asked to serve as a program officer in the Ecology office soon after I had moved to a new campus, and pleaded overwork and over commitment. In hindsight, that was shortsighted, at best.

I now consider the longer-term results of studies of ecosystem processes that were not addressed adequately by the IBP in its few years of operation. With the combined influence of several former IBP sites in the LTER, many of the key scientific players, and the gradual evolution of the LTER Network, several research studies are worthy of consideration. They appear next.

MAJOR RESEARCH FINDINGS IN THE LTER

There are several key patterns and processes in ecosystems that can be discerned only by long-term study, across a time frame of up to several decades. The following examples are illustrative of the sorts of research occurring in the LTER Network.

Biodiversity/Productivity Relationships

The relationship between biodiversity and ecosystem processes, such as net primary production, has been of great interest to ecologists. Across a range of phytoplankton, rotifers, cladocerans, copepods, macrophytes, and fish, all six taxa showed a significant quadratic response to increased annual primary productivity. This richness–productivity relationship for phytoplankton and fish was strongly dependent on lake area. For the average lake size in north-central North America, the highest diversity tended to occur in lakes with relatively low primary productivity, such as those in the NTL LTER sites and in the Experimental Lakes Area of Ontario (Dodson et al, 2000). This study exemplifies the strength of working from a long-term data set that is a hallmark of the LTER Network.

Experimental evidence from field and microcosm studies generally supports the concept that increasing species richness increases stability of ecosystem properties. Thus coefficient of variation of aboveground biomass decreased with increasing species richness. In a microcosm study, the standard deviation of carbon dioxide efflux from a microbial microcosm decreased with increasing species richness (Hooper et al., 2005).

"Soil processes appear to be primarily influenced by the functional characteristics of dominant species rather than by the number of species present" (Hooper et al., 2005). These processes include decomposition, soil organic matter dynamics, nutrient uptake by soil organisms, and nutrient retention. All of these are more strongly influenced by differences in functional traits (leaf chemistry, etc.) of the dominant plant species than by the diversity of plant species. Hooper et al. (2005) commented that "less is known about how the diversity of soil organisms affects rates of decomposition and nutrient cycling." This is a key point, deserving more study. Recent studies of synthesized soil food webs suggest that food web composition, rather than the diversity of the organisms within trophic levels, drives decomposition properties, with omnivory playing a key regulating role (Mikola and Setälä, 1998; Moore et al., 2004) and plant productivity (Laakso and Setälä, 1999).

Patterns of Invasive Species in Ecosystems

The impact of the introduction of nonnative species on native species populations has been a major source of concern for ecologists and conservation biologists for many decades (Elton, 1958; Wilcove et al., 1998). One of the major concerns of scientists in national networks in North America, including that of the LTER, is the increasingly widespread effect of invasive species, disease vectors, and pathogens that affect biodiversity, ecosystem function and services, and human health (Crowl et al., 2008). Among many keystone invasives, four key ones stand out: cheatgrass (*Bromus tectorum*), Gypsy moth (*Lymantria dispar*), the red imported fire ant (*Solenopsis invicta*), and the zebra mussel (*Dreissenia polymorpha*). The ranges of each of these span several time zones, and in one case (the zebra mussel) the potential range extends into southeastern Alaska (Crowl et al., 2008). The opportunities for studying the continent-wide spread of key invasives, in collaboration with the NEON network, are very great indeed (Crowl, 2008).

Studies in the LTER network have provided some insights from long-term manipulative experiments and inventories of species (Smith and Knapp 1999, 2001). Management activities (e.g., fire and grazing) do not have uniform effects on the ability of species to invade different ecosystems. The primary mechanism of concern relates to the dominant vegetation in a given ecosystem. If it is adapted to a given disturbance, then invasion is low, or minimal. North American grasslands were nitrogen-limited historically (Hooper and Johnson, 1999) and the dominant species thrived under these conditions. Removal of this limitation by various mechanisms resulted in a decline of the dominance of native grasses and enhanced the vulnerability of these ecosystems to invasion by nonindigenous species (Hobbie et al., 2003).

Some further examples of both LTER and non-LTER studies of the effects of invasive plants follow.

Eastern deciduous forests in North America have been invaded by two species of plants that are often dominant in the understory vegetation. *Berberis thunbergii* is a woody shrub that often forms dense thickets. *Microstegium vimineum*, a C_4 (warm season) grass, forms dense carpets. The two invasives cooccur often. In a series of laboratory and greenhouse experiments in New Jersey, Ehrenfeld et al. (2001) found that the soil under these plants was increased in available nitrate, and had elevated pH as well. The two invasive plants have different mechanisms to achieve a similar end result. *Berberis* combines large biomasses of N-rich roots with N-rich leaf litter, whereas *Microstegium* clumps combine small biomasses of N-rich roots with small biomasses of N-poor litter that leave much of the surface soil with few roots. Changing key chemical characteristics of soil—e.g., changed nitrate and pH—are undoubtedly only two of numerous ways in which invasive plant species alter the arena or playing field in contesting for dominance of patches of soil.

In the same research sites that were used by Ehrenfeld et al. (2001), Kourtev et al. (2002) measured alteration of microbial community structure and function by exotic plant species (Japanese barberry = *Berberis thunbergii* and Japanese stilt grass = *Microstegium vimineum*), compared to a co-occurring native species (blueberry = *Vaccinium* spp.). They found in both bulk and rhizosphere soils that phospholipid fatty acid (PLFA) profiles, enzyme activities, and substrate-induced respiration (SIR) profiles of microbial communities were significantly altered under the two exotic species. The PLFA profiles provided only an index of community structure rather than specific information about what species were active. A correlation of structure (PLFA) and function—namely, enzymes—showed that a particular set of species is associated with a particular pattern of enzyme activities but does not provide information about which of the species were responsible. Kourtev et al. (2002) found that profiles of enzymatic and catabolic capacity in the soil definitely differed with different microbial communities.

One of the more noted plant invasions of the past century in North America was that of the annual grass, *Bromus tectorum* L., which has a current range of 40,000,000 ha, notably in wide regions of Washington, Oregon, Idaho, and Utah. In the Snake River plains of Idaho, *Bromus tectorum* has increased the frequency of fire from once every 60–110 years to as often as once every 3–5 years. This has dramatic consequences for ecosystem conditions and processes, particularly relative to nitrogen cycling (D'Antonio and Hobbie, 2005).

Evans et al. (2001) measured litter biomass and C: N and lignin: N ratios to determine the effects on litter dynamics in a site in Utah that had been invaded in 1994. Long-term soil incubations (415 d) were used to measure potential soil microbial respiration and net N mineralization. Plant-available N was measured for two years with ion-exchange bags, and potential changes in rates of gaseous N losses were measured using denitrification enzyme activity. *Bromus* invasion significantly increased litter biomass, and its litter had significantly greater C:N and lignin:N ratios than did native species. The changes in litter quality and chemistry decreased potential rates of N mineralization in sites with *Bromus* by decreasing N available for microbial activity. Evans et al. (2001) suggest that *Bromus* may cause a short-term decrease in N loss by decreasing substrate availability and denitrification activity, but over the long term, N losses are likely to be greater in invaded sites because of increased fire frequency and greater N volatilization during fire. This mechanism, in conjunction with land use change, will set into play a set of positive feedbacks that will decrease N availability and alter species composition.

In a companion study to that of Evans et al. (2001), Belnap and Phillips (2001) studied the effects of invasion by *Bromus tectorum* in three study sites in the Canyonlands of southwestern Utah. They measured litter and soil changes in sites that had been dominated previously by *Hilaria jamesii*, a fall-active C_4 grass, and *Stipa comata* and *Stipa hymenoides*, predominantly spring-active C_3 species. Belnap and Phillips (2001) measured the abundances of a wide range of microbes, microarthropods, and macroarthropods under *Hilaria* and *Stipa* communities, as well as in those that had been invaded by *Bromus* in 1994. There were significant changes in numbers and diversity, due in part to changes in amounts and qualities of litter. In the *Bromus* invaded plots, litter quantity was 2.2 times higher in *Bromus* + *Hilaria* than in *Hilaria* alone, contrasted with *Stipa* and *Bromus*, which was 2.8 times greater than in the *Stipa* alone. Soil biota responded generally in opposite manners in the two perennial + annual grass plots. Active bacteria decreased in *Hilaria* vs. *Hilaria* + *Bromus*, and increased in *Stipa* vs. *Stipa* + *Bromus*. Most higher trophic-level organisms increased in Hilaria + Bromus relative to Hilaria alone, while decreasing in *Stipa* + *Bromus* relative to *Stipa* alone. The soil and soil foodweb characteristics of the newly invaded sites included (1) lower species richness and numbers of fungi and invertebrates, (2) greater numbers of active bacteria, (3) similar species of bacteria and fungi as those invaded over fifty years previously, (4) higher levels of silt (hence greater water holding capacity and soil fertility), and (5) a more continuous cover of living and dead plant material. The authors note that food web architecture can vary widely from what had existed previously within the same vegetation type, depending on the reactions to the invasive species relative to the previous uninvaded condition. Addition of a common resource can shift conditions significantly, and careful attention to the effects of species by season by site is definitely warranted. Further background on foodweb architecture and its role in ecosystem function is provided in Coleman et al. (2004) and Moore et al. (2004).

In general, numerous theoretical studies have usually supported Elton's (1958) biotic resistance hypothesis, in which more diverse communities better resist invading species (see Byers and Noonburg, 2003, and references cited therein). In a mathematical overview of more general aspects of biotic resistance to invasive species, Byers and Noonburg (2003) demonstrate that invasibility is influenced not only by the number of native species present, but also by the number of resources present in a given ecosystem. Building on a Lotka–Volterra competition model, Byers and Noonburg's model predicts that increasing invasibility with native diversity across large scales is the result of decreasing mean interaction strength as resources increase. The strength of the positive relationship between native and exotic species diversity and relative contribution of factors extrinsic to the community depend on whether niche breadth increases with the number of available resources. Interestingly, the same mechanism—the sum of interspecific competitive effects ($\Sigma\alpha_{ij}n_j$)—drives the opposite pattern of decreasing invasibility with native richness at small scales, because resource numbers are held constant. As a consequence, Byers and Noonburg (2003) conclude that Elton's biotic resistance hypothesis, interpreted as a small-scale phenomenon, is consistent with large-scale patterns in exotic species diversity.

Ecosystem Variance

The scale-dependency and magnitude of variance in ecosystem dynamics and population dynamics was compared across space and time at twelve LTER sites across a wide range of ecosystem types (Hobbie et al., 2003). In some instances, geomorphic processes varied and had a repercussion in the landscape. One example was movement of water across the landscape, which accounted for the largest amount of variance in patterns of temporal variability across a topographic gradient. The role of species diversity and its influence on variability of ecosystem processes has proven to be of great interest to ecologists.

Numerous factors influence the magnitude and stability of ecosystem properties, including climate, geography, and soil or sediment type. These abiotic controls interact with functional traits of organisms to control ecosystem properties (Hooper et al., 2005), with further feedbacks on biodiversity. Assuming that there is an increase in ecosystem function with increasing diversity, they could arise from two principal mechanisms: (1) Only one or a few species might have a large effect on any given ecosystem property. Increasing species richness increases the likelihood that these species would be present, and assumes that competitive success and high productivity are positively associated at the species level (Hooper et al., 2005; Tilman, 2001). (2) Species or functional richness could increase ecosystem properties through positive interactions among species. Two primary mechanisms for this are complementarity and facilitation, leading to the phenomenon of overyielding. All these effects are expected to show a similar saturating response as diversity increases (Hooper et al., 2005).

Implications of Long-Term Climate Trends

THE HANTAVIRUS STORY

If one goes online and searches the Centers for Disease Control's (CDC) Web site for "All about Hantaviruses," a fascinating story unfolds. In brief, in 1993, a young, physically fit Navajo man suffering from shortness of breath was rushed to a hospital in New Mexico and died soon afterward. An investigation of the etiology, or cause, of this disease by Dr. Bruce Tempest of the Indian Health Service located five young, healthy people who had all died after acute respiratory failure. A series of laboratory tests ruled out exposure to herbicides or bubonic plague or influenza, and toward some sort of virus. Samples of tissue from patients who had gotten the disease were sent to the CDC for thorough analysis. CDC scientists, after exhaustive tests, were able to link the pulmonary syndrome with a virus, a previously unknown type of Hantavirus. The disease was labeled Hanta Pulmonary Syndrome, or HPS. Researchers knew that other known Hantaviruses were transmitted to people by small mammals, such as mice and rats. They initiated a trapping program in the Four Corners area (where the four states of Arizona, New Mexico, Colorado and Utah intersect) and narrowed the target down to one species, the deer mouse (*Peromyscus maniculatus*). About 30 percent of the deer mice were infected, with a few other species showing lower occurrence of the infection. The next steps were to compare the frequency of occurrence of deer mice in "case" households versus "control" households where no one had gotten the disease. In essence, the linkage between small mammals, humans, and the Hantavirus were demonstrated and verified by CDC and scientists of the U.S. Army Medical Research Unit of Infectious Diseases. The CDC sings the praises of interagency cooperation, but does not specify the identity of the other agencies. Thereby hangs a tale.

The Sevilleta LTER Web site notes that "scientists at the CDC enlisted the aid of Sevilleta scientists in identifying ecological aspects of the epidemic of Hantavirus Pulmonary Syndrome, which had resulted in several dozens of deaths." Now we get to the intriguing part; biologists with the Sevilleta LTER and Canyonlands National Park were the only two groups of researchers who had long-term data on rodent populations in the southwestern region. The Sevilleta data showed large population increases in *Peromyscus* spp. during 1992 and early 1993. Rodent population fluctuations moved in phase with cycles in above average precipitation due to the 1992 El Niño and the mild winter of 1992–1993, which led to increased ecosystem productivity and subsequent rodent population explosions. These studies led to the development of rodent/ virus sampling strategies, models to predict potential disease outbreaks, and disease prevention plans for human populations. In fact, a team led by Robert Parmenter, working in collaboration with Dr. Terry Yates, of the University of New Mexico Natural History Museum, was able to track the existence of the Hantavirus back across more than 100 years, in the archived collections of *Peromyscus* specimens. This led to a successful application to the National Institutes of Health by Sevilleta LTER to become one of two major Hantavirus programs using large rodent enclosures to study the ecological basis for the transmission of Hantavirus in wild rodent populations. For more information on this fascinating story refer to Yates et al. (2002).

The take-home message from this example is abundantly clear: the collection of comprehensive field data and careful archiving, with suitable metadata (what the data are about, and their provenance) pays big dividends for the entire body of scientific researchers, and the wider human community as well. It really would behoove ecological researchers to more assiduously "get the message out" in wider communications. This need for communication transcends such wide-circulation journals such as the *Scientific American* and should include NOVA and other widely viewed television programs.

EFFECTS OF LARGE-SCALE CLIMATE DRIVERS

Numerous factors are involved in driving change in large-scale climatic phenomena. These include intense volcanic eruptions, the El Niño/ Southern Oscillation (ENSO), the North Atlantic Oscillation (NAO), and a few drivers in the North Pacific, such as variation in the strength of the Aleutian Low (Table 3.1, from Magnuson et al,, 2006b). The scientists in the North Temperate Lakes LTER have used long-term ice-on and ice-off data to determine relationships between the effects of rare events such as intense volcanic eruptions and the quasi-periodic oscillations of three to seven years in ENSO, or ones of longer time spans (NAO and the Aleutian low) (Magnuson et al., 2006b). As one might expect, Magnuson et al. gathered data on long-term ice data around the Northern Hemisphere in an LTER-funded international workshop held at the Trout Lake Station (Magnuson et al., 2000b). Ice-off dates in Wisconsin and the Great Lakes region are associated with at least four large-scale drivers in the South Pacific, North Pacific, and North Atlantic oceans (Table 3.1). The relation between ice-off on Lake Mendota and these drivers noted above is strongest for the NAO, accounting for 37% of the variation from 1879 to 1928 (Table 3.1). Other correlations, although weaker, are presented in the table as well. More importantly for global interest, differences in the strength of the relations between ice-off dates and the NAO and the Southern Oscillation Index (SOI) are found among such regions as Finland, Siberia, Switzerland, and Wisconsin, among years from 1871 to 1920 (Livingstone, 2000, cited in Magnuson et al., 2006a).

Table 3.1 *Relation of Ice-Off Dates to Large-Scale Climate Drivers*

Large-Scale Driver[a]	Years	Location	Relation to Ice-Off
ENSO	1900–1940	Canada and Eastern United States	Late with El Niño
ENSO	1940–1995	Canada and Eastern United States	Early with El Niño
ENSO	1942–1991	Lake Mendota, WI	Highest correlation with SOI $r^2 = 0.25$
NAO	1879–1928	Lake Mendota, WI	Highest correlation with NAO index $r^2 = 0.37$
PNA (Winter or Spring)	1969–1988	South Boreal and Temperate in North America	Correlation with index $r^2 = 0.09–0.20$
WP (Spring)	1969–1988	South Boreal and Temperate in North America	Correlation with index $r^2 = 0.07–0.18$
Intense Volcanic Eruption	1850s–1995	Five lakes in Northern Hemisphere, including Lake Mendota, WI	Delayed 1–4 days in second and/or third year after eruption

SOURCE: Magnuson 2002, see also Magnuson et al. 2004.

[a]ENSO = El Niño Southern Oscillation (SOI = Southern Oscillation Index); NAO = North Atlantic Oscillation; PNA = Pacific/North American Pattern; WP = West Pacific Pattern.

Watershed Ecosystem Analysis

The biggest challenge facing many ecosystem managers is the search for the best way to approach multiple-use. This has been a source of controversy for decades, largely because of the desired uses to which the lands are to be put by multiple stake-holders. Using small watersheds, usually <100 ha in area, serves as a convenient ecosystem size to studying how forests function in terms of energetics, and the cycling of nutrients and water. Among other findings, cross-ecosystem watershed studies have pointed out the important functions of woody debris in streams, including (1) creation of a more diverse aquatic habitat, (2) reduction of stream velocity, (3) provision of nutrients and substrate for biological activity, and (4) entrapment of sediment (Fisher and Likens, 1973; Webster et al., 1983, cited in Hornbeck and Swank, 1992).

As a result of watershed ecosystem studies in the Southern Appalachians, Webster et al. (1992) postulated a sequence of at least five phases of stream dynamics following logging or other disturbances (Fig. 3.2). In the initial phase, the energy base is shifted from lowered terrestrial organic matter to increased in-stream primary production; sediment production is increased due to road construction and other soil-disturbance activities; benthic organic matter is reduced due to low input and rapid breakdown; and there is a large phase of wood input associated with logging. In the second phase, sediment transport declines, but remains above predisturbance level due to the redistribution of material entering the stream during disturbance. Leaf inputs begin to increase and approach predisturbance levels in ten to twenty years, although leaf quality may be different. Woody material decreases due to rapid decay and, in some cases, through physical removal, and benthic organic matter continues to decline. In phase three, the energy base has fully returned to leaf inputs in twenty to thirty years, and regrowing vegetation is a source of small woody inputs to the stream. Accelerated sediment loss is likely to occur twenty to thirty years after logging due to loss of debris dams formed by small woody debris undergoing decomposition. Phase four, aggradation, begins when relatively large logs fall into the channel and provide the stability necessary to form debris dams, which stabilize sediment movement and collect particulate organic matter. It may take 100 years to reach the fifth phase of total recovery, including predisturbance levels of debris dams and benthic organic matter.

Based upon the preceding findings, it is possible to set up buffer strips in riparian areas. The widths are variable, from thirteen to thirty meters on each side of the stream, depending on how steep the terrain is (Hornbeck and Swank, 1992).

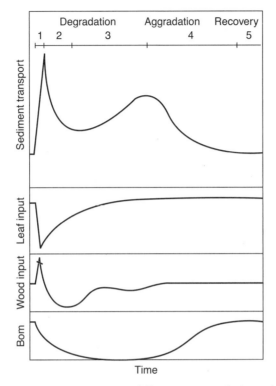

Figure 3.2   Trends in stream processes following streamside forest disturbance (from Webster et al., 1992; used with permission from the publisher).

Integrative Long-Term Experiments

The Andrews Log-Decomposition Experiment

The effects of log decomposition and dead wood on forest floor ecosystems have been of interest to ecologists for decades, certainly dating from the times of the IBP Biome studies. One of the prides and joys of long-term studies is the ability to establish the sorts of studies that could not be supported in any other research program. Such a study is the 200-year log decomposition study established at the H. J. Andrews site. Dr. Mark Harmon took the lead in establishing this study in 1985, with the ultimate objective being to measure the long-term processes of decomposition and immobilization of nutrients in the forest floor. Most litter decomposition studies occur for only a few years at most, with even the LIDET study running for no more than twenty years. Harmon developed a major literature review of the key processes involved in log decomposition, and enlisted USFS assistance in the logistics of setting up a large, comprehensive, well-replicated study (a total of 500 logs, distributed across six sites). This work grew out of previous studies of forest growth on permanent plots that had followed the growth of numerous trees across more than seventy years. This approach was designed to quantify the rates of loss, and the activities of organisms, in the five major classes of logs (Geier, 2007). There were many doubters about this seemingly overly long experiment, but after the experiment was in place, and being followed by scientists and managers, the real value of such a long-term experiment became readily apparent. It is important to note that these long-term studies of log decomposition were an extension in kind of the earlier research on the structural roles of wood in streams of Jim Sedell and his riparian studies group (Geier, 2007).

Addressing a more immediate concern—namely, quantification of the impacts of disturbance on net ecosystem productivity (NEP, the change in ecosystem carbon storage with time), Janisch and Harmon (2002) studied the influence of live tree and coarse woody debris (CWD) on NEP during secondary succession based on data collected along a 500-year chronosequence on the Wind River Ranger District in Southwest Washington state. Maximum live and total wood C stores of 319 Mg C ha^{-1}, respectively, were reached approximately 200 years post-disturbance. Decomposition rates (k) of CWD varied over threefold, from 0.013 to 0.043 per year for individual stands. Regenerating stands took 41 years to reach a mean live wood mass equivalent to the mean mass of CWD remaining after logging, 40 years to equal the mean CWD mass in 500-year-old forest, and more than 150 years to equal the mean total live and dead wood in an old-growth stand. With the average rotation age of eighty years in a stand managed for timber production, regenerating stands stored approximately half the wood mass of the 150- to 200-year-old stand. This has strong implications for the role of western forests in carbon storage, as the managed stands function as net sources, not sinks, of global carbon.

INTERSITE SYNTHESIS

Originally the LTER was site-driven, not a network. Both John Brooks and Tom Callahan were concerned that intersite comparisons be essential. The approach taken was incremental, and by and large, was very successful over a time span of one to two decades, as is developed in this section.

Research Coordinator

In 1988, NSF created a LTER Research Coordinator position at the Division of Environmental Biology and hired Caroline Bledsoe to encourage LTER cross-site research efforts. Caroline worked with the LTER Coordinating Committee in semiannual meetings to foster cross-site synthesis in the LTER network. These meetings, attended by the lead PI and another senior scientist from a given LTER site, have allowed for considerable exchange of ideas and developments that could be investigated on a trial basis and then adopted as part of the overall operational scheme if they proved successful. Dr. Bledsoe continues synthesis studies, with a project on belowground productivity by plant roots at several LTER and non-LTER sites. Entitled Distributed Research Environment for Analysis, Modeling, and Simulation, Using Integrated Technologies for Ecologists (DREAM SUITE), it includes collaboration on the use of various computer systems, and means to use them effectively in this research.

Intersite Synthesis

Intersite science was a high priority for NSF from the early days of the LTER program. This was emphasized by a meeting of the LTER Coordinating Committee held in Denver in November 1986. At that meeting John L. Brooks, Director of the Division of Environmental Biology at NSF, stated that the opportunities for new science lay in LTER Network science, not just in individual site science. In fact, expectations for network science would be a part of NSF evaluations of LTER (Jerry F. Franklin, pers. comm., Magnuson et al., 2006c). Brooks reinforced the concern that the Foundation would have spent a total of $15 million on eleven sites, and said, in effect, "What have we gotten from it?" (Magnuson et al., 2006c). Unfortunately, the amount of funding available for intersite synthesis always remained elusive. Site science tended to get top priority in allocating funding. This lack of funding was addressed several years later, as noted below.

In 1994, NSF announced a special competition for cross-site comparisons and synthesis at LTER and non-LTER sites and international research awards in response to the ten-year review of the LTER Program. Nine grants ranging from $109,353 to $200,000 were awarded to LTER and non-LTER U.S. sites and to sites in Ireland, Scotland, Costa Rica, Argentina, and Russia. NSF announced an open competition for LTER Network Office cooperative agreement. NSF announced the 1995 special competition for cross-site comparisons and synthesis at LTER and non-LTER sites. Thirteen awards ranging from $150,000 to $200,000 were made. The 1995 NSF/DOE/NASA/USDA Joint Program Awards, Terrestrial Ecology and Global Change (TECO), were announced. There were seven LTER recipients, including researchers at Bonanza Creek, Cedar Creek, Central Plains, Harvard Forest, H. J. Andrews, and Jornada. The following is a representative overview of some LTER intersite projects.

LIDET, CIDET, and DIRT

The LTER Network has enabled scores of researchers to pursue collaborative research in a wide variety of habitats, aquatic and terrestrial. The project that spanned the most sites (twenty-eight in toto, with seventeen in the LTER) was the Long-Term Intersite Decomposition

Experiment Team (LIDET). This project was established to determine the effects of substrate quality and macroclimate on decomposition and nutrient dynamics of leaves, wood, and fine roots (LIDET, 1995; Gholz et al., 2000; Kratz et al., 2003). The team consisted of site participants, scientists who model carbon, nitrogen, and phosphorus dynamics (e.g., Moorhead et al., 1999) and a central analysis group that performed chemical analyses and managed the data (Harmon et al., 1999). The influence of this network effort continues to reverberate across the decades. Parton et al. (2007) examined the patterns of N release from leaf litter across twenty-one sites in a ten-year time span. They concluded that the net N release was governed by initial tissue N concentration and mass remaining irrespective of climate, edaphic conditions or biota. Arid grasslands exposed to high UV radiation were an exception, with net N release being insensitive to initial N.

LIDET has a Canadian counterpart, Canadian Intersite Decomposition Experiment Team (CIDET), with a network of eighteen forested sites across Canada, coordinated by Dr. J. A. (Tony) Trofymow at the Pacific Forestry Research Centre, Victoria, British Columbia (Trofymow et al., 2002). They found that the rate of N release from the litters was not related to the original N concentration, perhaps due to the generally narrow range of N (0.59–1.28%) in the litters (Moore et al., 2006). Reasons for the differences between the Canadian and U.S. group results are not readily apparent, and require further study.

There are some long-term experiments in aboveground and belowground ecology, utilizing, in part, some of the International Long-term Ecological Research (ILTER) network of sites (the Andrews site and Harvard Forest are participants, as well as Bousson in Pennsylvania, and Sikfokut in Hungary) (Townsend et al., 2006). This comparative approach was considered but not acted on during the IBP. It enables us to answer questions across space and time. An example follows: What is the fate of plant detritus, or "litter," in soil systems? A network of long-term (decades), large-scale field experiments has been established across the North American continent to examine its fate. The Detritus Input and Removal and Transfer (DIRT) experiments were established by Nadelhoffer et al. (2004), drawing on the initial inspiration and results of Francis Hole and colleagues at the University of Wisconsin. Treatments consist of chronically altered aboveground and below-ground inputs in the following fashion: (1) double litter, (2) no roots (using trenched and root barrier containing plots), (3) no litter, (4) no inputs, and (5) O/A-less plots. This approach builds upon other (perhaps better-known, some IBP-inspired) long-term studies at Abisko (Sweden) and also Rothamsted (UK). What makes the DIRT studies intriguing is the fact that they have been replicated across different ecosystems and biomes, thus permitting ecologists to explore the generalities of some of the principles of decomposition across a wide range of biotic, climatic, and pedological conditions, as well as across decadal time spans.

LINX Project

Another successful cross-site study was the Lotic Intersite Nitrogen eXperiment (LINX), which added some non-LTER sites; some were IBP legacy (LTER) sites. The investigators used a standard experimental design and methodology, including following movement of ^{15}N-labeled substrates of small streams in a wide geographic range from the Alaskan tundra to temperate streams in Oregon and North Carolina, the south-western desert, and the Puerto Rican rain forest. The principal findings were that regardless of location, small streams are extremely important sites of nitrogen retention (Peterson et al., 2001). One principal contrib-uting factor to this result is that nitrogen uptake (15-N-ammonium) varied little across all eleven streams measured, reflecting metabolic compensation in streams, some of which have high autotrophic produc-tion where allochthonous (out of stream) inputs (Webster et al., 2003) are relatively low, and vice versa. This work continued across seventy-two streams and eight regions, measuring the effects of nitrate loading on downstream phenomena. Total biotic uptake and denitrification of nitrate increased with stream nitrate concentration, but the efficiency of biotic uptake and denitrification declines as concentration increases, reducing the proportion of in-stream nitrate that is removed from transport. This has strong implications for the effectiveness of in-stream capabilities for removing additional nitrates due to anthropogenic loading (Mulholland et al., 2008).

LINX was an important influence on the NEON network establishing cross-site stream experiments (STREON). This is discussed further in Chapter 4.

Smaller Multi-Site Studies

The LTER network has tended to support more wide-ranging multi-site comparative studies, as noted above. Smaller efforts, including two- or three-site studies, have proven more difficult to get funded. A small group of us from the Luquillo and Coweeta LTERs proposed a definitive study of the roles of microarthropods and fungi in leaf litter decomposition in tropical and temperate ecosystems. This was submitted to the Ecosystem Studies program office of NSF in late 1992 and went through three revisions, across two years, with numerous changes made to meet reviewers' criticisms. We eventually focused on a few key processes (decomposition and microarthropods' role in it), and streamlined the study to what two co-PIs and a postdoctoral fellow could carry out, or roughly $200,000 for three years. After deduction for overhead (indirect costs), this left approximately $144,000, which enabled us to study the breakdown of standard litters on all sites (CWT, LUQ, and La Selva on the Atlantic lowlands in Costa Rica), and native litters in each site, with and without naphthalene additions to repel arthropods in parts of each site. This study kept our postdoctoral fellow, Liam Heneghan, very busy indeed. We demonstrated strong effects of microarthropods on decomposition, but unexpectedly, the microarthropods had a much greater impact on decomposition in the two tropical sites compared with the temperate site at Coweeta (Heneghan et al., 1998; 1999a, 1999b). These results were further corroborated by Gonzalez and Seastedt (2001), who found that soil fauna had a disproportionately larger impact on decomposition and mineralization in wet tropical forest, when compared to similar studies in dry tropical and subalpine forests. For more information on soil microbial-soil biota and nutrient interactions in tropical sites, refer to the extensive studies of Vitousek and colleagues (Vitousek, 2004).

LTER MEETINGS

LTER Mini-Meetings

In 2002, NSF and LTER held a first annual Mini Symposium: LTER Network Major Research Accomplishments. The Network Information System Advisory Committee (NISAC) was formed.

In 2003, NSF and LTER held a second annual Mini Symposium: Integration of Geosciences and Social Science within the LTER Program: Progress and Prospects. LTER All Scientists' Meeting was held in Seattle, Washington.

In 2004, NSF and LTER held a third annual NSF-LTER Mini Symposium: LTER Research Informing Land Management. The LTER Network received a grant from NSF to conduct network-level strategic planning.

In 2005, NSF and LTER held a fourth annual Mini Symposium: Coastal Research in LTER. Mary Clutter retired as Assistant Director of the Directorate for Biological Sciences at NSF. Jim Collins was named to replace her. John Magnuson was chosen as interim chair. The first LTER Graduate Student Collaborative Research Symposium was held at Andrews Experimental Forest. In 2006, NSF and LTER held a fifth annual Mini Symposium: LTER and Global Change. An All Scientists' Meeting was held in Estes Park, Colorado. Peter Arzberger was named chair of the LTER National Advisory Board. In 2007, NSF and LTER held a sixth annual Mini Symposium: Cycles of Change in Social-Ecological Systems: Perspectives from Long-Term Ecological Research. This led to the development of a new ten-year research plan for the LTER.

All Scientists' Meetings

Looming high among the significant features of scientific interactions in the LTER are the All Scientists' Meetings, which began in Las Cruces, New Mexico, in 1981 and continued at three-yearly intervals afterward, including memorable ones at Lake Itasca in 1984, and Estes Park, Colorado, in 1993. More than 600 senior scientists and graduate students attend these gatherings and make presentations. With the steady increase in numbers of participants, larger and larger proportions of the presentations are given as posters. This reached a peak at the meeting in Seattle, WA, in September 2003. So many posters were being presented that two small ballrooms had to be pressed into service on two adjacent floors of the hotel we were meeting in. This was on a Saturday night. Despite the considerable influence of diversions in downtown Seattle, hundreds of participants went from one floor to the other and back again, providing an endlessly changing audience to hear the presentations of the authors and coauthors. These All Scientists' meetings have always been an order of magnitude more intense and enjoyable than the usual national scientific meetings, which often have more than one dozen concurrent oral sessions all competing for audiences across four to five days. One of the more noteworthy invited presentations that I ever heard at an All Scientists' Meeting (ASM) was given on the interaction between vegetation and climate at the landscape scale. At the 1993 ASM in Estes Park, Colorado, Bruce Hayden from the Virginia Coastal Reserve site of the University of Virginia showed that a significant amount of the "roughness" due to vegetation cover intercepts and interacts with winds impinging on the earth's surface. More specifically, evapotranspiration from land surfaces loads the atmosphere with water vapor, reducing the sensible heating of the surface layer of the atmosphere, and contributes up to 50 percent of the total precipitation across all continents. This notion was quite heretical in the early 1990s, but was foreshadowed by Tyndall in the nineteenth century and indeed by Christopher Columbus' son, Ferdinand, centuries earlier (Hayden,

1998). Hayden made the cogent observation that the level of realism incorporated by the abovementioned mechanisms would make climate models lacking this level of both detail and feedback mechanisms doomed to failure. This paper had a great impact on many of us, who had not thought much at the landscape-to-continent scale.

International Activities in the LTER

An International LTER Summit was held at Estes Park in September 1993. Argentina, Brazil, Australia, Canada, Chile, China, Costa Rica, France, Hungary, Mexico, Mongolia, New Zealand, Russia, Taiwan, the United Kingdom, and the United States were represented. The International LTER (ILTER) Network was established, and Jerry F. Franklin (U.S. LTER Chair) was elected ILTER Steering Committee Chair. LTER–Chinese Ecological Research Network (CERN) exchange/collaboration developed as well in 1993. The ILTER now comprises more than fifty countries, with some (e.g., China) having more than twenty across their vast extent.

SITE SYNTHESIS PUBLICATIONS

Beginning in 1994, Bruce Hayden was named Chair of the Publications Committee of the LTER. He and the committee contacted several publishers and arranged for the LTER Synthesis Volume series to be set up under the aegis of the Oxford University Press. In 1996, the LTER Network Publications Committee entered into a contractual agreement with Oxford University Press (OUP) to publish the "LTER Network Synthesis Series." The Palmer LTER site volume was published: Foundations for Ecological Research West of the Antarctic Peninsula (American Geophysical Union; Priscu, 1998).

A timetable to produce volumes involved several years, with the first volume produced by the Tallgrass Prairie group (Knapp et al., 1998). The volumes typically had long lag times before appearing in print. Finding a critical mass of authors who would make it a top priority was the main reason for this. This trend has continued into current times, but many more volumes have appeared in the last few years. These include the *Standard Soil Methods for Long-Term Ecological Research* volume (Robertson et al., 1999) and the Niwot site volume: *Structure and Function of an Alpine Ecosystem* (OUP; Bowman and Seastedt, 2001). The *Climate Variability and Ecosystem Response* volume followed (OUP; Greenland et al., 2003). Subsequent volumes published included the Bonanza Creek site: *Alaska's Changing Boreal Forest* (OUP [Chapin et al., 2005]), Jornada site: *Structure and Function of a Chihuahuan Desert Ecosystem* (OUP [Havstad et al., 2006]), *North Temperate Lakes LTER site: Long-Term Dynamics of Lakes in the Landscape* (OUP [Magnuson et al., 2006a]), and the Harvard Forest site volume: *Forests in Time. The Environmental Consequences of 1000 Years of Change in New England* (Foster and Aber, 2004; Yale University Press), and *Agrarian Landscapes in Transition: Comparisons of Long-Term Ecological & Cultural Change*, eds. Charles L. Redman and David R. Foster (2008) studied human interactions with agricultural land at six U.S. Long-Term Ecological Research sites.

Additional volumes include *Principles and Standards for Measuring Primary Production* (Fahey and Knapp, 2007) and the *Trends Folio* (now in progress, edited by Deb Peters). One international volume has appeared so far: Biodiversity in Drylands (Shachak et al., 2004). Additional volumes are in press, including *Disturbance, Response and Tropical Forest Dynamics: Long-Term Perspectives and Implications* (N. Brokaw et al., in press) and a Coweeta Disturbance and Recovery study (W. T. Swank and J. R. Webster, pers. comm.).

All of these books required several person-months of effort by the editors, and many person-weeks of writing by individual authors. Obtaining authorization from the LTER Coordinating Committee was quite an involved process, involving numerous meetings with scientists at the semi-annual meetings and the equally important authorization from the Network Office to fund the requisite planning meetings.

The following account provides an overview of the planning process involved in writing and editing the *Standard Soil Methods* volume. Senior scientists and graduate students alike were very concerned about making measurements across sites that were even closely comparable. Thus there was a clear and present need to standardize measurements of soil physics, chemistry, and biology. This required action by interested parties throughout the network, so a provisional outline was drawn up by Phil Robertson and circulated among co-PIs. Robertson assembled a group of coeditors, including Caroline Bledsoe, Phil Sollins, and myself. We proceeded to draw up a list of proposed topics and invited scientists within the LTER Network and outside it, as noted scientists in their areas of specialization, to write review papers.

There were skeptics who assumed that the reviewing and vetting process would be perfunctory. By the time we held an initial meeting of the invited authors and critiqued each other's papers, it became apparent that we needed in some cases to bring in new authors to provide greater coverage of the subject matter involved. This was particularly true in aspects of the root production and turnover papers, which required a wider spectrum of authors. Much to our gratification, the invitees agreed readily to participate in the rewriting process. A similar case has existed for other volumes in the synthesis series, with the review process being extensive and rigorous.

Comparison with the Track Record of the IBP Synthesis Volumes

In both the IBP and LTER, there has proved to be considerable inertia to overcome in order to produce a multi-authored and usually multi-editor volume. IBP volumes for North American biomes and also the international series were several years in gestation. Because of the wider time spans covered by the LTER volumes in most cases, the caliber and extent of synthesis has been considerably higher.

PUBLICATIONS FOR THE GENERAL PUBLIC

Several LTER children's books have been published as part of the LTER

Education and outreach effort. These include *My Water Comes from the Mountains*, about the Niwot Ridge LTER; *The Lost Seal*, about the McMurdo Dry Valleys LTER; *Student Work and Play*, a study of the Taiga biome produced as part of the Bonanza Creek Student LTER program; and *Sea Secrets*, published jointly by California Current Ecosystems LTER and Palmer LTER. Several more books are envisioned in this series, which is an essential part of the LTER outreach program.

ARCHIVING AND INFORMATION MANAGEMENT

One of the most important aspects of the LTER Network, required from the outset, was the need to archive data and to coordinate information management systems. This was perhaps the most difficult to implement as well, and underwent considerable development across the several decades of the LTER program. In the process of developing a successful information management system, the semiannual LTER Coordinating Committee meetings assumed an ever-increasing importance. These meetings, attended by the lead PI and another senior scientist from each LTER site, have allowed for considerable exchange of ideas and developments that could be investigated on a trial basis and then adopted as part of the overall operational scheme if they proved successful.

The Geographic Information Systems (GIS) working group analyzed the status of LTER Network technical supplements and assessed future technical needs (recommended enhanced Internet connectivity, individual site remote sensing capability, annual acquisition of remote sensing data, site archival storage capability, additional GPS units, enhanced site database software capabilities, automated field data collection). Global positioning systems (GPS) units were acquired for shared LTER site use, and GPS training was provided for representatives from all sites.

This aspect of the LTER is growing ever more rapidly and is the focal point of much of the Decadal Plan for the LTER (published in September 2007). Activities in the Decadal Plan are discussed extensively in the next section.

THE LEGACIES OF THE LTER PROGRAM

Including the role of the Forest Service and perhaps other agency sites and people in LTER, the program helps give continuity to long-term studies. In every LTER project that partners with the Forest Service and other Federal agencies, the land base and information management are greatly assisted by USFS managers, scientists, and the additional funding base.

Additional legacies of the LTER are discussed further in Chapter 4.

LTER PROGRAM REVIEWS

In 1983, NSF conducted a national review of the LTER Program. In 1989, NSF conducted a national LTER Program review. NSF commissioned a 10-Year Review of the LTER Program, chaired by Dr. Paul G. Risser. This review made several recommendations, principally concerning the role of a Network Office and the need for its expanded role in future years of LTER studies. It particularly emphasized the need for studying large-scale and cross-site patterns and processes, as well as anthropogenic influences on ecological systems.

In 1995, the LTER Coordinating Committee, at the request of NSF, developed an eight-year vision—LTER 2000—for the creation of a global environmental research network based upon approaches established in the LTER Program.

In 1999, the National Advisory Board reviewed the LTER Network. It found that the state of site-oriented research was very strong, but encouraged more explicit cross-site synthesis and a stronger emphasis on Cyberinfrastructure.

In 2001, NSF commissioned a 20-Year Review of the LTER Network (Harris and Krishtalka, 2002). This review concluded that the LTER community had identified several strategies for achieving synthesis science. This requires networked data acquisition, analysis, and testing by predictive models across increasingly broader phenomena.

This requires, in turn, the use of cross-domain approaches and interdisciplinary, collaborative teams. An essential component is that the

LTER program should become a research collaborator, conducting research along a seamless, integrated continuum from site-specific to cross-site to network- and systems-level ecological studies. They pointed out at this juncture that partnering with social scientists would pay big dividends in increasing understanding of the interrelationships and reciprocal impacts of natural and human ecosystems in order to inform environmental policy.

A logical outgrowth of the research modes noted above is that these collaborations will foster serendipitous science, which exploits unanticipated events, including disturbances, and scans multiple databases for emerging, unanticipated patterns and trends. The committee noted that the LTER program's informatics infrastructure should provide a "virtual portal" to LTER legacy data for investigators worldwide.

Interestingly, the committee recommended that new sites not be added to the LTER network until such expansion was justified in the strategic plan. They encouraged the LTER program to expand internationally by building on its collaborations with the ILTER network.

The Education and Outreach section of the review was quite explicit that much has been accomplished in graduate student education and training; also, the K–12-level Schoolyard LTER has also accomplished much in terms of outreach. They particularly supported the leveraging of funds by sites' pooling their programs and using modular programs that could be employed across several sites at once. We will revisit this aspect further in consideration of the prospects for the future of LTER into the fourth decade.

The committee urged that in the arena of public policy, the LTER program needs to assume a more "powerful and pervasive role" in informing environmental solutions at local, national and international levels. This has been approached in more of an ad hoc approach, with LTER scientists' being urged to meet with their representatives and senators and their staff to assist in more scientific inputs to environmental policy problems. This was also noted as way to better ensure greater support in future for such large-scale, long-term research programs.

The LTER program and budget came in for considerable scrutiny. To meet the goals outlined above, the committee urged that enhanced funding be given to the LTER network as rapidly as possible. Because of the increased funding for two sites that had the augmentation funding for socioeconomic studies, the need to achieve parity in funding for all sites was emphasized. The recommended informatics and biodiversity core activities were also listed as needing major attention in enhanced funding for all sites.

The need to foster LTER synthesis science was also held up as a major action item by the NSF. The committee urged that LTER proposal guidelines and review criteria be revised to integrate and balance site-specific and cross-site research and education; hold more frequent cross-disciplinary and cross-site competitions that invite participation from outside the LTER community; and increase the importance of data management and informatics in evaluating LTER site activities and proposals. To carry all of the above enhanced actions, the committee recommended that there be two NSF officers: a permanent officer and a rotator person. This last request has been noted by the NSF, but one of the major problems in NSF administration is getting enough (and adequate) personnel to staff the various ecosystem and LTER desks.

A more recent planning document, the Decadal Plan for LTER, was drawn up by co-PIs in the LTER Network in 2006 and was published in 2007. This document addresses several new initiatives that are envisioned for the next several years of the LTER program.

LOOKING FORWARD IN LTER

Prospects for the future, via new developments in major thematic areas, are very positive for the LTER Network. One of the major focuses of the Decadal Assessment document is to emphasize the areas of research collaboration by groups of LTERs within the broad scale of the LTER Network. This includes three groups: (1) managed lands, which focus on the sites most directly impacted by human land use, (2) cryoturbation studies, which involve the major polar ecosystem studies in polar regions, and (3) estuarine and marine studies, which incorporate the wide range of sites in these geographic categories.

An example of enhanced instrumentation that will prove useful in several LTER studies is "airborne spectranomics," by means of which forest canopy chemical and taxonomic diversity can be mapped (Asner and Martin, 2009). This is undoubtedly one of the areas that will be pursued in the NEON program that is discussed in Chapter 4. Combining spectral measurements with in situ studies of organic matter components and biota that accumulate in old-growth forest canopies (Nadkarni et al., 2002) promises to yield great benefits in future ecosystem studies.

Cyberinfrastructure (CI) Problems and Prospects: How to Facilitate
Communications between the Network Office and the LTER Sites

One of the continuing problems besetting the LTER Network—and, indeed, any large group of scientists who must maintain, nurture, and disseminate the contents of a data base—is how to successfully develop an "ecology of information" (sensu Nardi and O'Day, 1999). The stakes are high, because "to exchange data, communicate it, mine it, reuse it, and review it is essential to scientific productivity, collaboration, and discovery itself" (Gold, 2007a, 2007b). This system develops from a variety of partnerships to become "ecology of information," which is defined as "an interdependent system of people, practices, values and technologies in a particular local environment" (Nardi and O'Day, 1999). Much of these comments are well understood by members of the LTER Network. How can the necessary networking and exchange processes be facilitated? We have an example from researchers in oceanography—namely, scientists in the Palmer LTER and the United States Joint Global Ocean Flux Study (JGOFS) (Baker and Chandler, 2008).

As is true with all large ecosystems studies, approaches to studying the oceans are evolving to be more interdisciplinary and global. The scope of data management practices is similarly changing to involve both local and global communities as well as responding to broader scientific questions. How can the international LTER networks become a network of networks? More typical responsibilities for data capture and data use related to project needs have expanded to Web-based digital delivery systems. Thus, the transition from a scenario of local use to an augmented arrangement involves additional audiences who constitute reuse communities. This shift from individual data management to socially complex and highly mediated information management requires new practices—namely, organizational behaviors, semantic arrangements, and long-lived collections.

New ways of amalgamating efforts are required. Data flow, often perceived as linear, is often viewed as moving in a hierarchical fashion, from data source to project to repository to national archives to international archives. In fact, a more fruitful approach is to envision an information network as a nonlinear, complex system of often ill-defined relationships between local repositories and a larger-scale community web of institutional repositories, discipline-specific centers, and national archives. The form these independent entities take when joined together may be called a federation, or a network of networks. The process of federation involves networking techniques as well as conventions that scale for use across a range of collections and delivery systems. This leads to concerns for the need to define and negotiate their relations. Questions arise: How are systems federated? Who federates the networks? And (very important) what is required to sustain the federation?

Metadata (adequate description of the data and their provenance) have received much attention in the LTER, and will not be discussed more here. The need for integration, synthesis, and interoperability is equally important, with data interoperability being defined as the state of two or more files being comparable and therefore ready for data integration (Baker and Chandler, 2008). Putting the wealth of relevant experience at the working level in the research community has not been analyzed and organized to make it more readily available to researchers (NRC 1995 report, referenced in Baker and Chandler, 2008).

An example follows, from oceanographic research collaboration. The Palmer Station Long-Term Ecological Research program (Palmer

LTER) and the U.S. Joint Global Ocean Flux Study (JGOFS) have developed data management practices in close partnership with the scientific community. A brief synopsis summarizes their experiences across a decade of collaboration within a multi-investigator, interdisciplinary culture. Although both programs conducted research cruises that featured manually sampled biological and chemical data taken in close coordination with physical oceanographic measurements, the two programs progressed independently, but with common data practices developing in both programs. Palmer initially posted static text files online in the late 1990s. A decade later, to facilitate requests for data queriability and requirements for networking, a new Palmer information system, DataZoo, was launched to allow for online data access, strategic integration, and visualization. This system includes a tiered permission system that enables data provider participation in making data accessible. Interdependent sets of dictionaries describe data sets, while databases of term sets and personnel provide a flexible mechanism to capture and make visible information associated with both the datasets and the information system itself. Significantly, Palmer initiated an informatics focus in 2003 and developed an information management strategy in partnership with both the California Current Ecosystem (CCE) LTER site in 2004 and the California Cooperative Oceanic Fisheries Investigation (CalCOFI) program in 2006.

The U.S. JGOFS was initiated to study the global carbon cycle and associated elements in the context of how the oceans exchanged these elements with the atmosphere, sea floor, and continental boundaries. From 1988 onward, the JGOFS Steering Committee and U.S. NSF Ocean Sciences Division program managers recognized that a coordinated, multi-disciplinary, long-term research program would require a comprehensive data management strategy that addressed the needs of individual investigators and those of the overall program as well. A data manager was identified in 1988 and a Data Management Office (DMO) was created in 1994, complete with technical staff. A series of steps were taken to provide a "user-friendly" milieu for JGOFS system users, via the

Web, to generate custom data sets that match their research interests by combining multiple data sources "on the fly" (Baker and Chandler, 2008). As the JGOFS system moved from primarily process-oriented field studies to modeling, the data system was extended to include a customized Live Access Server. This process became all the more important as synthesis and model results, often global in scope, required a more graphically oriented user interface and extended visualization capabilities (Glover and Chandler, 2001, cited in Baker and Chandler, 2008).

Several data practices in common were identified. For both of them, data management was part of the planning process and was considered to be integral to the scientific research process, requiring close partnership with investigators. Both established centralized local depositories at the start of the project and then developed data policies addressing concerns of agencies, projects, and institutions. Sampling grids, event logs, and local dictionaries are three principal coordinating mechanisms that represent best practices in common in these two independent research programs. One final note: in both programs, custom dictionaries were constructed so as to provide dataset columns with unique, well-defined names and flexibility that accommodates tradition in local naming. Several innovations were developed in making data archiving and manipulation truly interoperable. Several information strategies were pursued with both short-term and long-term implementations (Baker and Chandler, 2008). Several of these management approaches have involved a "shift in culture" (Glover et al., 2006, cited in Baker and Chandler, 2008). Thus a published data policy that details data contribution requirements, data use, and acknowledgment of use serves to align expectations of all the user community members. This pays significant dividends when funding agencies begin to recognize the essential nature of data access and data sharing for the advancement of science.

It is useful to reimagine the entire earth system as studied by large groups of interdisciplinary researchers with information systems included explicitly. This integration creates a third component to the whole earth as an ecosystem, including human systems and environmental systems. Of course, over the long run, it is essential to include humans explicitly in the environmental systems sphere of interest and activity.

As we move further in the twenty-first century with enhanced data acquisition and management systems, perhaps it would be profitable for all concerned to work to develop common data management schemes with collaborators with the LTER, such as the U.S. Forest Service, the Agricultural Research Service, and other suitable federal entities.

NETWORKING INTERNATIONALLY IN THE AGE OF THE LTER: A CASE EXAMPLE WITH COMPARATIVE INSIGHTS FROM SIMILAR COLLABORATION IN THE IBP

The scientific community has tried to find many ways to bring colleagues together to discuss problems and concerns that need to be addressed. There has often been frustration at the size and impersonal nature of large national and international meetings that have attendees numbering in the thousands and a surfeit of possible sessions to attend. Smaller, targeted workshops that focus on just a few topics have been most fruitful over my academic career. One of the more fruitful small gatherings I ever participated in grew out of some initial meetings held in the middle 1980s. As with all good things, it required some overcoming of administrative inertia and even opposition to achieve success.

Beginning in the 1980s, numerous scientists worldwide have been interested in fostering research on basic processes occurring in tropical ecosystems, due in part to NSF's recognition of the need for a LTER tropical site competition. These efforts within North America have been supported by several agencies, primarily the National Science Foundation, the Rockefeller Brothers Foundation (for the Tropical Soil Biology and Fertility Program, or TSBF) (Woomer and Swift, 1994), and the Agency for International Development (AID). A workshop was held in Athens, Georgia, in November, 1985, on the topic "Tropical Soil Biology." This meeting led to further research interest in temperate and tropical comparisons of terrestrial carbon, nitrogen, sulfur, and phosphorus cycling (from a workshop in April 1986 funded by NSF) and the publication of a special issue of Biogeochemistry 5:1 (1988) on this topic.

Armed with the enthusiasm generated by the earlier meetings, a group of us, Ben Bohlool and Goro Uehara, both of the University of Hawaii, and I submitted a proposal to the Ecology Program of NSF on the topic "Dynamics of Tropical Soil Organic Matter." The proposal received very strong evaluations from Patrick Flanagan, Program Director of Ecology, and scientists who reviewed it, but the upper-level NSF administrators took one look at the location (Kahului, Maui) and saw "boondoggle." Apparently the location, which was near the headquarters buildings of the USAID-funded Nitrogen Fertilization by Tropical Agricultural Legumes (NiFTAL), gave the impression that this would be a vacation for scientists at the taxpayers' expense. We argued long and hard for the fact that Hawaii was a crossroads for world soil scientists and ecologists, and that the airfares for invited participants from Japan, New Zealand and Australia would be commensurately lower than having the meeting somewhere on the U.S. mainland. We also noted that Dr. Bohlool had found us a clean two-star motel that offered twin bed rooms for $39.95, or $20 per night per participant, less than half the most discounted hotel room rate that could be found in Athens, Georgia, or some other university town on the mainland. The NSF officials reluctantly admitted that we had done our homework, and gave approval for funding the workshop meeting. We held the intensive workshop on October 7–15, 1988. Our objectives were both straightforward and ambitious: to bring together a group of world-recognized authorities in organic matter studies, and to ascertain the principal areas where gaps remained in our knowledge.

To maximize the chances of success, we invited two or three lead authors to write a preliminary chapter prior to the meeting, so we would have something tangible to work with from the outset of the meeting. The topics covered were (1) constituents of organic matter in temperate and tropical soils, (2) soil organic matter as a source and a sink of plant nutrients, (3) interactions of soil organic matter and variable-charge clays, (4) biological processes regulating organic matter dynamics, (5) organic input management in tropical agroecosystems, (6) modeling soil organic matter dynamics, and (7) methodologies for assessing the quantity and quality of soil organic matter. Each chapter ended with conclusions and recommendations, followed by theme and research imperatives that we offered as suggested options for scientists in tropical countries.

After an initial plenary session to provide an overview of the topics, our workshop broke into seven working groups who wrote revisions and additions during mornings and evenings. The evening sessions usually wound up with a group of us singing folk songs around a beach fire, accompanied by Dr. Patrick Lavelle on the guitar. Afternoons were open for going to the beach. In midweek, we took a field trip to several sites along a transect from the windward (wet) to leeward (dry) sides of the island of Maui.

From the vantage point of twenty years after the meeting in Maui and production of the book (Coleman, Oades, and Uehara, 1989) less than one year later, what major impacts did such an expenditure of time, effort and resources produce? Both Cheryl Palm and Pedro Sanchez have been lifelong researchers on tropical soil organic matter and have worked in the Millennium Assessment project with colleagues in the Earth Institute of Columbia University. They commented that the approaches and methodologies covered in our book were useful to them in the past, and have continued to be of use to them to the present day. Goro Uehara noted that the book has been indispensable in educating students working in his tropical soil organic matter group at the University of Hawaii.

To handle synthesis meetings in the ecological sciences, the Division of Environmental Biology of the NSF created a national center for analysis and synthesis. A brief history of this innovative center is discussed next.

NATIONAL CENTER FOR ECOLOGICAL ANALYSIS
AND SYNTHESIS (NCEAS)

Although it is not an interdisciplinary research network per se, the role of NCEAS in promoting and facilitating synthesis activities in ecological research in North America and worldwide has been truly noteworthy. In the 1980s and earlier, those scientists who arranged to have interdisciplinary research groups from farflung locations on the globe meet on a common theme had a difficult time getting funds for these efforts from NSF Washington. Once one obtained funding, handling the logistical aspects, including travel, lodging, and so forth, often took person-months of time that was hard to support in one's own research group. All this changed when NCEAS was formed in the mid-1990s.

The Environmental Biology cluster at the National Science Foundation held a competition for a center for ecological analysis and synthesis in 1995, and by 1996 the winning group, from the University of California, Santa Barbara, began operations. It soon became evident that having offices in a building in downtown Santa Barbara on State Street would enhance the amenities, including numerous eating places and accessibility to nearby hotels and motels.

NCEAS was set up to bring a few senior investigators to spend sabbaticals there every year, and also to have a small cadre of postdoctoral fellows working on various projects. This mixture has been leavened with visiting synthesis groups, a few per month, working on projects that address various cutting-edge topics in any area of environmental biology, ranging from population and community to ecosystem ecology and global change research. The current budget is a bit over $2 million, which might seem large to any one investigator, but is quite a bargain when dispersed over a few hundred recipients per year. Numerous synthesis papers have appeared in *Ecology*, in *Frontiers in Ecology and the Environment*, and also in edited volumes. An example of a synergistic effect catalyzed by NCEAS is a synthesis of primary production in all of the LTER sites. This brought together personnel from North America and Europe, with high hopes of readily assembling a synthesis of abiotic and biotic factors involved in primary production. The bottom line was that data sets were not fully intercompatible, and the working group intensified its efforts to overcome the logistical challenges, proceeding to write up a very informative synthesis paper on that topic.

Another example illustrates the "outreach" component of NCEAS. A workshop entitled "Information Technology for the Decade of Synthesis: Data Synthesis in the Present and Future" was held at the September 2003 All Scientists' Meeting in Seattle, Washington. Some thirty-four scientists, students, and data managers participated in this workshop. Of those in attendance, 50 percent were LTER Information Managers or GIS Coordinators, 10 percent were from ILTER, 10 percent were students, 10 percent were collaborators, and 15 percent were LTER PIs. The remaining 5 percent were observers. The focus of the workshop was on tools that were being developed in order to integrate diverse data sets from individual site-based research programs in order to foster cross-site studies. The purpose of the workshop was to provide interaction between the information managers and the investigators to uncover what needs to go into the development of tools for scientific synthesis as well as what has gone into tools that have been developed.

Four approaches to software tools for data integration were presented, with discussion following. The presentations consisted of "Hand-Crafted Data Management: IT Tools Built to Last" (Greg Newman, Natural Resource Ecology Laboratory at Colorado State University), "Software Tools for Automated Metadata Creation, Metadata-Mediated Data Processing and Quality Control Analysis: Real-Time Processing Solutions for Real-Time Data" (Wade Sheldon, Georgia Coastal Ecosystem LTER), "Tools for Creating and Executing Scientific Workflows" (Chad Berkley, NCEAS), and "Southwest Environmental Information Network: Using EML to Mediate Data Discovery, Access, and Visualization" (Peter McCartney, Central Arizona Phoenix LTER).

The presenters discussed approaches to the development of new tools for scientific synthesis, as well as how the four following themes related to the development process:

1. What resources were available before development of the tool?
2. What was the need for the tool?
3. How much time was invested in order to develop the tool?
4. What level of scalability/portability does it have?

Each presenter noted the history and utility of the tools he had developed. The contributor from NCEAS, Chad Berkley, discussed the history of NCEAS's tool, Monarch, and how and why they wound up using another program called Ptolemy developed elsewhere. They have developed components to the already mature program (Ptolemy) that allow ingestion of a document that has metadata in a well-formed EML document. Ptolemy is a workflow model wherein "actors," or workflow steps, put data through processing while documenting each processing step, thus generating valuable metadata. The basic root of each of these tools appeared to be metadata. In order for any tool to work on a data set, the dataset must contain the ever-elusive data about the data. This is prima facie evidence of the interactive nature of NCEAS personnel and how the ecological community benefits from their efforts.

PROSPECTS FOR LTER'S FUTURE

As will become apparent in the next chapter, LTER and its networking capabilities are showing more and more promise for studying the phenomenon of connectivity in ecosystems, landscapes, and regions (Carpenter, 2008; Robertson, 2008). The consequences of living in an increasingly interconnected world, sensu Peters et al. (2008) are real, and lead inexorably toward a more explicitly national gridwork of sites that characterizes the nascent NEON network. We consider NEON and other networks in Chapter 4.

CHAPTER FOUR

The Future of Big Ecology: IGBP, AmeriFlux, NEON, and Other Major Initiatives

Anyone who has never made a mistake has never tried anything new.

Albert Einstein

This chapter presents an overview of the activities of various groups and networks conducting ecosystem studies. Some have had an extensive history, and others, such as the NEON program, were in their final establishment stages during 2009. This overview is followed by a discussion of current major initiatives in ecosystem science, including studies of ecosystem services and experimental studies of global change phenomena.

THE INTERNATIONAL GEOSPHERE–BIOSPHERE PROGRAM (IGBP)

In 1987 the International Council for Science (ICSU) initiated the International Geosphere–Biosphere Program (IGBP). This program was a logical outgrowth of the successful completion of the IGY (see Chapter 1), and the IBP (see Chapter 2). It has fostered interdisciplinary and international research infrastructures and networks of scientists who are focused on the ways in which human activities are impacting the Earth. IGBP is funded by many governmental funding bodies, including the International Group of Funding Agencies for Global Environmental Change (IGFA). Contributions from around fifty countries from all areas of the globe help support IGBP, which is directed by a Scientific Committee comprised of ICSU-appointed members and administered by a Secretariat hosted by the Royal Swedish Academy of Sciences. Regionally, IGBP operates through IGBP or Global Change National Committees. IGBP studies the interactions between biological, chemical, and physical processes and human systems. The IGBP has served as one of the major mechanisms for international collaboration on global change research.

IGBP research is comprised of a suite of nine research projects focused on the major Earth System components (land, ocean, atmosphere) and the interfaces between them and system-wide integration (Earth System modeling and paleoenvironmental studies). IGBP research has three goals, to understand (1) the interactive physical, chemical and biological processes that define Earth System dynamics, (2) the changes that are occurring in these dynamics, and (3) the role of human activities in these changes subsystems, and their response to climate impacts.

Fast-Track Initiatives

Operating on a short three- to four-year time-frame, IGBP has a series of Fast-Track Initiatives (FTI), including Ocean Acidification over

Time, and The Role of Fire in the Earth System. Completed FTIs include (1) the Global Iron Cycle, which analyzed and reviewed the global dust/iron cycle, cutting across conventional boundaries, bringing together terrestrial, atmospheric and aquatic professionals, who do not usually work together, and (2) the Global Nitrogen Cycle, under the name of the International Nitrogen Initiative, whose overall goal is to optimize nitrogen's beneficial role in sustainable food production, and to minimize negative effects on human health and the environment resulting from food and energy production. Some future FTIs include (1) plant functional classification with the goal of improving large-scale vegetation models that are needed for global and regional assessments (including IPCC and future biodiversity assessments) and improved Earth system modeling and (2) the State of the Earth 2030–2050, which will analyze and describe what the Earth might be like one generation from now, based on expert knowledge from a wide range of disciplines. All of the programs noted above are quite costly, with an overall budget for the U.S. contribution of $1.2 billion, and rising. It has been a godsend for encouraging research collaboration (Mooney, 1998).

In order to strengthen research collaboration, IGBP, along with DIVERSITAS, the International Human Dimensions Programme on Global Environmental Change (IHDP), and the World Climate Research Programme (WCRP), have formed the Earth System Science Partnership (ESSP). This association of programs provides a framework for addressing issues of global sustainability such as water resources, food production, human health, and the global carbon and other elemental cycles.

Global Change and Terrestrial Ecosystems (GCTE)

Several programs that were begun early in the IGBP program were concluded ten to fifteen years later. One of these was Global Change and Terrestrial Ecosystems (GCTE). This program addressed the questions of how global change will affect terrestrial ecosystems, and what the feedbacks to the physical climate system will be? Two edited volumes of papers were produced in this program: Walker and Steffen (1996) and Walker et al. (1999).

Two of the steering committee members of GCTE, Hal Mooney (an ecosystem physiologist) and Hank Shugart (a systems ecologist who has become more of an evolutionary ecologist), had been involved with the IBP (Kwa, 2005). Jerry Melillo, a biogeochemist from the Ecosystems Center, Woods Hole, Massachusetts, and long-term LTER participant in the Harvard Forest project served as an ex officio member, and was an advisor to the steering committee. Working in interdisciplinary fashion from within the system, the ecologists were able to interact effectively with the other earth sciences, and to make the concept of "global" evolve over the decades, to include more of a whole-system, ecological orientation (Kwa, 2005).

Some of the more noteworthy findings in the GCTE include an early foreshadowing of the impact of global change on crop production and the distribution of forests worldwide. Although yield increases of 20–40 percent by most major crops with a doubling of ambient carbon dioxide concentrations were forecast, the very significant impacts of changes in carbon stored in boreal and forest soils, with much greater emission of global greenhouse gases including methane and CO_2 were estimated to more than offset the increases in crop yields (Tinker and Ingram, 1996). Global biogeochemical cycles were summarized in a comprehensive terrestrial ecosystem model by Melillo et al (1993), but net changes in pools and fluxes due to interactive effects could not be assessed at that time (Walker, 1996) These concerns are amplified by trends noted in the Alaskan Boreal Forest, where permafrost is more unstable, leading to losses of stored organic carbon and slowed growth of black spruce with increasing temperature regimes. This would be partially offset by the more rapid growth of white spruce and birch, which are predicted to move into colder regions as they gradually warm (Hinzman et al., 2006). These questions are more capable of being addressed now in the nascent NEON program, which is reviewed later in this chapter.

Species differences between ecosystems are explained in part by gap models as the consequence of competitive relationships. However, the structural differences between ecosystems from polar regions to the tropics are dominated more by larger-scale disturbance processes that are initiated locally and subsequently spread across landscapes. These contagious processes include abiotic ones such as fire, storm, and water, and biotic processes such as insect outbreaks and large mammal herbivory (Holling et al., 1996). An example of the time and space scales and their relationship to some of the processes that structure the boreal forest in Fig. 4.1 (Holling et al., 1996) shows how contagious mesoscale disturbance processes furnish a linkage between macroscale atmospheric processes and microscale landscape processes.

A more general concern exists about the relationship between species composition of an ecosystem and their roles in ecosystem function and dynamics. Research in this area was reviewed briefly in

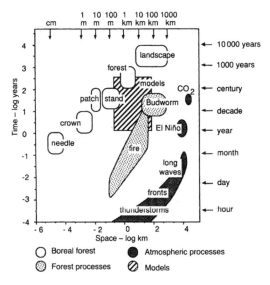

Figure 4.1. Time and space scales of the boreal forest, and their relationship to some of the processes which structure the forest. Contagious mesoscale disturbance processes provide a linkage between macroscale atmospheric processes and microscale landscape processes (from Holling et al., 1996; used with permission from Cambridge University Press).

Chapter 3. For useful overviews of climate change and biodiversity, see Wolters et al. (2000) and Lovejoy and Hannah (2005); for biodiversity and ecosystem services in soils and sediments, see Hansen (2000; Wall (2004); and Coleman (2008).

Holling et al. (1995) produced a synthesis of boreal forest, marine, freshwater and savannah ecosystems. The principal conclusion was that the number of species involved in the structuring set of processes that determines the functional diversity was a subset of all the species present. The species that do not notably affect the ecosystems were proposed to be "passengers," relative to the more influential "drivers" (sensu Walker, 1992). In summary Holling et al. (1996) make the case that only a small set of species and self-organizing processes made up of biotic and physical processes are likely critical in forming the structure and overall behavior of ecosystems. These small groups of species establish sets of relationships, each of which dominates over a definable range of scales in space in time. Each set includes several species of plants animals and microbes, with each species having similar but overlapping influence to give functional redundancy (Holling et al, 1996). This early work led to a series of later papers on the importance of species diversity and ecosystem processes (Mooney, 1998; Naeem, 2002; Tilman, 2001; and Wolters et al., 2000).

AMERIFLUX AND OTHER FLUX NETWORKS

The AmeriFlux network, comprising more than 100 sites, was established in 1996 by several federal agencies (Department of Energy, Department of Commerce, Department of Agriculture [USDA–Forest Service], the National Aeronautics and Space Administration, and the National Science Foundation). The network provides continuous observations of ecosystem level exchanges of carbon dioxide, water, energy, and momentum spanning a range of time scales from diurnal, synoptic, seasonal, to interannual. It is currently composed of sites from North, Central, and South America. Each site consists of one or more towers, from which eddy covariance measurements are made to determine carbon, water, and energy fluxes.

The objectives of AmeriFlux are to quantify spatial and temporal variation in carbon storage in plants and soils, and exchanges of carbon, water, and energy in major vegetation types across a range of disturbance histories and climatic conditions in the Americas. The network thus advances knowledge of processes regulating carbon assimilation, respiration, and storage, and linkages between carbon, water, energy and nitrogen through measurements and modeling.

These studies allow scientists to measure magnitudes of carbon storage and exchanges of energy, CO_2 and water vapor in a wide range of disturbed and undisturbed terrestrial ecosystems. Questions are addressed that include how spatial and temporal variability are influenced by vegetation type, phenology, changes in land use, management and disturbance history, and what the effects of these factors are. More importantly for global change research, what is the causal link between climate and the exchanges of energy, CO_2, and water vapor for major vegetation types, and how do seasonal and interannual climate variability and anomalies influence fluxes?

Scientific Findings in AmeriFlux

Scientific findings are published in the international refereed literature and cover an array of top-ranking journals in meteorology, oceanography, and ecological journals. One recent example draws on research results from the AmeriFlux network and also a sister network in Europe, EuroFlux. Davidson et al. (2002) examined the total belowground carbon allocation (TBCA) in thirty-three sites worldwide. A regression analysis of data from mature forests produced the following relationship: annual respiration = 287 + 2.80 × annual litterfall. This regression slope indicates, on average, that soil respiration is roughly three times aboveground litterfall-C, which further implies that TBCA is roughly twice annual aboveground litterfall-C. Among only mature temperate hardwood forests, however, the correlation between litterfall and soil respiration was poor, and the correlation among years for a single site also poor. Forest age is an important factor, because the regression slope for data from young forests is steeper (possibly indicating a proportionally greater TBCA), and the necessary assumption of steady-state for these calculations is more problematic for the younger forests. The authors provide further examples of caveats using this approach, but the synthesis is most impressive.

FLUXNET: An International Collaborative Network

FLUXNET is a global network of over 140 micrometeorological flux measurement sites that measure the exchanges of carbon dioxide, water vapor, and energy between the biosphere and atmosphere. The vegetation under study includes temperate conifer and broadleaved (deciduous and evergreen) forests, tropical and boreal forests, crops, grasslands, chaparral, wetlands, and tundra. Sites exist on five continents with latitudinal distributions ranging from 70 degrees north to 30 degrees south (Baldocchi et al., 2001).

SCIENTIFIC FINDINGS IN FLUXNET

Findings to date include (1) net CO_2 exchange of temperate broadleaved forests increases by about 5.7 g C m^{-2} d^{-1} for each additional day that the growing season is extended, as is expected during global climate change, (2) the sensitivity of net ecosystem CO_2 exchange to sunlight doubles if the sky is cloudy rather than clear, (3) the spectrum of CO_2 flux density exhibits peaks at timescales of days, weeks, and years, and a spectral gap exists at the month timescale, (4) the optimal temperature of net CO_2 exchange varies with mean summer temperature, and (5) stand age affects carbon dioxide and water vapor flux densities (Baldocchi et al., 2001). This sort of international collaboration certainly rivals that of any other network groups, and the prospects for continued success in this field seem bright indeed.

NEON: THE NATIONAL ECOLOGICAL
OBSERVATORY NETWORK

Introduction to the Formation of NEON

For decades, biologists have looked enviously at the wide array of large instrumentation that has been deployed in research in the physical sciences, including astronomy. Until recently, ecologists have never requested any funding from the NSF Major Research Equipment and Facilities Construction (NSF-MREFC) program. From the time he went to serve as head of the Biological Sciences Division of NSF in 1998, Dr. Bruce Hayden, with the encouragement of Dr. Mary Clutter, Assistant Director for Biological, Behavioral and Social Sciences, worked on a plan to establish an infrastructural network of environmental sensors that would work in a coordinated nationwide fashion. It was to be a distributed array of environmental sensors akin to that of a large array employed in astronomical research observatories. Dr. Clutter dubbed this national observatory network "NEON," and the somewhat catchy name stayed with it ever since. Numerous workshops were held at various locations around the USA between 2000 and 2002, chaired by Scott Collins of the NSF; these were followed by additional town meetings and workshops organized by Jeff Goldman of the American Institute of Biological Sciences (AIBS). Scientists were asked to formulate key questions about science, management, and other topics that could be addressed by such a network. Upon the award of the initial NEON grant, some 150 scientists, engineers and educators were asked to formulate key questions that could be addressed by such a network. In addition, domains were forming and had meetings to advise on how NEON should be structured and function. Some 1,300 persons participated in these discussions. The questions addressed included concerns about climate change and land use impacts, invasive species, biodiversity, biogeochemistry and ecohydrology, and disease ecology. These concerns have been summarized by Crutzen and Steffen (2003), who note that the inhabitants of the biosphere are now in an "Anthropocene Era."

Lists were made of the sorts of equipment needed to address the questions under the supervision of Liz Blood, who had recently been hired at NSF to help organize this first large-ecological instrumentation platform.

The National Science Board, which advises NSF on all major funding projects, raised questions about the appropriateness of such an array for the facilities program, and a study was conducted by a National Research Council committee to consider how NEON might be configured in a timely manner (Tilman, 2003). The National Research Council committee noted:

> Existing large-scale research programs, such as the National Atmospheric Deposition Program/National Trends Network, Global Energy and Water Cycle Experiments, and Moderate Resolution Imaging Spectroradiometer, have focused mostly on the physical and geochemical aspects of environmental change. To complement those programs, research should focus on the fundamental biological processes that underlie climate change and biogeochemical cycles and other important human-driven environmental change, such as introduction of invasive species, emerging diseases, and the loss of biodiversity.

For further overviews of NEON, see Field et al. (2006) and Keller et al. (2008).

A brief history of NEON to date (mid- 2009) is as follows: to give it more of a "standalone" nature and ensure its longer-term continuity, NEON, Inc., a 501(c)3 nonprofit corporation, was formed to develop and implement the nationwide NEON network. NEON, Inc., a consortium of universities and other groups, has organized a board of directors consisting of seventeen scientists and businesspeople from a wide range of disciplines, with Jim MacMahon as chair. The eighteen-member Science, Technology, and Education Committee is chaired by Chris Field. The staff of NEON, with headquarters in Boulder, Colorado, is led by Dave Schimel as chief executive officer. The chief of science is Michael Keller, and Tony Beasley is chief operating officer.

Of the persons listed above, it is noteworthy that Jim MacMahon is an alumnus of the Desert IBP. His roles in Biome synthesis were mentioned in Chapter 2. Dave Schimel is a post-IBP Ph.D. graduate of Colorado State University, having obtained his doctorate on nitrogen cycling with Bob Woodmansee, one of the modeling postdoctorals with George Innis in the Grassland Biome. He worked for many years as a biogeochemist with the National Center for Atmospheric Research (NCAR), in Boulder, Colorado. Although it may be premature to speculate in this fashion, there seems to be a strong thread of interdisciplinary research history that stretches across several decades, from the IBP in the 1970s to the present. Of the members of the board of directors, four (John Blair, Deborah Goldberg, Jerry Melillo, and Debra Peters) are also senior scientists with LTER sites within the LTER Network.

With the generally flat funding for NSF across the years of the George W. Bush administration, the NEON program made slow but steady headway. The case was made that the scientific community lacks observing systems that collect the range of variables needed for a complete view of ecosystem responses to environmental stressors, particularly those associated with global climate change. Thus NEON is planned as a continental-scale research platform for measuring and forecasting the impacts of the key questions noted above. The NEON manipulative experiments are designed to inform ecological forecast models that accurately anticipate future conditions. Although this is a very "tall order" indeed, it builds on the experience garnered since the pioneering large-scale modeling efforts involved in the IBP programs forty years earlier. It is important to note that NEON provides an observing platform, and the scientific community will determine how and what experiments and analyses will be done.

There is a significant coming together of researchers in a wide range of environmental disciplines, noting the strong need for a continent-wide scale of ecological measurements. Thus a group of scientists, mostly from the LTER Network, noted the need for and possibility for studying the key drivers and consequences of connectivity acting across

BOX 4.1. *NEON Network*

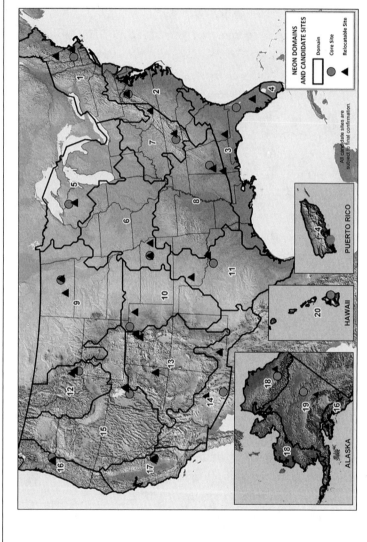

Figure 4.2. Nationwide map of NEON Network, with twenty domains (used with permission from NEON, Inc.).

NEON Core sites

	Domain Name	Candidate Core Wildland Site	Lat.(N)	Long.(W)
1	Northeast	Harvard Forest	42.4	72.3
2	Mid-Atlantic Res. Center	Smithsonian Conserv.	38.9	78.2
3	Southeast	Ordway Biol. Sta.	29.7	82.0
4	Atlantic Neo-Trop.	Guánica Forest	18.0	66.8
5	Great Lakes Res. Ctr., Trout Lake Biol. Station	Univ. Notre Dame Environ	46.2	89.5
6	Prairie Peninsula	Konza Prairie Biol. Sta.	39.1	96.6
7	Appalachians/Cumberland Plateau	Oak Ridge Nat'l. Environ. Research Park	35.6	84.2
8	Ozarks Complex	Talladega Nat'l. Forest	32.9	87.4
9	Northern Plains	Woodworth Field Sta.	47.1	99.3
10	Central Plains	C. P. Expt'l. Range	40.8	104.7
11	Southern Plains	Caddo-LBJ Nat'l. Grassl.	33.4	97.6
12	Northern Rockies	Yellowstone North. Range	45.1	110.7
13	Southern Rockies	Niwot Ridge	40.0	105.6
14	Desert Southwest	Santa Rita Exptl. Range	31.8	110.9
15	Great Basin	Onaqui-Benmore Expt. Sta.	40.2	112.5
16	Pac. Northwest	Wind River Exptl. Forest	45.8	121.9
17	Pac. Southwest	San Joaquin Expt. Range	37.1	119.7
18	Tundra	Toolik Lake Res. Nat. Area	68.6	149.6
19	Taiga Watershed	Caribou-Poker Creek Res.	65.2	147.5
20	Pacific Tropical Wet Forest Unit	Hawaii ETF Laupahoehoe	19.9	155.3

temporal and spatial scales (Peters et al., 2008). They proposed a "network of networks," which would take advantage of existing research facilities and cyberinfrastructure, such as those used by the LTER Network, with a view toward the possibility of collaboration with nascent networks with new technologies, such as that being developed in NEON.

Unlike the IBP and even the LTER, NEON is set up with the United States partitioned into twenty ecoclimatic domains that have been selected to represent the ecological and climate diversity of the continental United States and key island possessions. The domains were determined through the use of an algorithm developed by W.W. Hargrove and F. M. Hoffman (Keller et al., 2008). The map (Fig. 4.2) shows the boundaries that indicate the composite statistical analysis developed by NEON, Inc., and NSF to study changes over the next thirty years. The array of twenty core and forty relocatable sites are envisioned with one or more strategies for analysis of climate change impacts (C), land use impacts (L), and biological invasion (I) (Fig. 4.2). The NEON observing systems include ground-based deployment of three types: core, relocatable, and mobile. Each domain is planned to host a fully instrumented core site in a wildland area. Each domain will have two relocatable units to study intensively impacted ecosystems. NEON mobile systems (on vehicles or towed) will be deployed to study sudden changes in the landscape such as wildfires or the emergence of an invasive species. These mobile platforms are also envisioned to be usable for educational and outreach purposes (Lowman et al., 2009).

NEON Science Packages

There are four basic science packages of equipment to measure the environmental variables of interest: (1) The Fundamental Instrument Unit (FIU) will observe physical and chemical climate, soil properties, and carbon fluxes. The FIU will be fixed towers in wildland or managed areas, co-located with soil and aquatic sensor arrays. The FIU will be used in all three versions: core, relocatable, and mobile. (2) The Fundamental Sentinel Unit (FSU) supports measurements of organisms, soil, hydrology, and aquatic processes conducted by local field workers, supervised by local scientists and specialists in regional biota. The organisms surveyed include a range of small mammals, birds, fish, mosquitoes, ground beetles, microbes, and vegetation. FSU observations will be made at all three types of sites. (3) The Airborne Observation Platform (AOP) consists of an aircraft-mounted hyperspectral instrument and waveform LiDAR employed to collect the three-dimensional distribution of plant canopies and topographic data. This hyperspectral instrument is state of the art and enables the measurement of the chemistry going on in the complete depth of whatever canopy the instrument is scanning. For example, it allows the calculation of net primary production, chlorophyll content, H_2O stress, and so forth. Data from these instruments will provide the capability to scale from sites to whole ecoregions. Of the three airborne packages, one will be reserved for investigator-driven experiments, focusing on targets of opportunities and other PI-initiated studies. Sensors 2 and 3 will be used to pursue programmatic "context-driven" objectives, some of them monitoring key ecosystem variables at various times during the year in each domain to track seasonal changes and other large-scale dynamics. (4) The Land Use Analysis Package (LUAP) will provide an interface to satellite and geographic data and will support a comprehensive analysis and assessment of patterns, change and drivers of land use, cover, and management. The LUAP provides geographical information to scientists in the ecological community via an interface that will provide suitable data from remote sensing imagery as well as those from governmental and private archival sources.

It is important to note that forty of the sixty locations can be moved (usually once every five years). Thus a wide range of phenomena (e.g., insect outbreaks, follow-up measurements after fires) can be followed over time, and new research questions can be added in response to event-driven changes.

NEON Experiments

There are two sorts of national experiments envisioned, derived from the National Research Council recommendation to focus on climate change and nitrogen-deposition accelerators: (1) The Stream Experimental and Observational Network (STREON) will feature nutrient manipulation in small streams. These experiments will measure water chemistry, stream metabolism, and key biological components, including microbes, algae, and fish in one of the first sets of comparative studies. STREON, developed by Walter Dodds from Konza LTER and Pat Mulholland from Oak Ridge National Laboratory, is a direct outgrowth of the nationwide LINX project mentioned in Chapter 3. It will include coordinated experimental and observational studies to examine how nutrient loading, species losses, and hydrologic change impact the structure and function of North American streams regionally and continentally. The comparative stream sites (reaches) will be placed in each of the twenty domains distributed across the United States, including Alaska, Hawaii, and Puerto Rico. Sensors will be located upstream and downstream of a reach at each site to examine material flux budgeting and estimates of rates of net nutrient transformations and metabolism. STREON will feature ten experimental sites where long-term nutrient-enrichment experiments will be integrated with manipulations of consumer species to simulate effects of species losses. Additional biological measurements will characterize consumer and nutrient effects, such as how they are altered by natural variability caused by floods and drought.

The Global Change Experiment (GCE) will manipulate carbon dioxide concentrations and terrestrial temperature. It will observe the impacts of accelerated rates of global change on ecosystem, population and changes in vegetational structure over decadal time periods. This study, proposed by Alan Knapp, Melinda Smith, and others will not be funded by NEON directly, but funds will be sought elsewhere.

NEON Data Products and Cyberinfrastructure

NEON is investing considerable effort into Cyberinfrastructure (CI) that will transform data acquired from the four basic science packages into information that will be used for next-generation ecological forecasting. This effort requires considerable forward planning, so that raw data are transformed into different levels of data products through a set of algorithms that are well documented. Taking the initial suite of data products, NEON will define the mathematical, statistical, and computational requirements for the algorithms that compute them. The algorithms will be developed in the scientific community as an integral part of ongoing research activities. The NEON CI is being designed to be both adaptable and robust. There will be inevitably increases in workloads, so the design will utilize scalable industry-standard products where possible, as well as having clearly defined interfaces between data preprocessing, product generation, and product distribution. Provisions will be made to capture and maintain metadata, including provenance information. Data quality will be assessed at each step of the data acquisition and subsequent manipulation and processing.

Forecasting

One of the principal goals of NEON is the ability to extrapolate to areas not sampled by NEON facilities, but where at least partial or gridded information is available. The NEON Web site provides a forecasting framework in a diagram (Fig. 4.3) that addresses the ways in which major processes and variables of concern are used to inform regional and continental forecasts. This is a tall order, and one which the greater ecological community would do well to follow—and, where possible, participate in this continent-wide experiment. Perhaps the NEON managers will provide frequent updates on what is occurring in the course of the

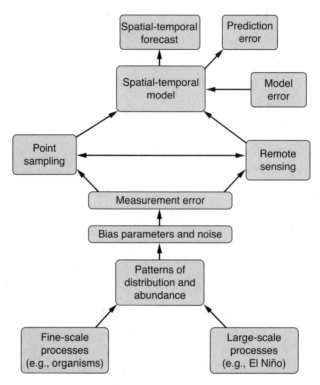

Figure 4.3. Forecasting framework for NEON Network. The forecasting framework in the figure enables the use of NEON information products to address much larger regions than those directly sampled at core and relocatable sites. It uses a quantitative statistical approach to combining information from distinct but related field and laboratory experiments that informs regional and continental forecasts (used with permission from NEON, Inc.).

measurements and archiving of the large streams of data that will be flowing in. This would address concerns of Congress about the availability and accessibility to research findings that are of interest to the general public. This leads into the final area of interest in NEON: that of education.

NEON and Education

To enhance the diversity and educational opportunities for all groups, including minorities, and to understand, use, and benefit from NEON resources, an education and outreach component will be supported via partnerships with professional societies, various governmental agencies, educational institutions, and community organizations. NEON is different from other national science programs by having goals to launch platforms for ecological research and education simultaneously in a manner that should improve ecological forecasting. This goal will be achieved by fostering collaboration between educators and CI engineers to design user-appropriate interfaces, data processing, search services, and other technologies. The overall plan is that ecologists, the public, policymakers, students, teachers, and other groups will be able to benefit from, and also contribute to, NEON data streams, products, and learning experiences (Lowman et al., 2009). An example of a collaborative effort involving NEON is the work of the National Institute of Invasive Species Science (NIISS), a consortium of organizations that relies on citizen-science monitoring and reporting of invasive species. NIISS is developing a Global Detection and Monitoring system that allows users to browse, upload, download, and analyze data on invasive species of all taxa. Members of the public trained to follow research protocols collect field data. Working jointly, NEON and NIISS could build a national program of geographically distributed "human sensors" that would complement the array of physical–chemical sensors distributed nationally by NEON (Lowman et al., 2009).

NEON's Prospects for the Future

When NEON passes its final design review in August 2009, it will become the first research initiative in the biological sciences to be considered by the NSF Major Research Equipment and Facilities Fund (MREFC). Once this hurdle is past, it will be launched on a thirty-year trajectory to further explore the problems and prospects of "Big Ecology."

It is worth noting that full-time scientists and staff of NEON, like its predecessor IBP, are predominantly young, just beginning their careers and willing to give this innovative program a try (Alan P. Covich, pers.

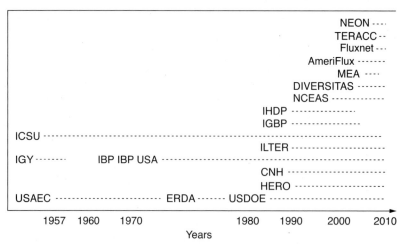

Figure 4.4. Timelines of Programs in Big Ecology. USAEC = U.S. Atomic Energy Commission, later ERDA = Energy Research and Development Agency, and subsequently USDOE = U.S. Department of Energy; ICSU = International Council of Scientific Unions, later simplified to International Council of Science; IBP = International Biological Program; HERO = Human-Environment Regional Observatory; CNH = Dynamics of Coupled Natural and Human Systems; IGBP = International Biosphere Geosphere Program; IHDP = International Human Dimensions Program. For other acronyms, please see the Chapter 4 text.

comm.). This young cohort bodes well for NEON's future, because if the participants are carefully chosen and given a chance to experience the expected ontogeny, or unfolding, of this ambitious project, the long-term benefits to them and to ecosystem science should be considerable.

For a summarization of all of the major programs considered in this book on "Big Ecology," see Fig. 4.4, which presents a timeline of the various programs from the IGY and IBP onward, up to and including NEON.

EXPANDING THE SOCIOECONOMIC BASIS FOR LONG-TERM STUDIES

Expansion of the socioeconomic basis for long-term studies is another promising legacy of the initial forays into broader coverage that the LTER and other networks are ideally suited for. When one thinks back over the approaches used four decades ago, the emphasis was still primarily on relatively "pristine" systems. Looking from the 1920s onward, the course of "big Ecology," sensu Blair (1977), has proceeded through several saltatory (stepwise) increments, beginning with the IGY, IBP, and early AEC programs on to LTER, the Human-Environment Regional Observatory (HERO), and the National Center for Ecological Analysis and Synthesis (NCEAS). This could well lead into a transformative approach to large-scale science—namely, the Integrative Science for Society and Environment (ISSE), which proposes to move socioecological research to a new level of synthesis and integration (Collins et al., 2007). The ISSE is a logical outgrowth from the Millennium Ecosystem Assessment (2005), which was conducted to meet demand from decision makers for scientific information regarding consequences of changes in ecosystems for human well-being (Carpenter et al., 2006a). Although the intended audience was decision makers, scientists became concerned with gaps in data and knowledge that became evident in the course of the assessment. These included numerous gaps in the quantitative links between ecosystem processes, ecosystem services, and human well-being. Thus the capacity to integrate information at multiple scales, from local sites, to regions, and onward to national and international networks appeared as a key need. Despite the efforts of LTER and ILTER, better long-term data were needed on land use change, desertification, changes in distributions of wetlands, standing stocks and flows of living resources, and trends in human reliance on ecosystem services (Carpenter et al., 2006b).

This grew out of widespread interest in research to better document the provisioning of ecosystem services—namely, food, fuel, fiber, fresh water, natural biochemicals, and genetic resources (Daily, 1997). These, in turn, lead to regulating services, which are benefits that people obtain from natural regulation of air quality, climate, erosion, disease, soil, and water quality. Cultural services are nonmaterial benefits that people obtain from the aesthetic, educational, recreational, and spiritual aspects of ecosystems (Collins et al., 2007).

The reason for the concern and interest is clear: the changes in key ecological and sociological drivers of environmental change are quite evident over the last several decades—namely, the rapid increases in mean global temperatures, and the rapid increases in human population and rapidly increasing energy use, with its attendant increases in atmospheric CO_2 concentrations (Fig. 4.5). The top plot of changes in global mean temperatures shows the continuous rise from a mean zero between 1961 and 1990 up to the present. The bottom hockey team diagram shows the conjoint increases in human population, resource consumption (e.g., energy use), atmospheric carbon dioxide concentration, and N availability over the last 150 years.

The consequences of unprecedented environmental changes are several, and widespread across the earth. For North America alone, they include changes in albedo in the Arctic, forest fragmentation and consequent species loss in the Pacific Northwest, increased fire frequency across southern Canada, nitrogen pollution in the southwest, shrub encroachment in the intermountain West, sediment losses throughout the Midwest and subsequent hypoxia in the Gulf of Mexico, and nitrogen saturation across much of the southeastern and northeastern regions of the United States. Indeed, the conduct of integrated studies of coupled human and natural systems has revealed new and complex patterns and processes, some of them counterintuitive, when compared to more traditional studies by social or environmental scientists separately. This discovery proved to be equally true for systems in developing and developed countries across several continents.

Some examples of socioenvironmental interactions worldwide include Kristianstads Vattenrike (a semi-urban wetland and agricultural landscape in southern Sweden) and the Wolong nature preserve in Sichuan Province in Southwest China. Upon formation of the forest conservation program in 2001 for local residents of Wolong to monitor illegal harvesting of bamboo (primary food for the giant panda) for fuelwood, many households decided to split into smaller ones to more effectively garner subsidies (20–25 percent of the average household income)

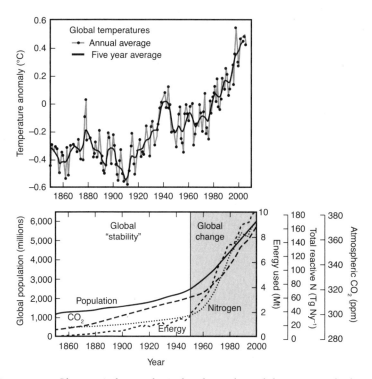

Figure 4.5.   Changes in key ecological and sociological drivers over the last
150+ years. (Top) A plot of changes in global mean temperature based on
instrumental records compiled by the Climatic Research Unit of the
University of East Anglia and the Hadley Centre of the UK Meteorological
Office (Brohan et al, 2006). Following IPCC protocols, zero is the mean
temperature from 1961 to 1990. This figure recreates the controversial hockey
stick diagram in Mann et al. (1998, 1999). (Bottom) A new hockey team
diagram that along with temperature shows changes in human population,
resource consumption (energy), atmospheric CO_2 concentration, and N
availability over the last 150 years (Smith et al., 2009). Population data are
from the U.S. Census Bureau (www.census.gov), energy consumption from the
U.S. Department of Energy Information Administration (www.eia.doe.gov),
total reactive N from Galloway et al. (2003), and atmospheric CO_2
concentrations from the Carbon Dioxide Information Analysis Center
(CIDAC, http://cdiac.esd.ornl.gov; figure from Collins et al., 2007, used with
permission from the LTER Network office).

given to households as part of the program. The household proliferation and concomitant reduction in household size increased demand for fuelwood and land for home construction. An example of the centuries-long lag legacy is in the Kristianstads Vattenrike in Scania county, southern Sweden, where the wetland system is maintained only by continued grazing over centuries. To improve ecosystem properties, an intentional participatory process mobilized stakeholders laying the groundwork for a shift from conventional management to adaptive co-management (Liu et al., 2007). The main take-home lesson is that past couplings of human and natural phenomena often have several-decade to centuries-long time lags, so working from an extensive chronological data base is absolutely essential (Liu et al., 2007).

ECOSYSTEM SERVICES AND THEIR ROLES IN DECISION MAKING

There has been concern among ecologists that ecosystem services—namely, clean air, water, soil stabilization, and so forth—be explicitly considered in the costs of doing business in the industrialized world. These concerns have been expressed eloquently by Daily (1997), Daily and Ellison (2002), and Daily et al. (2009). In the first decade of the twenty-first century, groups of interdisciplinary scientists have been working, not only within the LTER Network but also in many countries around the world, to apply ecological and socioeconomic principles to work to retain the biodiversity and ecosystem services of entire ecoregions. Some examples are presented next.

One of the more important ecosystem services is crop pollination by wild bees. Investigating the role of tropical forest remnants as sources of pollinators to surrounding coffee crops in Costa Rica, Ricketts (2004) found that forest fragments, more so than riparian strips of forest, provided the necessary diversity of bees to provide adequate pollination services. To enable country-wide support for ecosystem services, the World Bank, with financing from the Global Environment Facility, has developed pilot programs for generating biodiversity conservation and carbon sequestration services (payment to local landowners [Pagiola et al., 2005; Sanchez-Azofeifa et al., 2007]). This requires further follow-up and active monitoring on the ground, as noted in several case examples described by Jack et al. (2008). The lessons learned are further highlighted by Chazdon et al. (2009), who note that not only multidisciplinary but also participatory approaches are needed to involve stakeholders (the local inhabitants) in successful enhancement of biodiversity conservation that also promotes sustainable livelihoods.

There are more than 150 ecosystem payment schemes existing in China, which has realized belatedly that wholesale deforestation of vast areas of the interior have resulted in the accumulation of large amounts of silt in major rivers and dams, such as the enormous dam in the Three Gorges region to the west of Beijing. The Chinese government has instituted a reforestation plan for vast regions of its interior to assist in flood control. There is a ban on logging in the wide expanses of Yunnan Province, in southwest China, above Laos. The ban is quite contentious, with many stakeholder groups fighting it (Gretchen Daily, pers. comm.).

The integrity of the municipal water supply of New York City, which is used by upwards of 9 million people, was under threat from the encroachment of large numbers of summer homes being erected during the 1980s in watersheds of the Catskill Mountains, the major source of New York's water supply. The cost of physical filtration at the user end was estimated to be $6–8 billion, with annual maintenance costs of $300–500 million, which would be required as a permanent cost of providing clean water. In contrast, employing "natural capital," at the source, including buying tracts of riparian lands for buffers, and upgrading sewage treatment plants, and providing incentives to farmers to protect river banks from erosion by cattle and poor farming practices in the upstate watershed cost only $1.5 billion, a fraction of the physical engineering approach. Interestingly, with the efforts of conservation groups and local farmers contending with real estate developers on the other side, the natural capital approach was chosen, and New York continues

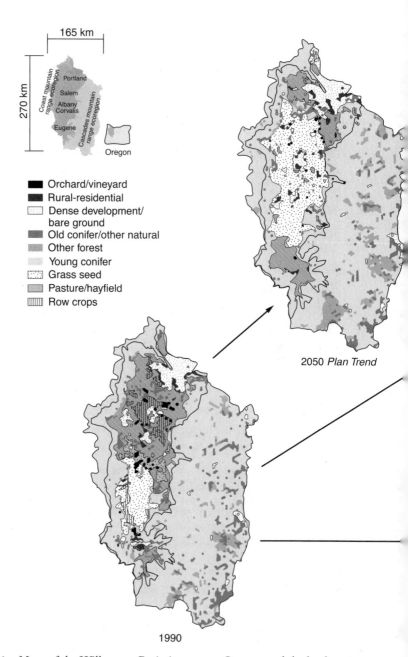

165 km

270 km

Coast mountain range ecoregion

Portland
Salem
Albany
Corvalis
Cascades mountain range ecoregion
Eugene

Oregon

■ Orchard/vineyard
■ Rural-residential
☐ Dense development/
   bare ground
■ Old conifer/other natural
■ Other forest
  Young conifer
⋯ Grass seed
▨ Pasture/hayfield
▥ Row crops

2050 *Plan Trend*

1990

Figure 4.6. Maps of the Willamette Basin in western Oregon, and the land-use/land-cover (LU/LC) patterns for 1990 and, under the three, LU/LC change scenarios for 2050. A 500-ha hexagon is the spatial unit used in the LU/LC pattern maps.

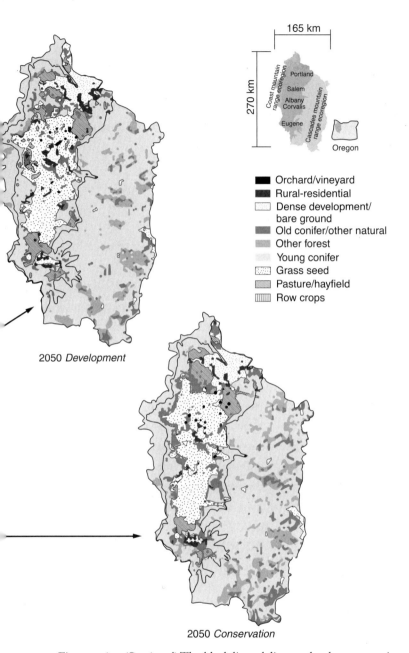

165 km

270 km

Coast mountain range ecoregion

Portland
Salem
Albany
Corvalis
Eugene

Cascades mountain range ecoregion

Oregon

■ Orchard/vineyard
▓ Rural-residential
▢ Dense development/
   bare ground
▩ Old conifer/other natural
▨ Other forest
░ Young conifer
⸪ Grass seed
▨ Pasture/hayfield
▥ Row crops

2050 *Development*

2050 *Conservation*

Figure 4.6. *(Continued)* The black lines delineate the three ecoregions that intersect the Basin. From west to east, the ecoregions are the Coast Range, the Willamette Valley, and the Cascades Range (redrawn from Nelson et al., 2009, with permission from the Ecological Society of America).

to have ample amounts of clean, unmetered water provided using natural capital (Daily and Ellison, 2002). Ongoing research among ecologists and economists continues to make this example one of the most studied cases of using ecosystem services as a way to increase options in resolving large-scale issues (Heal et al., 2005).

A more recent collaborative study used a combined approach, including spatially explicit modeling, to more effectively forecast the interplay between conservation and land use in the Willamette Basin of Oregon. The modeling tool, Integrated Valuation of Ecosystem Services and Tradeoffs (InVEST) was used to predict changes in ecosystem services, biodiversity/conservation, and commodity production levels between 1990 and 2050 (Fig. 4.6, Nelson et al., 2009). Using stakeholder-defined scenarios of land-use/land-cover (LU/LC) change, Nelson et al. (2009) found that scenarios that scored high for a variety of ecosystem services (clean water, control of downstream flooding, climate regulation, and soil fertility) also had high scores for biodiversity, leading to the conclusion that there was little tradeoff between biodiversity conservation and ecosystem services. Scenarios with more development had higher commodity production values, but with ensuing lower levels of biodiversity conservation and ecosystem services (Fig. 4.7, Nelson et al., 2009). By including payments for carbon sequestration, this tradeoff was alleviated. The approach used here—quantifying ecosystem services in a spatially explicit fashion and analyzing tradeoffs between them—is a significant advance in improving natural resource decision making, one that will convince stakeholders from a wide range of backgrounds.

A diametrically opposed example, also from western Oregon, has a longer history, but went awry badly several decades ago. The Bull Run watershed, a 65,000-acre (>26,300 ha) pristine woodland northwest of Mount Hood, provides the principal source of drinking water for the metropolitan region of Portland, Oregon. It was set aside as a National Forest Reserve by President Harrison in 1892, with access further limited under the Bull Run Trespass Act, signed into law by President Theodore Roosevelt, on April 28, 1904. For the next sixty years, it remained almost inviolate, but then was subjected to logging with increasing intensity, including salvage logging after a windstorm in December 1983, leading to major runoff problems during massive flooding in 1996. In contrast to the forward-looking examples noted above in the greater Willamette Valley, the Bull Run watershed was the victim of furtive and occasionally mis-leading policies by timber organizations and the USDA Forest Service (Larson, 2009). It will require decades of regrowth to return to a more fully functional natural filter and source of water for a large metropolitan area. For more details on measuring the economic value of restoring eco-system services in an impaired riber basin, see Loomis and others (2000).

The real take-home message from this work on ecosystem services is that the ultimate challenge in conjoint ecosystem and social science

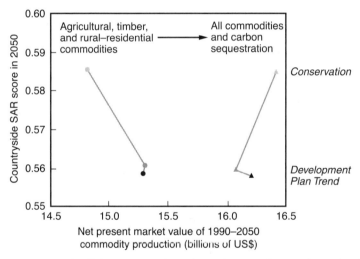

Figure 4.7. Tradeoffs between market values of commodity production and biodiversity conservation on the landscape between 1990 and 2050, excluding (circles) and including (triangles) the market value of carbon sequestration (social value of carbon is assumed to be equal to the market value of seques-tered carbon). The x axis measures the total discounted value of commodities, and the y axis measures the biodiversity (i.e., countryside species–area relation-ship) score for 2050 (from Nelson et al., 2009, used with permission from the Ecological Society of America).

studies is in adequately anticipating human actions across landscapes across several years' time. As Gretchen Daily (pers. comm.) pointedly observed: "the chemical and biological science is reasonably straightforward; the real 'rocket science' is on the human side of the equation." This brings us back to the role of new directions for LTER and multidisciplinary studies. The real future for cutting-edge research on major issues like climate change lies with programs such as ISSE noted above, and their specific interdigitation with other major networks such as NEON.

GLOBAL CHANGE EXPERIMENTAL STUDIES, NOW AND IN THE FUTURE

Ecosystems influence climate in many ways, along numerous pathways. This influence is achieved primarily by changing the energy, water, and greenhouse-gas balance of the atmosphere. As a consequence, mitigating carbon as in the Kyoto protocol, while important, only partially addresses the more-encompassing aspects of ecosystem-climate interactions (Chapin et al., 2008). Thus, the cooling of climate resulting from carbon sequestration by plants may be partially offset by reduced land albedo, which increases solar energy absorption and warms the climate. The relative importance of these effects varies with spatial scale and latitude. Chapin et al. (2008) suggest that consideration of multiple interactions and effects could lead to several novel climate-mitigation strategies, including greenhouse-gas reductions, reduced desertification in arid zones, and reduced deforestation in the tropics. As noted earlier in this chapter, issues involving equity are a central challenge in developing regional, as well as global strategies to mitigate climate change. For a succinct overview of carbon sequestration scenarios in terrestrial and aquatic ecosystems, see Lal (2009).

Examples of Ecosystem Feedbacks under Global Change Conditions

Some examples of recent studies of ecosystem feedbacks and processes follow. Arctic and alpine ecosystems will experience shifts in plant growth forms (cryptogams, deciduous and evergreen dwarf shrubs, graminoids and forbs) with climate change. These plants have relatively low functional redundancy, which may have cascading effects on consumers and net carbon exchange, requiring careful study well into the future (Wookey et al., 2009). In marshlands, there is the possibility of a transient gain in elevation of marsh levels with increased atmospheric CO_2. A two-year study of elevated CO_2 (ambient + 340 ppm) accelerated soil elevation gain by 3.9 mm y^{-1} (Langley et al., 2009). In a two-year plant–soil mesocosm experiment, with a constant 3.5°C increase in experimental vs. controls mesocosms, little change was measured in soil respiration and changes in aboveground plant biomass. However, numerous soil faunal groups and soil fungi increased significantly, indicating that shifts toward a fungal food web under conditions of soil warming need to be incorporated into more long-term global C models (Briones et al., 2009). Both of the latter studies occurred over a relatively short time frame, and caveats as noted below must be made to follow experimentally and by modeling, the changes expected over decadal time spans.

International Collaboration on Global Change Studies: TERACC

The international research coordination network "Terrestrial Ecosystem Response to Atmospheric and Climatic Change" (TERACC) was established in 2001. Encompassing 135 sites in twenty-five countries, TERACC has focused on using experimental manipulations and models to understand ecosystem responses to single and multiple facets of global change (Rustad, 2008). The goals of TERACC are threefold: (1) to integrate and synthesize existing whole-ecosystem research on ecosystem response to individual drivers of global change, (2) to foster new research on whole-ecosystem responses to the combined effects of elevated atmospheric CO_2, warming, and other aspects of global change (see Chapin et al., 2008), and (3) to promote better communication and integration between experimentalists and modelers (Rustad, 2008).

Some examples of long-term experiments over a wide range of variables considered under the rubric of Global Change are reviewed by Rustad (2008).

Experimental Studies of the Consequences of Global Warming

ECOSYSTEM WARMING EXPERIMENTS

A series of ecosystem warming experiments have been pursued at more than two dozen sites worldwide. The initial results showed that warming of whole ecosystems or soils in them from 0.3 to 6.0°C. significantly increased soil respiration rates by 20 percent, net N mineralization rates by 46 percent, and plant productivity by 19 percent (Rustad et al., 2001). However, in one of the longest-running experiments of them all, at Harvard Forest in Petersham, Massachusetts, some counterintuitive results occurred. The expected trends, of increased soil respiration, occurred in the first four years. However, by 2000, ten years after the initiation of the experiments, soil respiration in the experimental and control plots no longer differed. This project has continued through 2004 (Jacqueline Mohan, pers. comm., cited in Rustad, 2008) and indeed up to the present. Melillo et al. (2002) suggested that the reduced response in the warmed plots was due to the depletion of labile carbon compounds (e.g., simple sugars and amino acids), which may be more temperature sensitive than more recalcitrant heterocyclic compounds.

PRECIPITATION MANIPULATION EXPERIMENTS

A classic example of ecosystem state change or development occurred in one of the longest-running precipitation manipulation experiments known. Begun in 1991, supplemental water was added to meet plant water demand in a tall grass prairie ecosystem at the Konza Prairie LTER site. Over the first eight years of the study, water availability limited ANPP in six, and supplemental water increased ANPP by approximately 25 percent in the irrigated plots compared to the controls. The response was due to physiological changes in the dominant plant species, big bluestem, Andropogon *scoparius* (Knapp et al., 2001). However, in the next five years (1999–2003), supplemental water increased by approximately 70 percent compared to the control, a response due to an increased cover of *Panicum virgatum*—hence a change in community composition (A. Knapp, pers. comm., cited in Rustad, 2008).

WHOLE-RIVER NUTRIENT ADDITION EXPERIMENTS

Phosphorus additions were made during four summers in the late 1980s and early 1990s to an Arctic fourth-order stream, the Kuparuk River, by a research team at the Arctic LTER site, north of the Brooks Range and above the Arctic Circle. Both algal biomass and productivity increased, and chlorophyll accumulated on the river bottom in the first two summers. This "bottom-up" response occurred in the riverine food web early on, but was modified in years 3 and 4 by a strong "top-down" feedback of insects grazing on epilithic algae and by competitive exclusion of black flies by caddisflies (Peterson et al., 1993). Carbon and nitrogen stable tracer studies indicated that the measured increases in insect and fish growth were largely due to increases in production of epilithic algae, showing a true cascade in the riverine food web. This riverine experimental study was continued for several more years, and the contributions were compared as to those internal or autochthonous to it, derived from net primary production by algae and cyanobacteria, versus external, allochthonous sources. Sources of organic matter were both coarse and fine particulate organic matter, and also dissolved organic matter (DOM). This latter fraction was a significant fraction (5–10 percent) of terrestrial NPP in the watershed (Harvey et al., 1997). This latter finding is fraught with consequences for longer-term global change phenomena.

In a set of experiments following Dissolved Organic Carbon (DOC) from peatlands in upland watersheds in the United Kingdom over twelve years' time, Freeman et al. (2001) measured a 65 percent increase in DOC concentrations over that time period. This was traced to the increased phenol oxidase activity which increased by up to 36 percent over a 10°C rise in temperature (Q_{10} = 1.36), accompanied by a 33 percent increase in DOC and an even greater increase of phenolic compounds from organic matter stored in the peatland soils (Freeman et al., 2001). The take-home message from these studies is clear: a key terrestrial store of carbon is being increasingly being translocated into the oceans. This land–water linkage needs further follow-up, and the LTER and NEON networks are ideally suited to further measure these changes, which are cause for concern as we see global biogeochemical changes unfolding before us.

SOME TAKE-HOME LESSONS FROM

LONG-TERM, MULTI-FACTOR EXPERIMENTS

One of the classical examples of multiple-factor experiments is the Jasper Ridge Global Change Experiment in the Santa Cruz Mountains of California. Rustad (2008) provides a succinct summary of several counterintuitive findings in this now eleven-year experiment (it began in 1998). Suffice it to say that shifts in plant and microbial species and associated changes in productivity and a warming-induced increase in growing season soil moisture were all interesting "surprises" to occur in more than a decade. It is also somewhat sobering to realize that the ratio of multi-factor to single-factor experiments in TERACC (25 vs. 124), and the fact that the majority are in grassland or low-stature ecosystems, is proof positive that fully replicated multi-factor experiments are both logistically and financially challenging (Rustad, 2008). This leads to some key recommendations for the successful pursuit of unified multidisciplinary approaches to studying global change phenomena in terrestrial ecosystems: (1) better integration is needed between experiments and models, (2) stable and increased support is required for these studies, (3) explicit inclusion of biodiversity, disturbance, and extreme events is needed in both experiments and models, (4) there must be consideration of timing and intensity of global change factors in experiments and models, (5) evaluation of potential thresholds or "tipping points" is needed, and (6) increased support is needed for model–model and model–experiment interactions (Rustad, 2008).

A further consideration of possibly changed influences of the El Niño/ Southern Oscillation (ENSO) should have some bearing on long-term multi-factorial experiments. The post-1940 period alone accounts for 30 percent of extreme ENSO years observed since 1525. Thus there is a possibility that ENSO operates differently under global warming when compared to preindustrial eras (Gergis and Fowler, 2009).

THOUGHTS ON ECOSYSTEM ENERGETICS AT A GLOBAL SCALE

One of the legacies of the brothers Odum is the need to be global, and in as holistic a fashion as possible. A recent analysis of the environmental impact of civilization provides some sobering estimates of what can be expected from so-called "green power," or the usage of energy from alternative energy sources (solar, wind, hydrothermal, tidal power, and thermohaline circulation). All of the foregoing can provide no more than 10 percent of the current or future human global energy demands. Even if this estimate is overly pessimistic, perhaps only one-fourth of future human energy needs, at current demand levels, can be met by alternative energy sources. The current direct energy consumption, from fossil and nuclear sources, is 15×10^{12} W, and is still dwarfed by the primary productivity of ecosystems worldwide (Makarieva et al., 2008).

One of the major lessons that must be realized by the world community is the need not only to work "smarter" (using cogeneration of fuel for electricity and heating of homes, as is widely practiced in Scandinavia), but to reduce net nonrenewable energy consumption. An inevitable result of major increases in fission fuel sources for electricity generation (including adequate storage of waste fission products) is that the entire process requires more fossil fuel subsidies than the energy it generates (Odum, 1971, 1983, 2007), and the wider public needs to be aware of this. When one adds in the continued waste heat loads from nuclear sources, this option becomes even less sustainable (Makarieva et al., 2008). Fusion energy remains as elusive now as it was several decades ago. The waste heat from that source is probably less, but it also needs to be considered in global energy scenarios.

PROSPECTS FOR THE FUTURE OF ECOSYSTEM SCIENCE

Global Change in Marine Ecosystems

Coming from a terrestrial ecosystem background, my coverage of global change phenomena in aquatic systems has been rather light. The longer-term concerns about the effects of ocean acidification are worthy of consideration. The effects of increasing temperature and CO_2-related ocean chemistry indicate that significant acidification will occur with continued absorption by the oceans. Viewed across animal groups and phyla, Portner (2008), a physiologist, suggests that there will be a narrowing of tolerance windows, as many of the invertebrates have little flexibility to respond to such changes. The biogeographical consequences for these organisms and their interactions will be profound, indeed.

"Big Ecology" Compared with Other Big Science Programs

When viewed through the lens of three to four decades since the heyday of the IBP Biome programs, several features stand out. The main point that comes across is the sheer magnitude of the accomplishments by only a few hundred scientists working in concert over four decades. The second thought is: how much more could have been accomplished had there been a more concerted effort to involve a greater number of scientists, and to educate several hundred more graduate students, during that period. When viewing oral and poster paper sessions at the annual meetings of the Ecological Society of America, the predominant mode still seems to be that of pre-IBP—namely, one or two faculty members and a similar number of graduate students. A countervailing tendency, with several more specialized meetings, has developed over the past one to two decades. Such groups as the American Geophysical Union, Conservation Biology, North American Benthological Society, Restoration Ecology, and Soil Ecology Society are all very active and publish in a wide range of international journals.

In spite of some of the concerns indicated above, the scientific activity in the area of global change and "big ecology" is very large indeed. A search of ISI using global change and nutrient cycling as key words yielded more than 1,200 refereed publications in the five-year period between 2004 and 2008 (mid-June, 2009).

There is some inverse logic at play here. The really large collaborative group studies in science with twenty or more authors seem to be focused on large, but narrowly focused questions: the human genome, studies in astronomy, interplanetary exploration, and biochemical syntheses. In contrast, ecological topics tend to have only a few authors, but the numbers of collaborators are increasing over time, as noted in the references cited section of this book.

As was noted earlier, the NEON program is developing rapidly, and is bidding to become the environmental equivalent of a large telescope for environmental science. Will it really become a darling of the scientific community? Proof positive of a change in attitude of the public would be the presentation of a few NEON-produced programs on widely viewed series like NOVA, on the Public Television Network. There are numerous programs on Mars exploration, the search for life and water, and so forth, on that planet's surface and or crust, with hundreds of scientists devoting years of effort to their study. There seems to be nothing commensurate so far for either LTER or NEON in mass media coverage.

Among the general public there seems to be little appreciation of the fact that the number of problems and unknowns regarding the environment on Earth and its future over the next few decades is infinitely more complex and challenging than anything that is being studied in the extraterrestrial sphere. One way to address this lack of attention and support is to encourage the production of NOVA specials, and books for schoolchildren and the general public. The latter aspect has been addressed by several LTER projects—notably, the McMurdo, Baltimore, and Niwot LTERs as noted in Chapter 3.

A "BIG ECOLOGY" RETROSPECTIVE

Future Scenarios for "Big Ecology" and Comparisons with Other "Big Science" Projects

It is apparent that big ecology is alive and well. More programs are in place and operating than ever before in the history of ecosystem science. The amount of uncertainty about funding for long-term ecological studies, with the exception of the ongoing efforts of the LTER program, makes it difficult to forecast trends in future support. However, there seem to be an increasing number of researchers who are interested in and actively participating in such large programs.

When one considers the array of large non-ecosystem science projects in existence today, the group efforts of the IBP, LTER, and even NEON pale in comparison. For example, the Jet Propulsion Laboratory in Pasadena, or the assemblages of scientists in seismology networks and the Human Genome Project involve greater numbers of personnel than ones we have considered in this book (Shrum et al., 2007). In all the cases noted above, there are legacies of project formation that carry over into future collaborations. The uncertainties of funding play key roles in how the organizations are formed and operated (Shrum et al., 2007).

The IBP played a role in establishing "big ecology," along with the ongoing support from the AEC in the early years. Once the LTER came along, it proceeded to increase gradually, by adding sites in phases over more than a generation and more than thirty years. NEON has taken nearly ten years to reach a critical mass of personnel and research efforts, but this timeframe is about typical for large groups of scientists developing and pursuing major research projects (Knorr Cetina, 1999). Interestingly, the IBP and NEON projects are similar in their drawing upon a pool of relatively young investigators, who are willing to try out a new project possibly entailing some risks in its early stages (David S. Schimel comments, via Alan Covich, pers. comm.). Apart from reviews by Kwa (1987, 1989, 2005, 2006) on the IBP and IGBP and by Bocking (1995, 1997), there have been few studies of how programs in "big ecology" have been established and evolved over time, providing a system ontogeny, as it were.

Concluding Remarks

When viewed through the prism of forty-plus years' reflection upon the field of ecosystem science, much excitement was generated in the development of many process-level models and research projects. Model-experiment interactions were an outgrowth of the IBP and perhaps its biggest legacy, and are what impels the field of "big ecology" forward in the twenty-first century. It has been an extraordinary experience to live through. The ontogeny of "big ecology" has been fascinating to observe and participate in. I hope that at least some of my enthusiasm, and that of my colleagues, has been evident in the writing of this history.

REFERENCES

Anderson, J. M., and A. Macfadyen (eds.). 1976. *The Roles of Terrestrial and Aquatic Organisms in Decomposition Processes*. Oxford: Blackwell. 474 p.

Andersson, F. 2010. "Ecosystem Science," Chapter 2. In G. I. Ågren, F. O. Andersson (eds.). *Terrestrial Ecosystem Science—Theoretical and Empirical Approaches and Their Applications* [manuscript].

Andrén, O., T. Lindberg, K. Paustian, and T. Rosswall (eds.). 1990. "Ecology of Arable Land. Organisms, Carbon and Nitrogen Cycling." *Ecological Bulletins* 40. Copenhagen. 222 p.

Andrews, R., D. C. Coleman, J. E. Ellis, and J. S. Singh. 1974. "Energy Flow Relationships in a Shortgrass Prairie Ecosystem" (22–28). In *Proceedings, 1st International Congress of Ecology*, The Hague, September 9–14, 1974.

Appel, T. A. 2000. *Shaping Biology*. The National Science Foundation and American Biological Research, 1945–1975. Baltimore: Johns Hopkins Press. 393 p.

Asner, G. P., and R. E. Martin. 2009. "Airborne Spectranomics: Mapping Canopy Chemical and Taxonomic Diversity in Tropical Forests." *Frontiers in Ecology and the Environment* 7:269–276.

Auerbach, S. I. 1958. "The Soil Ecosystem and Radioactive Waste Disposal to the Ground." *Ecology* 39:522–529.

Auerbach, S. I., R. L. Burgess, and R. V. O'Neill. 1977. "The Biome Programs: Evaluating an Experiment." *Science* 195:902–904.

Azam, F., T. Fenchel, J. G. Field, J. S. Gray, L. A. Meyerreil, and F. Thingstad. 1983. "The Ecological Role of Water-Column Microbes in the Sea." *Marine Ecology-Progress Series* 10:257–263.

Baker, K. S., and C. L. Chandler. 2008. "Enabling Long-Term Oceanographic Research: Changing Data Practices, Information Strategies and Informatics." *Deep-Sea Research* II 55 :2132–2142.

Baker, K. S., B. Benson, D. L. Henshaw, D. Blodgett, J. Porter, and S. C. Stafford. 2000. "Evolution of a Multi-Site Network Information System: The LTER Information Management Paradigm." *BioScience* 50:963–983.

Baldocchi, D., and 26 co-authors. 2001. FLUXNET: A New Tool to Study the Temporal and Spatial Variability of Ecosystem-Scale carbon Dioxide, Water Vapor, and Energy Flux Densities." *Bulletin of the American Meteorological Society* 82:2415–2434.

Barrett, G. W., T. L. Barrett (eds.). 2001. *Holistic Science: The Evolution of the Georgia Institute of Ecology (1940–2000).* New York: Taylor & Francis. 366 p.

Bazilevich, N. I., A. V. Drozdov, and L. E. Rodin. 1971. "World Forest Productivity: Its Basic Regularities and Relationship with Climatic Factors" (345–353). In P. Duvigneaud (ed.). *Productivity of Forest Ecosystems.* Proceedings of the Brussels symposium. Paris: Unesco.

Behan-Pelletier, V. M., and S. B. Hill. 1983. "Feeding Habits of Sixteen Species of Oribatei (Acari) from an Acid Peat Bog, Glenamoy, Ireland." *Revues d' Ecologie et de Biologie du Sol* 20:221–267.

Belanger, D. O. 2006. *Deep Freeze: The United States, the International Geophysical Year, and the Origins of Antarctica's Age of Science.* Boulder: University Press of Colorado. 494 p.

Belnap, J., and S. L. Phillips. 2001. "Soil Biota in an Ungrazed Grassland: Response to Annual Grass (*Bromus tectorum*) Invasion." *Ecological Applications* 11:1261–1275.

Bernhard-Reversat, F., C. Huttel, and G. Lemee. 1972. "Some Aspects of the Seasonal Ecologic Periodicity and Plant Activity in an Evergreen Rain Forest of the Ivory Coast" (217–234). In P. M. Golley and F. B. Golley (eds.). *Tropical Ecology with an Emphasis on Organic Productivity.* Athens, GA: International Society of Tropical Ecology, International Association for Ecology, Indian National Science Academy.

Berthet, P. 1972. *Soil Fauna and Decomposition Processes.* Report of IBP/PT Theme 8 Meeting. July 1972. Louvain, Belgium. 174 p.

Berthet, P., and G. Gerard. 1970. "Miscellaneous Information Concerning Methods of Studying the Productivity of Edaphic Acarines" (189–193).

In J. Phillipson (ed.). *Methods of Study in Soil Ecology*. Proceedings of Symposium. Paris: IBP-Unesco.

Blair, W. F. 1977. *Big Biology: The US/IBP*. Stroudsburg, PA: Dowden, Hutchinson & Ross. 261 p.

Bliss, L. C. 1977. "Introduction" (1–11). In L. C. Bliss (ed.). *Truelove Lowland: Devon Island, Canada—A High Arctic Ecosystem*. Edmonton: University of Alberta Press. 714 p.

Bliss, L. C., O. W. Heal, and J. J. Moore (eds.). 1981. *Tundra Ecosystems: A Comparative Analysis*. IBP Publication No. 25. Cambridge, UK: Cambridge University Press. 813 p.

Bocking, S. 1995. "Ecosystems, Ecologists, and the Atom: Environmental Research at Oak Ridge National Laboratory." *Journal of the History of Biology* 28:1–47.

Bocking, S. 1997. *Ecologists and Environmental Politics: A History of Contemporary ecology*. New Haven, CT: Yale University Press. 271 p.

Botkin, D. B. (convenor). 1977. *Long-Term Ecological Measurements: Report of a Conference*. Woods Hole, MA, March 16–18, 1977. Division of Environmental Biology, National Science Foundation, Washington, DC.

Bowen, S. (ed.). 1972. *Proceedings 1972 Tundra Biome Symposium*. U.S. IBP Tundra Biome Report, July 1972. Hanover, NH: USA-CRREL.

Bowman, W. D. 2001. "Introduction: Historical Perspective and Significance of Alpine Ecosystem Studies" (3–12). In W. D. Bowman and T. R. Seastedt (eds.). *Structure and Function of an Alpine Ecosystem*. New York: Oxford University Press.

Breymeyer, A. I., and G. M van Dyne (eds.). 1980. *Grasslands, Systems Analysis, and Man*. IBP Publication No. 19. Cambridge, UK: Cambridge University Press. 950 p.

Brian, M. V., and J. Pętal. (eds.). 1972. *Productivity Investigations on Social Insects and Their Role in Ecosystems*. Ecologia Polska 20, 184 p.

Briones, M. J. I., N. J. Ostle, N. R. McNamara, and J. Poskitt. 2009. "Functional Shifts of Grassland Soil Communities in Response to Soil Warming." *Soil Biology & Biochemistry* 41:315–322.

Brohan, P., J. J. Kennedy, I. Harris, S. F. B. Tett, and P. D. Jones. 2006. "Uncertainty Estimates in Regional and Global Observed Temperature Changes: a New Dataset from 1850." *Journal of Geophysical Research* 111: D 12106. DOI: 10.1029/2005JD006548 (viewed June 2009).

Brokaw N. L. V., T. A. Crowl, A. E. Lugo, W. H. McDowell, F. N. Scatena, R. B. Waide, and M. R. Willig (eds.). In press. *Disturbance, Response and Tropical Forest Dynamics: Long-Term Perspectives and Implications*. Oxford University Press.

Brown, J., P. C. Miller, L. L. Tieszen, and F. L. Bunnell. (eds.). 1980. *An Arctic Ecosystem: The Coastal Tundra at Barrow, Alaska*. Stroudsburg, PA: Dowden, Hutchinson & Ross. 571 p.

Bunnell, F. L. 1973. "Theological Ecology; Or, Models and the Real World." *Forestry Chronicle* 49:167–171.

Burgess, R. L. 1981. "United States," Chapter 5 (67–101). In E. J. Kormondy and J. F. McCormick (eds.). *Handbook of Contemporary Developments in World Ecology*. Westport, CT: Glenwood Press.

Byers, J. E., and E. G. Noonburg. 2003. "Scale Dependent Effects of Biotic Resistance to Biological Invasion." *Ecology* 84:1428–1433.

Caldwell, M. M., and L. B. Camp. 1974. "Below Ground Productivity of Two cool desert Communities." *Oecologia* 17:123–130.

Caldwell, M. M., L. L. Tieszen, and M. Fareed. 1974. "The Canopy Structure of Tundra Plant Communities at Barrow, Alaska and Niwot Ridge, Colorado." *Arctic and Alpine Research* 6:151–159.

Callahan, J. T. 1984. "Long Term Ecological Research." *BioScience* 34:363–367.

Callahan, J. T. 1991. "Long-Term Ecological Research in the United States: A Federal Perspective" (9–21). In P. G. Risser (ed.). *Long-Term Ecological Research: An International Perspective*. SCOPE 47. Chichester, UK: John Wiley & Sons.

Carpenter, S. R. 2008. "Emergence of Ecological Networks." *Frontiers in Ecology and the Environment* 6:228.

Carpenter, S. R., R. DeFries, T. Dietz, H. A. Mooney, S. Polasky, W. V. Reid, and R. J. Scholes. 2006a. "Critical Research Needs Revealed by the Millennium Ecosystem Assessment." [unpublished manuscript].

Carpenter, S. R., R. C. Lathrop, P. Nowak, E. M. Bennett, T. Reed, and P. A. Saranno. 2006b. "The Ongoing Experiment: Restoration of Lake Mendota and Its Watershed" (236–256). In J. J. Magnuson, T. K. Kratz, and B. J. Benson (eds.). *Long-Term Dynamics of Lakes in the Landscape*. New York: Oxford University Press.

Chapin, F. S. III, M. W. Oswood, K. Van Cleve, L. A. Viereck, D. L. Verbyla, and M. C. Chapin (eds.). 2005. *Alaska's Changing Boreal Forest*. New York: Oxford University Press. 354 p.

Chapin, F. S. III, J. T. Randerson, A. D McGuire, J. A. Foley, and C. B. Field. 2008. "Changing Feedbacks in the Climate-Biosphere System." *Frontiers in Ecology and the Environment* 6:313–320.

Chazdon, R. L., C. A. Harvey, O. Komar, D. M. Griffith, B. G. Ferguson, M. Martinez-Ramos, H. Morales, R. Nigh, L. Soto-Pinto, M van Breugel, and S. M. Philpott. 2009. "Beyond Reserves: A Research Agenda for

Conserving Biodiversity in Human-Modified Tropical Landscapes." *Biotropica* 41:142–153.

Clarholm, M. 1985. "Possible Roles for Roots, Bacteria, Protozoa and Fungi in Supplying Nitrogen to Plants" (355–363). In A. H. Fitter, D. Atkinson, D. J. Read, and M. B. Usher (eds.). *Ecological Interactions in Soil: Plants, Microbes and Animals.* Oxford: Blackwell.

Clark, F. E. 1977. "Internal Cycling of ^{15}N in Shortgrass Prairie." *Ecology* 58:1322–1333.

Clark, F. E., and E. A. Paul. 1970. "The Microflora of Grassland." *Advances in Agronomy* 22:375–435.

Cole, C. V., G. S. Innis, and J. W. B. Stewart. 1977. "Simulation of Phosphorus Cycling in Semiarid Grasslands." *Ecology* 58:1–15.

Coleman, D. C. 1970. "Nematodes in the Litter and Soil of El Verde Rain Forest," Chapter E-7 (E-103–E-104). In H. T. Odum and R. F. Pigeon (eds.). *A Tropical Rain Forest: A Study of Irradiation and Ecology at El Verde, Puerto Rico.* USAEC TID-24270.

Coleman, D. C. 1976. "A Review of Root Production Processes and Their Influence on Soil Biota in Terrestrial Ecosystems" (417–434). In J. M. Anderson and A. Macfadyen (eds.). *The Role of Terrestrial and Aquatic Organisms in Decomposition Processes.* Oxford: Blackwells.

Coleman, D. C. 1994. "The Microbial Loop Concept as Used in Terrestrial Soil Ecology Studies." *Microbial Ecology* 28:245–250.

Coleman, D. C. 2008. "From Peds to Paradoxes: Linkages between Soil Biota and Their Influences on Ecological Processes." *Soil Biology & Biochemistry* 40:271–289.

Coleman, D. C., and J. T. McGinnis. 1970. "Quantification of Fungus: Small Arthropod Food Chains in the Soil." *Oikos* 21:134–137.

Coleman, D. C., and A. Sasson (coords.). 1980. "Decomposers Subsystem," Chapter 7 (609–655). In A. Breymeyer and G. Van Dyne (eds.). *Grasslands, Systems Analysis, and Man.* IBP Publication No. 19. London: Cambridge University Press.

Coleman, D. C., and W. B. Whitman. 2005. "Linking Species Richness, Biodiversity and Ecosystem Function in Soil Systems." *Pedobiologia* 49:479–497.

Coleman, D. C., D. A. Crossley Jr., and P. F. Hendrix. 2004. *Fundamentals of Soil Ecology,* 2nd ed. San Diego: Elsevier Academic Press. 386 p.

Coleman, D. C., J. M. Oades, and G. Uehara (eds.). 1989. *Dynamics of Soil Organic Matter in Tropical Ecosystems.* Honolulu: University of Hawaii Press. 249 p.

Coleman, D. C., C. P. P. Reid, and C. V. Cole. 1983. "Biological Strategies of Nutrient Cycling in Soil Systems." *Advances in Ecological Research* 13:1–55.

Coleman, D. C., R. Andrews, J. E. Ellis, and J. S. Singh. 1976. "Energy Flow and Partitioning in Selected Man-Managed and Natural Ecosystems." *Agro-Ecosystems* 3:45–54.

Coleman, D. C., M. D. Hunter, J. Hutton, S. Pomeroy, and L. Swift Jr. 2002. "Soil Respiration from Four Aggrading Forested Watersheds Measured over a Quarter Century." *Forest Ecology and Management* 157:247–253.

Collins, S. L., S. M. Swinton, C. W. Anderson, B. J. Benson, J. Brunt, T. Gragson, N. B. Grimm, M. Grove, D. Henshaw, A. K. Knapp, G. Kofinas, J. J. Magnuson, W. McDowell, J. Melack, J. C. Moore, L. Ogden, J. H. Porter, O. J. Reichman, G. P. Robertson, M. D. Smith, J. Vande Castle, and A. C Whitmer. 2007. "Integrated Science for Society and the Environment: A Strategic Research Initiative." Publication #23 of the U.S. LTER Network. LTER Network Office, Albuquerque, New Mexico, USA. 35 p. (www.lternet .edu/planning/).

Coughenour, M. B., J. E. Ellis, D. M. Swift, D. L. Coppock, K. Galvin, J. T. McCabe, and T. C. Hart. 1985. "Energy Extraction and Use in a Nomadic Pastoral Ecosystem." *Science* 230:619–625.

Coupland, R. T. (ed.). 1979. *Grassland Ecosystems of the World: Analysis of Grasslands and Their Uses*. IBP Publication No. 18. Cambridge, UK: Cambridge University Press. 401 p.

Coupland, R. T., J. R. Willard, E. A. Ripley, and R. L. Randell. 1975. "The Matador Project" (19–50). In T. W. M. Cameron and L. W. Billingsley (eds.). *Energy Flow: Its Biological Dimensions: A Summary of the IBP in Canada, 1964–1974*. The Royal Society of Canada, Ottawa.

Covich, A. P., M. C. Austen, F. Bärlocher, E. Chauvet, B. J. Cardinale, C. L. Biles, P. Inchausti, O. Dangles, M. Solan, M. O. Gessner, B. Statzner, and B. Moss. 2004. "Role of Biodiversity in the functioning of Freshwater and Marine Ecosystems. *BioScience* 54:767–775.

Cox, T. L., W. F. Harris, B. S. Ausmus, and N. T. Edwards. 1978. "The Role of Roots in Biogeochemical Cycles in an Eastern Deciduous Forest." *Pedobiologia* 18:264–271.

Craige, B. J. 2001. *Eugene Odum. Ecosystem Ecologist and Environmentalist*. Athens: University of Georgia Press. 226 p.

Cromack, K. Jr., P. Sollins, W. C. Graustein, K. Speidel, A. Todd, F. Spycher, C. Y. Li, and R. L. Todd. 1979. "Calcium Oxalate Accumulation and Soil

Weathering in Mats of the Hypogeous Fungus *Hysterangium crassum.*" *Soil Biology & Biochemistry* 11:463–468.

Cromack, K. Jr., B. L. Fichter, A. M. Moldenke, J. A. Entry, and E. R. Ingham. 1988. "Interactions between Soil Animals and Ectomycorrhizal Fungal Mats." *Agriculture, Ecosystems and Environment* 24:161–168.

Crossley, D. A. Jr. 1963. "Use of Radioactive Tracers in the Study of Insect-Plant Relationships" (43–54). In *Radiation and Radioisotopes Applied to Insects of Agricultural Importance.* Vienna: International Atomic Energy Agency.

Crowcroft, P. 1991. *Elton's Ecologists.* Chicago, IL: University of Chicago Press. 177 p.

Crowl, T. A., T. O. Crist, R. R. Parmenter, G. Belovsky, and A. E. Lugo. 2008. "The Spread of Invasive Species and Infectious Disease as Drivers of Ecosystem Change." *Frontiers in Ecology and the Environment* 6:238–246.

Crutzen, P. J., and W. Steffen. 2003. "How Long Have We Been Living in the Anthropocene Era?" *Climatic Change* 61:251–257.

D'Antonio, C. M., and S. E. Hobbie. 2005. "Plant Species Effects on Ecosystem Processes: Insights from Invasive Species" (65–84). In D. F. Sax, J. J. Stachowicz, and S. D. Gaines (eds.). *Species Invasions. Insights into Ecology, Evolution, and Biogeography.* Sunderland, MA: Sinauer.

Daily, G. C. 1997. "Valuing and Safeguarding Earth's Life-Support Systems" (365–375). In G. C. Daily (ed.). *Nature's Services: Societal Dependence on Natural Ecosystems.* Island Press, Washington, DC.

Daily, G. C., and K. Ellison. 2002. *The New Economy of Nature: The Quest to Make Conservation Profitable.* Washington, DC: Island Press. 260 p.

Daily, G. C., S. Polasky, J. Goldstein, P. M Kareiva, H. A. Mooney, L. Pejchar, T. H. Ricketts, J. Salzman, and R. Shallenberger. 2009. "Ecosystem Services in Decision Making: Time to Deliver." *Frontiers in Ecology and the Environment* 7:21–28.

Davidson, E. A., K. Savage, P. Bolstad, D. A. Clark, P. S. Curtis, D. S. Ellsworth, P. J. Hanson, B. E. Law, Y. Luo, K. S. Pregitzer, J. C. Randolph, and D. Zak. 2002. "Belowground Carbon Allocation in Forests Estimated from Litterfall and IRGA-Based Soil Respiration Measurements." *Agricultural and Forest Meteorology* 113:39–51.

Dodd, J. L., W. K. Lauenroth, and R. K. Heitschmidt. 1982. "Effects of Controlled SO_2 Exposure on Net Primary Production and Plant Biomass Dynamics." *Journal of Range Management* 35:572–579.

Dodson, S. I., S. E. Arnott, and K. L. Cottingham. 2000. "The Relationship in Lake Communities between Primary Productivity and Species Richness." *Ecology* 81:2662–2679.

Duvigneaud, P. (ed.). 1971. *Productivity of Forest Ecosystems*. Proceedings of the Brussels symposium. Paris: Unesco. 707 p.

Duvigneaud, P., and S. Denayer-De Smet. 1971. "Cycle of the Biogenic Elements in the Forest Ecosystems of Europe (Chiefly Deciduous Forests)" (527–542). P. Duvigneaud (ed.). *Productivity of Forest Ecosystems*. Proceedings of the Brussels symposium. Paris: Unesco.

Dyer, M. I., and U. G. Bokhari. 1976. "Plant-Animal Interactions: Studies of the Effects of Grasshopper Grazing on Blue Grama Grass." *Ecology* 57:762–772.

Edmonds, R. L. (ed.). 1974. "An Initial Synthesis of Results in the Coniferous Forest Biome, 1970–1973." Bulletin No. 7, Coniferous Forest Biome, University of Washington, Seattle. 245 p.

Edmonds, R. L. 1982. "Introduction" (1–27). In R. L. Edmonds (ed.). *Analysis of Coniferous Forest Ecosystems in the Western United States*. Stroudsburg, PA: Hutchinson Ross.

Edwards, N. T., and W. F. Harris. 1977. "Carbon Cycling in a Mixed Deciduous Forest Floor." *Ecology* 58:431–437.

Ehrenfeld, J. G., P. Kourtev, and W. Huang. 2001. "Changes in Soil Functions Following Invasions of Understory Plants in Deciduous Forests." *Ecological Applications* 11:1287–1300.

Ellenberg, H. (ed.). 1971a. *Integrated Experimental Ecology: Methods and Results of the German Solling Project*. Ecological Studies 2. Heidelberg: Springer. 214 p.

Ellenberg, H. 1971b. "The Solling Project, an IBP/PT Integrated Project in the Federal Republic of Germany" (667–670). In P. Duvigneaud (ed.). *Productivity of Forest Ecosystems*. Proceedings of the Brussels symposium. Paris: Unesco.

Elliott, E. T., D. C. Coleman, and C. V. Cole. 1979. "The Influence of Amoebae on the Uptake of Nitrogen by Plants in Gnotobiotic Soil" (221–229). In J. L. Harley and R. S. Russell (eds.). *The Soil-Root Interface*. London: Academic Press.

Elliott, E. T., R. V. Anderson, D. C. Coleman, and C. V. Cole. 1980. "Habitable Pore Space and Microbial Trophic Interactions." *Oikos* 35:327–335.

Ellis, J. E., and D. M. Swift. 1988. "Stability of African Pastoral Ecosystems: Alternate Paradigms and Implications for Development." *Journal of Range Management* 41:450–459.

Elton, C. S. 1958. *The Ecology of Invasions by Animals and Plants*. London: Methuen/Wiley. 181 p.

Evans, D. D., and J. L. Thames (eds.). 1981. *Water in Desert Ecosystems*. Stroudsburg, PA: Dowden, Hutchinson & Ross. 280 p.

Evans, F. C. 1956. "Ecosystem as the Basic Unit in Ecology." *Science* 123: 1127–1128.

Evans, R. D., R. Rimer, L. Sperry, and J. Belnap. 2001. "Exotic Plant Invasion Alters Nitrogen Dynamics in an Arid Grassland." *Ecological Applications* 11:1301–1310.

Fahey, T. J., and A. K. Knapp (eds.). 2007. *Principles and Standards for Measuring Primary Production.* LTER Network Series. New York: Oxford University Press. 288 p.

Fenchel, T. 1975. "Quantitative Importance of Benthic Microfauna of an Arctic Tundra Pond." *Hydrobiologia* 46:445–464.

Field, C., R. DeFries, D. Foster, et al. 2006. "Integrated Science and Education Plan for the National Ecological Observatory Network." www.neoninc.org/documents/ISEP_2006Oct23.pdf.

Fisher, S. G., G. E. Likens. 1973. "Energyflow in Bear Brook, New Hampshire: An Integrative Approach to Stream Ecosystem Metabolism." *Ecological Monographs* 43: 421–439.

Foster, D. R., and J. D. Aber (eds.). 2004. *Forests in Time: The Environmental Consequences of 1,000 Years of Change in New England.* New Haven, CT: Yale University Press. 477 p.

Franklin, J. F., D. W. Goodall, and D. E. Reichle (eds.). 1975. *Productivity of World Ecosystems.* Washington, DC: National Academy of Sciences. 166 p.

Fraser, R. 1957. *Once Round the Sun: The Story of the International Geophysical Year.* New York: Macmillan Co. 160 p.

Freckman D. W. (ed.). 1982a. *Nematodes in Soil Ecosystems.* Austin: University of Texas Press. 206 p.

Freckman, D. W. 1982b. "Parameters of the Nematode Contribution to Ecosystems" (81–97). In D. W. Freckman (ed.), *Nematodes in Soil Ecosystems.* Austin: University of Texas Press.

Freckman, D. W., and R. Mankau. 1986 "Abundance, Distribution, Biomass, and Energetics of Soil Nematodes in a Northern Mojave Desert Ecosystem." *Pedobiologia* 29:129–142.

Freckman, D. W., and R. A. Virginia. 1989. "Plant-Feeding Nematodes in Deep-Rooting Desert Ecosystems." *Ecology* 70:1665–1678.

Freeman, C., C. D. Evans, D. T. Monteith, B. Reynolds, and N. Fenner. 2001. "Export of Organic Carbon from Peat Soils." *Nature* 412:785.

French, N. R. (ed.). 1979. *Perspectives in Grassland Ecology.* "Results and Applications of the US/IBP Grassland Biome Study." New York: Springer-Verlag. 204 p.

Galloway, J. N., J. D. Aber, J. W. Erisman, S. P. Seitzinger, R. W. Howarth, E. B. Cowling, and B. J. Cosby. 2003. "The Nitrogen Cascade." *BioScience* 53:341–356.

Gaudinski, J. B., S. E. Trumbore, E. A. Davidson, and S. Zheng. 2000. "Soil Carbon Cycling in a Temperate Forest: Radiocarbon-Based Estimates of Residence Times, Sequestration Rates and Partitioning of Fluxes." *Biogeochemistry* 51:33–69.

Gaudinski, J. B., S. E. Trumbore, E. A. Davidson, A. C. Cook, D. Markewitz, and D. D. Richter. 2001. "The Age of Fine-Root Carbon in Three Forests of the Eastern United States Measured by Radiocarbon." *Oecologia* 129: 420–429.

Geier, M. G. 2007. *Necessary Work: Discovering Old Forests, New Outlooks, and Community on the H.J. Andrews Experimental Forest, 1948–2000*. General Technical Report PNW-GTR-687. Portland, OR: USDA, Forest Service, Pacific Northwest Research Station. 357 p.

Gergis, J. L., Fowler, and A. M. 2009. "A History of ENSO Events since AD 1525: Implications for Future Climate Change." *Climatic Change* 92:343–387.

Gholz, H. L., D. Wedin, S. Smitherman, M. E. Harmon, and W. J. Parton. 2000. "Long-Term Dynamics of Pine and Hardwood Litter in Contrasting Environments: Toward a Global Model of Decomposition." *Global Change Biology* 6:751–765.

Gibson, J. H., and W. F. Blair. 1977. "The Biome Programs." *Science* 195: 822–823.

Glover, D. M., C. L. Chandler. 2001. "An Update on Data Management in US JGOFS." *USJGOFSNews*. US JGOFS Planning Offic, Woods Hole, MA. 11(3), 16.

Gold, A. 2007a. "Cyberinfrastructure, Data and Libraries, Part 1: A Cyberinfrastructure Primer for Librarians." *D-Lib Magazine* 13 (9–10). www.dlib.org/dlib/september07/gold/09gold-pt.1.html.

Gold, A. 2007b. "Cyberinfrastructure, Data and Libraries, Part 2: Libraries and the Data Challenge: Roles and Actions for Libraries." *D-Lib Magazine* 13 (9–10). www.dlib.org/dlib/september07/gold/09gold-pt.2.html.

Golley, F. B. 1993. *History of the Ecosystem Concept in Ecology: More Than the Sum of the Parts*. New Haven, CT: Yale University Press. 254 p.

Golley, F. B. 2001. "Establishing the Network" (38–67). In G. W. Barrett and T. L. Barrett (eds.). *Holistic Science: The Evolution of the Georgia Institute of Ecology (1940–2000)*. New York: Taylor & Francis.

Golley, P. M., and F. B. Golley (eds.). 1972. *Tropical Ecology with an Emphasis on Organic Productivity*. Athens, GA: International Society of Tropical Ecology, International Association for Ecology, Indian National Sci. Academy. 418 p.

Gonzalez, G., and T. R. Seastedt. 2001. "Soil Fauna and Plant Litter Decomposition in Tropical and Subalpine Forests." *Ecology* 82:955–964.

Gragson, T. L., and M. Grove. 2006. "Social Science in the Context of the Long Term Ecological Research Program." *Society and Natural Resources* 19:93–100.

Greenland, D., D. G. Goodin, and R. C. Smith. (eds.). 2003. *Climate Variability and Ecosystem Response at Long-Term Ecological Research Sites*. LTER Network Series. New York: Oxford University Press. 480 p.

Grimm, N. B., D. Foster, P. Groffman, J. M. Grove, C. S. Hopkinson, K. J. Nadelhoffer, D. E. Pataki, and D. P. C. Peters. 2008. "The Changing Landscape: Ecosystem Responses to Urbanization and Pollution across Climatic and Societal Gradients." *Frontiers in Ecology and the Environment* 6:264–272.

Hagen, J. B. 1992. *An Entangled Bank: The Origins of Ecosystem Ecology*. New Brunswick, NJ: Rutgers University Press. 245 p.

Hall, C. A. S. (ed.). 1995. *Maximum Power: The Ideas and Applications of H.T. Odum*. Niwot: University Press of Colorado. 393 p.

Hansen, R. A. 2000. "Diversity in the Decomposing Landscape" (203–219). In D. C. Coleman and P. F. Hendrix (eds.). *Invertebrates as Webmasters in Ecosystems*. Wallingford, UK: CAB International.

Harmon, M. E., K. J. Nadelhoffer, and J. M. Blair. 1999. "Measuring Decomposition, Nutrient Turnover, and Stores in Plant Litter" (202–240). In G. P. Robertson, D. C. Coleman, C. S. Bledsoe, and P. Sollins. (eds.). *Standard Soil Methods for Long Term Ecological Research*. New York: Oxford University Press.

Harris, W. F., P. Sollins, N. T. Edwards, B. E. Dinger, and H. H. Shugart. 1975. "Analysis of Carbon Flow and Productivity in a Temperate Deciduous Forest Ecosystem" (116–122). In J. F. Franklin, D. W. Goodall, and D. E. Reichle (eds.). *Productivity of World Ecosystems*. Washington, DC: National Academy of Sciences.

Harris, W. F., and L. Krishtalka (co-chairs). 2002. "Long-Term Ecological Research Program: Twenty-Year Review—A Report to the National Science Foundation." Arlington, VA: National Science Foundation. 39 p.

Harvey, C. J., B. J. Peterson, W. B. Bowden, L. A. Deegan, J. C. Finlay, A. E. Hershey, and M. C. Miller. 1997. "Organic Matter Dynamics in the Kuparuk

River, a Tundra River in Alaska, USA." *Journal of the North American Benthological Society* 16:18–23.

Hautaluoma, J. E., and R. G. Woodmansee. 1994. "New Roles in Ecological Research and Policy Making." *Ecology International Bulletin* 21:1–10.

Havstad, K. M., L. F. Huenneke, and W. H. Schlesinger (eds.). 2006. *Structure and Function of a Chihuahuan Desert Ecosystem*. LTER Network Series. New York: Oxford University Press. 492 p.

Hayden, B. P. 1998. "Ecosystem Feedback on Climate at the Landscape Scale." Philosophical Transactions of the Royal Society London. *B-Biological Sciences* 353:5–18.

Head, G. C. 1970. "Methods for the Study of Production in Root Systems" (151–157). In J. Phillipson (ed.). *Methods of Study in Soil Ecology*. Proceedings of Symposium. Paris: IBP-Unesco.

Heal, G. M., E. B. Barbier, K. J. Boyle, A. P. Covich, S. P. Gloss, C. H. Hershner, C. M. Pringle, et al. 2005. *Valuing Ecosystem Services: Toward Better Environmental Decision Making*. Washington, DC: National Academy Press. 277 p.

Heal, O. W., and D. F. Perkins. 1976. "IBP Studies on Montane Grassland and Moorlands." Philosophical Transactions of the Royal Society London. *B-Biological Sciences* 274:295–314.

Healey, I. N. 1970. "The Study of Production and Energy Flow in Populations of Soft-Bodied Microarthropods" (175–182). In J. Phillipson (ed.). *Methods of Study in Soil Ecology*. Proceedings of Symposium. Paris: IBP-Unesco.

Heneghan, L., D. C. Coleman, X. Zou, D. A. Crossley Jr., and B. L. Haines. 1998. "Soil Microarthropod Community Structure and Litter Decomposition Dynamics: A Study of Tropical and Temperate Sites." *Applied Soil Ecology* 9:33–38.

Heneghan, L., D. C. Coleman, X. Zou, D. A. Crossley Jr., B. L. Haines. 1999a. "Soil Microarthropod Contributions to Decomposition Dynamics: Tropical–Temperate Comparisons of a Single Substrate." *Ecology* 80:1873–1882.

Heneghan, L., D. C. Coleman, D. A. Crossley Jr., X. Zou. 1999b. "Nitrogen Dynamics in Decomposing Chestnut Oak (*Quercus prinus* L.) in Mesic Temperate and Tropical Forest." *Applied Soil Ecology* 13:169–175.

Hinzman, L. D., L. A. Viereck, P. C. Adams, V. E. Romanovsky, and K. Yoshikawa. 2006. "Climate and Permafrost Dynamics of the Alaskan Boreal Forest" (39–61). In F. S. Chapin III, M. W. Oswood, K. Van Cleve, L. A. Viereck, D. L. Verbyla, and M. C. Chapin (eds.). 2005. *Alaska's Changing Boreal Forest*. New York: Oxford University Press.

Hobbie, J. E. (ed.). 1975. *Limnology of Tundra Ponds.* Stroudsburg, PA: Dowden, Hutchinson and Ross. 514 p.

Hobbie, J. E., T. Traaen, P. Rublee, J. P. Reed, M. C. Miller, and T. Fenchel. 1980. "Decomposers, Bacteria and Microbenthos" (340–387). In J. E. Hobbie (ed.). *Limnology of Tundra Ponds.* Stroudsburg, PA: Dowden, Hutchinson and Ross.

Hobbie, J. E., S. R. Carpenter, N. B. Grimm, J. R. Gosz, and T. R. Seastedt. 2003. "The US Long Term Ecological Research Program." *BioScience* 53:21–32.

Holding, A. J., O. W. Heal, S. F. MacLean Jr., and P. W. Flanagan (eds.). 1974. *Soil Organisms and Decomposition in Tundra.* Stockholm: Tundra Biome Steering Committee. 398 p.

Holling, C. S., D. W. Schindler, B. Walker, and J. Roughgarden. 1995. "Biodiversity in the Functioning of Ecosystems: An Ecological Primer and Synthesis" (44–83). In C. Perrings, K.-G. Mäler, C. Folke, C. S. Holling, and P.-O. Jansson (eds.). *Biodiversity: Ecological and Economic Foundations.* Cambridge, UK: Cambridge University Press.

Holling, C. S., G. Peterson, P. Marples, J. Sendzimir, K. Redford, L. Gunderson, and D. Lambert. 1996. "Self-Organization in Ecosystems: Lumpy Geometries, Periodicities and Morphologies" (346–384). In B. H. Walker and W. Steffen (eds.). *Global Change and Terrestrial Ecosystems.* Cambridge, UK: Cambridge University Press.

Hooper, D. U., and L. Johnson. 1999. "Plant Response to Herbivory and Belowground Nitrogen Cycling." *Ecology* 71:1040–1049.

Hooper, D. U., F. S. Chapin III, J. J. Ewel, A. Hector, P. Inchausti, S. Lavorel, J. H. Lawton, D. M. Lodge, M. Loreau, S. Naeem, B. Schmid, H. Setälä, A. J. Symstad, J. Vandermeer, and D. A. Wardle. 2005. "Effects of Biodiversity on Ecosystem Functioning: A Consensus of Current Knowledge." *Ecological Monographs* 75:3–35.

Hornbeck, J. W., and W. T. Swank. 1992. "Watershed Ecosystem Analysis as a Basis for Multiple-Use Management of Eastern Forests." *Ecological Applications* 2:238–247.

Hunt, H. W. 1977. "A Simulation Model for Decomposition in Grasslands." *Ecology* 58:469–484.

Hutchinson, G. E. 1944. Nitrogen in the Biogeochemistry of the Atmosphere." *American Scientist* 32:178–195.

Hutchinson, G. E. 1950. "Survey of Contemporary Knowledge of Biogeochemistry. 3. The Biogeochemistry of Vertebrate Excretion." *Bulletin of the American Museum of Natural History* 96. 554 p.

Hutchinson, G. E. 1957. *A Treatise on Limnology*, vol. 1. New York: John Wiley & Sons. 1030 p.

Ingham, R. E., J A. Trofymow, E. R. Ingham, and D. C. Coleman. 1985. "Interactions of Bacteria, Fungi, and Their Nematode Grazers: Effects on Nutrient Cycling and Plant Growth." *Ecological Monographs* 55: 119–140.

Innis, G. S. (ed.). 1978. *Grassland Simulation Model*. Ecological Studies 26. Heidelberg: Springer-Verlag. 298 p.

Innis, G. S., I. Noy-Meir, M. Godron, and G. M. Van Dyne. 1980. "Total-System Simulation Models" (759–797). In A. I. Breymeyer and G. M. Van Dyne (eds.). 1980. *Grasslands, Systems Analysis, and Man*. IBP Publication No. 19. Cambridge, UK: Cambridge University Press.

Jack, B. K., C. Kousky, and K. R. E. Sims. 2008. "Designing Payments for Ecosystem Services: Lessons from Previous Experience with Incentive-Based Mechanisms." *Proceedings of the National Academy of Sciences of the USA* 105:9465–9470.

Janisch, J. E., and M. E. Harmon. 2002. "Successional Changes in Live and Dead Wood Carbon Stores: Implications for Net Ecosystem Productivity." *Tree Physiology* 22:77–89.

Jeffers, J. N. R. (ed.). 1972. *Mathematical Models in Ecology*. Oxford: Blackwell. 398 p.

Johnson, D. W., and D. W. Cole. 2005. "Nutrient Cycles in Conifer Forests" (427–450). In F. Andersson (ed.). *Coniferous Forests*. Amsterdam: Elsevier.

Johnson, D. W., D. W. Cole, C. S. Bledsoe, K. Cromack, R. L. Edmonds, S. P. Gessel, C. C. Grier, B. N. Richards, and K. A. Vogt. 1982. "Nutrient Cycling in Forests of the Pacific Northwest" (186–232). In R. L. Edmonds (ed.). *Analysis of Coniferous Forest Ecosystems in the Western United States*. Stroudsburg, PA: Hutchinson Ross.

Johnson, P. L., and W. T. Swank. 1973. "Studies of Cation Budgets in the Southern Appalachians on Four Experimental Watersheds with Contrasting Vegetation." *Ecology* 54:70–80.

Kaplan, J. (Chairman). 1956. *Proposed United States Program for the International Geophysical Year 1957–58*. National Academy of Sciences, National Research Council, Washington, DC.

Keller, M., D. S. Schimel, W. W. Hargrove, and F. M. Hoffman. 2008. "A Continental Strategy for the National Ecological Observatory Network." *Frontiers in Ecology and the Environment* 6:282–284.

Kitazawa, Y. 1971. "Biological Regionality of the Soil Fauna and Its Function in Forest Ecosystem Types" (485–498). In P. Duvigneaud (ed.). *Productivity of Forest Ecosystems*. Proceedings of the Brussels symposium. Paris: Unesco.

Knapp, A. K., J. M. Briggs, D. C. Hartnett, and S. L. Collins (eds.). 1998. *Grassland Dynamics: Long-Term Ecological Research in Tallgrass Prairie*. LTER Network Series. New York: Oxford University Press. 364 p.

Knapp, A. K., J. M. Briggs, and J. K. Koelliker. 2001. "Frequency and Extent of Water Limitation to Primary Production in a Mesic Temperate Grassland." *Ecosystems* 4:19–28.

Knorr Cetina, K. 1999. *Epistemic Cultures: How the Sciences Make Knowledge*. Cambridge, MA: Harvard University Press. 329 p.

Kourtev, P. S., J. G. Ehrenfeld, and M. Häggblom. 2002. "Exotic Plant Species Alter the Microbial Community Structure and Function in the Soil." *Ecology* 83:3152–3166.

Kratz, T. K., L. Deegan, M. E. Harmon, and W. K. Lauenroth. 2003. "Ecological Variability in Space and Time: Insights Gained from the US LTER Program." *BioScience* 53:57–67.

Kuhn, T. S. 1996. *The Structure of Scientific Revolutions*, 3rd ed. Chicago: University of Chicago Press. 214 p.

Kwa, C. 1987. "Representations of Nature Mediating between Ecology and Science Policy: The Case of the International Biological Programme." *Social Studies of Science* 17:413–442.

Kwa, C. 1989. *Mimicking Nature: The Development of Systems Ecology in the United States, 1950–1975*. Doctoral dissertation. Free University of Amsterdam. 157 p.

Kwa, C. 2005. "Local Ecologies and Global Science: Discourses and Strategies of the International Geosphere-Biosphere Programme." *Social Studies of Science* 35:923–950.

Kwa, C. 2006. "The Programming of Interdisciplinary Research through Informal Science-Policy Interactions." *Science and Public Policy* 33:457–467.

Laakso, J., and H. Setälä. 1999. "Sensitivity of Primary Production to Changes in the Architecture of Belowground Food Webs." *Oikos* 87:57–64.

Lal, R. 2009. "Sequestering Atmospheric Carbon Dioxide." *Critical Reviews in Plant Science* 28:90–96.

Langley, J. A., K. L. McKee, D. R. Cahoon, J. A. Cherry, and J. P. Megonigal. 2009. "Elevated CO_2 Stimulates Marsh Elevation Gain, Counterbalancing Sea-Level Rise." *Proceedings of the National Academy of Sciences of the USA* 106:6182–6186.

Larson, C. E. 1971. "Not in Retrospect" (xiii–xvi). In D. J. Nelson (ed.). *Radionuclides in Ecosystems*. Proceedings of the Third National Symposium on Radioecology, Oak Ridge, TN. CONF-710501. Springfield, VA: NTIS. 1242 pp.

Larson, D. W. 2009. "The Battle of Bull Run." *American Scientist* 97:182–184.

Lauenroth, W. K., and E. M. Preston (eds.). 1984. *The Effects of SO$_2$ on a Grassland: A Case Study in the Northern Great Plains of the United States.* Ecological Studies 45. New York: Springer-Verlag. 207 p.

Leetham, J. W., T. J. McNary, J. L. Dodd, and W. K. Lauenroth. 1982. "Response of Soil Nematodes, Rotifers and Tardigrades to 3 Levels of Season-Long Sulfur-Dioxide Exposures." *Water, Air and Soil Pollution* 17:343–356.

LIDET (Long-Term Intersite Decomposition Team). 1995. "Meeting the Challenge of Long-Term, Broad-Scale Ecological Experiments." Publication No. 19. Seattle, WA: LTER Network Office. 23 pp.

Likens, G. E., F. H. Bormann, R. S. Pierce, J. S. Eaton, and N. M. Johnson. 1977. *Biogeochemistry of a Forested Ecosystem.* New York: Springer-Verlag. 146 p.

Little, M. A., N. Dyson-Hudson, R. Dyson-Hudson, J. E. Ellis, K. A. Galvin, P. W. Leslie, and D. M. Swift. 1990. "Ecosystem Approaches in Human Biology: Their History and a Case Study of the South Turkana Ecosystem Project" (389–434). In E. F. Moran (ed.). *The Ecosystem Approach in Anthropology: From Concept to Practice.* Ann Arbor: University of Michigan Press.

Liu, J., T. Dietz, S. R. Carpenter, M. Alberti, C. Folke, E. Moran, A. N. Pell, P. Deadman, T. Kratz, J. Lubchenco, E. Ostrom, Z. Ouyang, W. Provencher, C. L. Redman, S. H. Schneider, and W. W. Taylor. 2007. "Complexity of Coupled Human and Natural Systems." *Science* 317:1513–1517.

Livingstone, D. M. 2000. "Large-Scale Climatic Forcing Detected in Historical Observations of Lake Ice Break Up." Verhandungen Internationale. *Vereinigung für Limnologie* 27: 2775–2783.

Loomis, J., P. Kent, L. Strange, K. Fausch, and A. P. Covich. 2000. "Measuring the Total Economic Value of Restoring Ecosystem Services in an Impaired River Basin: Results from a Contingent Valuation Survey." *Ecological Economics* 33:103–117.

Lotka, A. J. 1925. *Elements of Physical Biology.* Baltimore: Williams and Wilkins. Reprinted as *Elements of Mathematical Biology.* 1956. New York: Dover. 465 p.

Loucks, O. L. 1979. *Long-Term Ecological Research: Concept Statement and Measurement Needs.* Summary of a workshop. June 25–27, 1979. Indianapolis: The Institute of Ecology. 27 p.

Loucks, O. L. 1986. "The United States' IBP: An Ecosystems Perspective after Fifteen Years," Chapter 19 (390–405). In N. Polunin (ed.). *Ecosystem Theory and Application.* New York: John Wiley & Sons.

Loucks, O. L., M. A. Little, and P. L. Jamison. 1974. *U.S. Participation in the International Biological Program.* Report No. 6 of the U.S. National Committee for the International Biological Program. Washington, DC: National Academy of Sciences. 166 p.

Lovejoy, T. E., and L. Hannah (eds.). 2005. *Climate Change and Biodiversity*. New Haven, CT: Yale University Press. 418 p.

Lowman, M., C. D'Avanzo, and C. Brewer. 2009. "A National Ecological Network for Research and Education." *Science* 323:1172–1173.

Lugo, A. E. 1995. "A Review of Dr. Howard T. Odum's Early Publications: From Bird Migration Studies to Scott Nixon's Turtle Grass Model" (3–10). In C. A. S. Hall (ed.). *Maximum Power: The Ideas and Applications of H. T. Odum*. Niwot: University Press of Colorado.

Macfadyen, A. 1963a. *Animal Ecology: Aims and Methods*. London: Pitman. 344 p.

Macfadyen, A. 1963b. "The Contribution of the Microfauna to Total Soil Metabolism" (1–17). In J. Doeksen and J. van der Drift (eds.). *Soil Organisms*. Amsterdam: North-Holland Pub. Co..

MacLean, S. F. Jr. 1974. "Primary Production, Decomposition, and the Activity of Soil Invertebrates in Tundra Ecosystems: A Hypothesis" (197–206). In A. J. Holding, O. W. Heal, S. F. MacLean Jr., and P. W. Flanagan (eds.). 1974. *Soil Organisms and Decomposition in Tundra*. Stockholm: Tundra Biome Steering Committee.

MacMahon, J. A., and D. J. Schimpf. 1981. "Water as a Factor in the Biology of Desert Plants" (114–171). In D. D. Evans and J. L. Thames (eds.). *Water in Desert Ecosystems*. Stroudsburg, PA: Dowden, Hutchinson & Ross.

Magnuson, J. J. 2002. "Signals from Ice Cover Trends and Variability. Fisheries in a Changing Climate." (3–14) In vol. 32. American Fisheries Society Symposium, Bethesda, Maryland. American Fisheries Society.

Magnuson, J. J., B. J. Benson, and T. K. Kratz. 2004. "Patterns of Coherent Dynamics within and between Lake Districts at Local to Intercontinental Scales." *Boreal Environmental Research* 9:359–369.

Magnuson, J. J., T. K. Kratz, B. J. Benson (eds.). 2006a. *Long-Term Dynamics of Lakes in the Landscape*. LTER Network Series. New York: Oxford University Press. 464 p.

Magnuson, J. J., B. J. Benson, J. D. Lenters, D. M. Robertson. 2006b. "Climate-Driven Variability and Change" (123–150). In J. J. Magnuson, T. K. Kratz, and B. J. Benson (eds.). *Long-Term Dynamics of Lakes in the Landscape*. LTER Network Series. New York: Oxford University Press.

Magnuson, J. J., B. J. Benson, T. K. Kratz, D. E. Armstrong, C. J. Bowser, A. C. C. Colby, T. W. Meinke, P. K. Montz, K. E. Webster. 2006c. "Origin, Operation, Evolution, and Challenges" (280–322). In J. J. Magnuson, T. K.

Kratz, and B. J. Benson (eds.). *Long-Term Dynamics of Lakes in the Landscape.* LTER Network Series. New York: Oxford University Press.

Makarieva, A. M., V. G. Gorshkov, and B. L. Li. 2008. "Energy Budget of the Biosphere and Civilization: Rethinking Environmental Security of Global Renewable and Non-Renewable Sources." *Ecological Complexity* 5: 281–288.

Mann, M. E., R. S. Bradley, and M. K. Hughes. 1998. "Global-Scale Temperature Patterns and Climate Forcing over the Past Six Centuries." *Nature* 392:779–787.

Mann, M. E., R. S. Bradley, and M. K. Hughes. 1999. "Northern Hemisphere Temperatures during the Past Millennium: Inferences, Uncertainties, and Limitations." *Geophysical Research Letters* 26:759–762.

Margalef, R. 1968. *Perspectives in Ecological Theory.* Chicago, IL: University of Chicago Press. 111 p.

Margalef, R. 1997. *Our Biosphere.* Oldendorf, Germany: Ecology Institute. 176 p.

Marr, J. W. 1961. "Ecosystems of the East Slope of the Front Range in Colorado." *University of Colorado Studies, Series in Biology* 8:1–134.

Marshall, J. K. (ed.). 1977. *The Belowground Ecosystem: A Synthesis of Plant Associated Processes.* Range Sci. Dep. Sci. Ser. No. 26. Fort Collins: Colorado State University.

McGraw, D. P. *Millennial Biology: A History of the NSF Biology Directorate, 1975–2005.* In preparation.

McIntosh, R. P. 1985. *The Background of Ecology: Concept and Theory.* Cambridge, UK: Cambridge University Press. 383 p.

McLaughlin, J. W., and S. A. Phillips. 2006. "Soil Carbon, Nitrogen, and Base Cation Cycling 17 Years after Whole-Tree Harvesting in a Low-Elevation Red Spruce (*Picea rubens*)-Balsam Fir (*Abies balsamea*) Forested Watershed in Central Maine, USA." *Forest Ecology & Management* 222:234–253.

Melillo, J. M., A. D. McGuire, D. W. Kicklighter, B. Moore III, C. J. Vorosmarty, and A. L Schloss. 1993. "Global Climate Change and Terrestrial Net Primary Production." *Nature* 363:234–240.

Melillo, J. M., P. A. Steudler, J. D. Aber, K. Newkirk, H. Lux, F. P. Bowles, C. Catricala, A. Magill, T. Ahrens, and S. Morrisseau. 2002. "Soil Warming and Carbon-Cycle Feedbacks to the Climate." *Science* 298:2173–2176.

Mikola, J., and H. Setälä. 1998. "No Evidence of Trophic Cascades in an Experimental Microbial-Based Food Web." *Ecology* 79:153–164.

Millennium Ecosystem Assessment. 2005. *Ecosystems and Human Well-Being: Synthesis.* Washington, DC: Island Press. 137 p.

Misra, R., and B. Gopal (eds.). 1968. "Proceedings of the Symposium on Recent Advances in Tropical Ecology, Part II" (377–771). Varanasi, India: International Society for Tropical Ecology.

Mitchell, R., R. A. Mayer, and J. Downhower. 1976. "Evaluation of 3 Biome Programs." *Science* 192:859–865.

Mooney, H. A. (ed.). 1977. *Convergent Evolution in Chile and California.* Stroudsburg, PA: Dowden, Hutchinson & Ross, Inc. 224 p.

Mooney, H. A. 1998. *The Globalization of Ecological Thought.* Excellence in Ecology 5. Oldendorf/Luhe, Germany: Ecology Institute. 150 p.

Mooney, H. A. 1999. "On the Road to Global Ecology." *Annual Review of Energy and the Environment* 24:1–31.

Moore, J. C., E. L. Berlow, D. C. Coleman, P. C. de Ruiter, Q. Dong, A. Hastings, N. C. Johnson, K. S. McCann, K. Melville, P. J. Morin, K. Nadelhoffer, A. D. Rosemond, D. M. Post, J. L. Sabo, K. M. Scow, M. J. Vanni, and D. H. Wall. 2004. "Detritus, Trophic Dynamics, and Biodiversity." *Ecology Letters* 7:584–600.

Moore, T. R., J. A. Trofymow, C. E. Prescott, J. Fyles, B. D. and Titus. 2006. "Patterns of Carbon, Nitrogen and Phosphorus Dynamics in Decomposing Foliar Litter in Canadian Forests." *Ecosystems* 9:46–62.

Moorhead, D. L., W. S. Currie, E. B. Rastetter, W. J. Parton, M. E. Harmon, 1999. "Climate and Litter Quality Controls on Decomposition: An Analysis of Modeling Approaches." *Global Climate Change* 13:575–589.

Mulholland, P. J., and 30 co-authors. 2008. "Stream Denitrification across Biomes and Its Response to Anthropogenic Nitrate Loading." *Nature* 452:202–205.

Nadelhoffer, K., R. Boone, R. Bowden, J. Canary, J. Kaye, P. Micks, A. Ricca, W. McDowell, and J. Aitkenhead. 2004. "The DIRT Experiment: Litter and Root Influences on Forest Soil Organic Matter Stocks and Function" (300–315). In D. W. Foster and J. Aber (eds.). *Forests in Time.* New Haven, CT: Yale University Press.

Nadkarni, N., D. Schaefer, T. J. Matelson, and R. Solano. 2002. "Comparison of Arboreal and Terrestrial Soil Characteristics in a Lower Montane Forest, Monteverde, Costa Rica." *Pedobiologia* 46:24–33.

Naeem, S. 2002. "Ecosystems Consequences of Biodiversity Loss: The Evolution of a Paradigm." *Ecology* 83:1537–1552.

Nardi, B. A., and V. L. O'Day. 1999. *Information Ecologies: Using Technology with Heart.* Cambridge, MA: MIT Press. 232 p.

National Science Foundation. 1977. "Experimental Ecological Reserves: A Proposed National Network." Directory for Biology, Behavioral and Social Sciences, Division of Environmental Biology, Washington, DC.

Nelson, D. J. (ed.). 1971. *Radionuclides in Ecosystems: Proceedings of the Third National Symposium on Radioecology.* Oak Ridge, TN. CONF-710501. Springfield, VA: NTIS. 1242 pp.

Nelson, E., G. Mendoza, J. Regetz, S. Polasky, H. Tallis, D. R. Cameron, K. M. A. Chan, G. C. Daily, J. Goldstein, P. M. Kareiva, E. Lonsdorf, R. Naidoo, T. H. Ricketts, and M. R. Shaw. 2009. "Modeling Multiple Ecosystem Services, Biodiversity Conservation, Commodity Production, and Tradeoffs at Landscape Scales." *Frontiers in Ecology and the Environment* 7:4–11.

Odishaw, H., and S. Ruttenberg. (eds.). 1958. *Geophysics and the IGY: Proceedings of the Symposium at the Opening of the International Geophysical Year.* American Geophysical Union of the National Academy of Sciences. Geophysical Monograph No. 2, Washington, DC. 210 p.

Odum, E. P. 1953. *Fundamentals of Ecology,* 1st ed. Philadelphia, PA: Saunders. 384 p.

Odum, E. P. 1969. "The Strategy of Ecosystem Development." *Science* 164:260–270.

Odum, E. P., and G. W. Barrett. 2005. *Fundamentals of Ecology,* 5th ed. Belmont, CA: Thomson Brooks/Cole. 598 p.

Odum, H. T. 1971. *Environment, Power, and Society.* New York: Wiley–Interscience. 331 p.

Odum, H. T. 1983. *Systems Ecology: An Introduction.* New York: Wiley & Sons. 644 p.

Odum, H. T. 2007. *Environment, Power, and Society for the Twenty-First Century: The Hierarchy of Energy.* New York: Columbia University Press. 418p.

Odum, H. T., and A. Lugo. 1970. "Metabolism of Forest Floor Microcosms" (I-35–I-56). In H. T. Odum and R. F. Pigeon (eds.). 1970. *A Tropical Rain Forest: A Study of Irradiation and Ecology at El Verde, Puerto Rico.* USAEC TID-24270. Springfield, VA.

Odum, H. T., and E. P. Odum. 1955. "Trophic Structure and Productivity of a Windward Coral Reef Community on Eniwetok Atoll." *Ecological Monographs* 25:291–320.

Odum, H. T., and R. F. Pigeon (eds.). 1970. *A Tropical Rain Forest: A Study of Irradiation and Ecology at El Verde, Puerto Rico.* USAEC TID-24270. Springfield, VA. 1659 p.

Odum, H. T., and C. F. Jordan. 1970. "Metabolism and Evapotranspiration of the Lower Forest in a Giant Plastic Cylinder" (I-165–I-189). In H. T. Odum and R. F. Pigeon (eds.). *A Tropical Rain Forest: A Study of Irradiation and Ecology at El Verde, Puerto Rico.* USAEC TID-24270. Springfield, VA.

Odum, H. T., A. Lugo, G. Cintrón, and C. F. Jordan. 1970. "Metabolism and Evapotranspiration of Some Rain Forest Plants and Soil" (I-103–I-164). In H. T. Odum and R. F. Pigeon (eds.). *A Tropical Rain Forest: A Study of Irradiation and Ecology at El Verde, Puerto Rico.* USAEC TID-24270. Springfield, VA.

Olson, J. S. 1963. "Energy-Storage and Balance of Producers and Decomposers in Ecological-Systems." *Ecology* 44:322–331.

O'Neill, R. V. 1976. "Ecosystem Persistence and Heterotrophic Regulation." *Ecology* 57:1244–1253.

O'Neill, R. V., and A. W. King. 1998. "Homage to St. Michael; Or, Why Are There So Many Books on Scale?" (3–15). In D. L. Peterson and V. T. Parker (eds.). *Ecological Scale. Theory and Applications.* New York: Columbia University Press.

Orians, G. H., and O. T. Solbrig (eds.). 1977. *Convergent Evolution in Warm Deserts.* Stroudsburg, PA: Dowden, Hutchinson & Ross, Inc. 333 p.

Pace, M. L., and P. M. Groffman. 1998. "Needs and Concerns in Ecosystem Science" (1–6). In M. L. Pace and P. M. Groffman (eds.). *Success, Limitations, and Frontiers in Ecosystem Science.* New York: Springer-Verlag.

Pace, M. L., P. M. Groffman (eds.). 1998. *Success, Limitations, and Frontiers in Ecosystem Science.* New York: Springer-Verlag. 499 p.

Pagiola, S., P. Agostini, J. Gobbi, C. de Haan, M. Ibrahim, E. Murgueitio, E. Ramirez, M. Rosales, and J. P. Ruiz. 2005. "Paying for Biodiversity Conservation Services: Experience in Colombia, Costa Rica, and Nicaragua." *Mountain Research and Development* 25:206–211.

Parton, W., W. L. Silver, I. C. Burke, L. Grassens, M. E. Harmon, W. S. Currie, J. Y. King, E. C. Adair, L. A. Brandt, S. C. Hart, and B. Fasth. 2007. "Global-Scale Similarities in Nitrogen Release Patterns during Long-Term Decomposition." *Science* 315:361–364.

Patten, B. C. 1971–1976. *Systems Analysis and Simulation in Ecology,* vols. 1–4. New York: Academic Press.

Paustian, K., L. Bergstrom, P.-E. Jansson, and H. Johnsson. 1990. "Ecosystem Dynamics" (153–180). In O. Andrén, T. Lindberg, K. Paustian, and T. Rosswall (eds.). *Ecology of Arable Land. Organisms, Carbon and Nitrogen Cycling.* Ecological Bulletins 40. Copenhagen.

Persson, T. 1980. (ed.). *Structure and Function of Northern Coniferous Forests.* Ecological Bulletins 32. Stockholm. 609 p.

Peters, D. P. C., P. M. Groffman, K. J. Nadelhoffer, N. B. Grimm, S. L. Collins, W. K. Michener, and M. A. Huston. 2008. "Living in an Increasingly-Connected World: A Framework for Continental-Scale Science." *Frontiers in Ecology and the Environment* 6:229–237.

Petersen, H. 1995. "Energy Flow and Trophic Relations in Soil Communities: State of Knowledge Two Decades after the International Biological Programme" (111–130). In C. A. Edwards, T. Abe, and B. R. Striganova (eds.). *Structure and Function of Soil Communities.* Japan: Kyoto University Press.

Petersen, H. A., and M. Luxton. 1982. "A Comparative Analysis of Soil Fauna Populations and Their Role in Decomposition Processes." *Oikos* 39:287–388.

Peterson, B. J., L. Deegan, J. Helfrich, J. E. Hobbie, M. Hullar, B. Moller, T. E. Ford, A. Hershey, A. Hiltner, G. Kipphut, M. A. Lock, D. M. Fiebig, V. McKinley, M. C. Miller, J. R. Vestal, R. Ventullo, and G. Volk. 1993. "Biological Responses of a Tundra River to Fertilization." *Ecology* 74:653–672.

Peterson, B. J., W. M. Wollheim, P. J. Mulholland, J. R. Webster, J. L. Meyer, J. L. Tank, E. Marti, W. B. Bowden, H. M. Valett, A. E. Hershey, W. H. McDowell, W. K. Dodds, S. K. Hamilton, S. Gregory, and D. D. Morrall. 2001. "Control of Nitrogen Export from Watersheds by Headwater Streams." *Science* 292:86–90.

Petrusewicz, K. (ed.). 1967. *Secondary Productivity of Terrestrial Ecosystems* (Principles and Methods). Panstwowe Wydawnictwo Naukowe, Polish Academy of Sciences, Warsaw and Krakow, 579 p.

Petrusewicz, K., and A. Macfadyen. 1970. *Productivity of Terrestrial Animals: Principles and Methods.* IBP Handbook No. 13. Philadelphia: F.A. Davis Co. 190 p.

Phillipson, J. 1964. "A Miniature Bomb Calorimeter for Small Biological Samples." *Oikos* 15:130–139.

Phillipson, J. (ed.). 1970. *Methods of Study in Soil Ecology.* Proceedings of Symposium. IBP-Paris: Unesco. 303 p.

Pomeroy, L. R. 1970. "The Strategy of Mineral Cycling." *Annual Review of Ecology and Systematics* 1:171–190.

Pomeroy, L. R. 1974. "The Ocean's Food Web, a Changing Paradigm." *BioScience* 24:499–504.

Portner, H.-O. 2008. "Ecosystem Effects of Ocean Acidification in Times of Ocean Warming: A Physiologist's View." *Marine Ecology-Progress Series* 373:203–217.

Priscu, J. (ed.). 1998. *Ecosystem Dynamics in a Polar Desert: The McMurdo Dry Valleys, Antarctica.* Washington, DC: American Geophysical Union. 369 p.

Reichle, D. E. (ed.). 1970. *Analysis of Temperate Forest Ecosystems*. Ecological Studies 1. Heidelberg: Springer-Verlag. 304 p.

Reichle, D. E. 1971. "Energy and Nutrient Metabolism of Soil and Litter Invertebrates" (465–477). In P. Duvigneaud (ed.). *Productivity of Forest Ecosystems*. Proceedings of the Brussels symposium. Paris: Unesco.

Reichle, D. E. 1975. "Advances in Ecosystem Analysis." *BioScience* 25:257–264.

Reichle, D. E. (ed.). 1981. *Dynamic Properties of Forest Ecosystems*. I.B.P. Publication No. 23. Cambridge, UK: Cambridge University Press. 683 p.

Reichle, D. E., and D. A. Crossley Jr. 1965. Radiocesium Dispersion in a Cryptozoan Food Web. *Health Physics* 11:1375–1384.

Reichle, D. E., B. E. Dinger, N. T. Edwards, W. F. Harris, and P. Sollins. 1973. "Carbon Flow and Storage in a Forest Ecosystem" (345–365). In G. M. Woodwell and E. V. Pecan (eds.). *Carbon and the Biosphere*. Atomic Energy Commission, Springfield, VA.

Reuss, J. O., and G. S. Innis. 1977. "A Grassland Nitrogen Flow Simulation Model." *Ecology* 58:379–388.

Ricketts, T. H. 2004. "Tropical Forest Fragments Enhance Pollinator Activity in Nearby Coffee Crops." *Conservation Biology* 18:1262–1271.

Robertson, G. P. 2008. "Long-Term Ecological Research: Re-inventing Network Science." *Frontiers in Ecology and the Environment* 6:281.

Robertson, G. P., D. C. Coleman, C. S. Bledsoe, and P. Sollins (eds.). 1999. *Standard Soil Methods for Long-Term Ecological Research*. LTER Network Series. New York: Oxford University Press. 462 p.

Rodin, L. E., and N. I. Bazilevich. 1967. *Production and Mineral Cycling in Terrestrial Vegetation*. English ed. (Transl. Scripta Technica Ltd., Fogg, G. E., Ed.). London: Oliver & Boyd. 288 p.

Rodin, L. E., and N. N. Smirnov (eds.). 1975. *Resources of the Biosphere*, vol. 1 [Russian]. Leningrad: Nauka Publishers. 337 p.

Rosenberg, O., and S. Jacobson. 2004. "Effects of Repeated Slash Removal in Thinned Stands on Soil Chemistry and Understorey Vegetation." *Silva Fennica* 38, 133–142.

Rosswall, T., and O. W. Heal (eds.). 1974. *Structure and Function of Tundra Ecosystems*. Ecological Bulletins No. 20. Stockholm. 450 p.

Rundel, P. W., and A. C. Gibson. 1996. *Ecological Communities and Processes in a Mojave Desert Ecosystem: Rock Valley, Nevada*. Cambridge, UK: Cambridge University Press. 369 p.

Rustad, L. E. 2008. "The Response of Terrestrial Ecosystems to Global Climate Change: Towards an Integrated Approach." *Science of the Total Environment* 404:222–235.

Rustad, L. E., J. Campbell, G. M. Marion, R. J. Norby, M. J. Mitchell, A. E. Hartley, J. H. C. Cornelissen, and J. Gurevitch. 2001. "A Meta-Analysis of the Response of Soil Respiration, Net N Mineralization, and Aboveground Plant Growth to Experimental Ecosystem Warming." *Oecologia* 126: 543–562.

Rychert, R., J. Skujins, D. Sorensen, and D. Porcella. 1978. "Nitrogen Fixation by Lichens and Free-Living Microorganisms in Deserts" (20–30). In N. E. West and J. J. Skujins (eds.). *Nitrogen in Desert Ecosystems*. East Stroudsburg, PA: Dowden, Hutchinson & Ross.

Ryszkowski, L. 1982. "Obituary, Kazimierz Petrusewicz." *Acta Theriologica* 27:161–165.

Sanchez-Azofeifa, G. A., A. Pfaff, J. A. Robalino, and J. P. Boomhower. 2007. "Costa Rica's Payment for Environmental Services Program: Intention, Implementation, and Impact." *Conservation Biology* 21:1165–1173.

Satoo, T. 1971. "Primary Production Relations of Coniferous Forests in Japan" (191–205). In P. Duvigneaud (ed.). *Productivity of Forest Ecosystems*. Proceedings of the Brussels symposium. Paris: Unesco.

Schultz, V., and A. W. Klement Jr. (eds.). 1961. *Radioecology: Proceedings of the First National Symposium on Radioecology Held at Colorado State University, Fort Collins, CO*. Washington, DC: Reinhold and American Institute of Biological Sciences. 746 p.

Shachak, M., J. R. Gosz, S. T. A. Pickett, and A. Perevolotsky (eds.). 2004. *Biodiversity in Drylands: Toward a Unified Framework*. LTER Network Series. New York: Oxford University Press. 368 p.

Shaver, G. R., and W. D. Billings. 1975. "Root Production and Root Turnover in a Wet Tundra Ecosystem." *Ecology* 56:401–409.

Shrum, W., J. Genuth, and I. Chompalov. 2007. *Structures of Scientific Collaboration*. Cambridge, MA: The MIT Press. 280 p.

Singh, J. S. 1968. "Net Aboveground Community Productivity in the Grasslands at Varanasi" (631–654). In R. Misra (ed.). *Proceedings of Symposium on Recent Advances in Tropical Ecology*. Varanasi, India.

Singh, J. S., and D. C. Coleman. 1974. "Distribution of Photo-Assimilated Carbon-14 in the Root System of a Shortgrass Prairie." *Journal of Ecology* 62:389–395.

Singh, J. S., and R. Misra. 1969. "Diversity, Dominance, Stability, and Net Production in the Grasslands at Varanasi, India." *Canadian Journal of Botany* 47:425–427.

Sistla, S., O. Sala, J. Mohan, J. Blanchard, F. Bowles, and J. Melillo. 2006. "Reversible Separation of Root Respiration from Total Soil Respiration." LTER All

Scientists' Meeting poster. (www.lternet.edu/asm/2006/posters/poster .php?poster_id=171).

Smith, M. D., and A. K. Knapp. 1999. "Exotic Plant Species in a C_4-Dominated Grassland: Invasibility, Disturbance, and Community Structure." *Oecologia* 120:605–612.

Smith, M. D., and A. K. Knapp. 2001. "Size of the Local Species Pool Determines Invisibility of a C_4-Dominated Grassland." *Oikos* 92:55–61.

Smith, M. D., A. K. Knapp, and S. L. Collins. 2009. "A Framework for Addressing Ecosystem Dynamics in Response to Chronic Resource Alterations Induced by Global Change." *Ecology.* 90:2279–2289.

Smith, M. H., E. P. Odum, and R. R. Sharitz. 2001. "Savannah River Ecology Laboratory: A Model for a Cooperative Partnership between a University and the Federal Government" (93–127). In G. W. Barrett and T. L. Barrett (eds.). *Holistic Science: The Evolution of the Georgia Institute of Ecology (1940–2000).* New York: Taylor & Francis.

Smolik, J. D., and J. K. Lewis. 1982. "Effect of Range Condition on Density and Biomass of Nematodes in a Mixed Prairie Ecosystem." *Journal of Range Management* 35:657–663.

Sollins, P., C. C. Grier, K. Cromack Jr., F. Glenn, and R. Fogel. 1980. "The Internal Nutrient Cycle of an Old-Growth Douglas-Fir Stand in Western Oregon." *Ecological Monographs* 50:261–285.

Stout, J. D. 1963. "The Terrestrial Plankton." *Tuatara* 11:57–65.

Sullivan, W. 1961. *Assault on the Unknown: The International Geophysical Year.* New York: McGraw-Hill. 460 p.

Swank, W. T., and D. A. Crossley Jr. (eds.). 1988. *Forest Hydrology and Ecology at Coweeta.* Ecological Studies, vol. 66. New York: Springer-Verlag. 469 p.

Swank, W. T., J. L. Meyer, and D. A. Crossley Jr. 2001. "Long-Term Ecological Research: Coweeta History and Perspectives" (143–163). In G. W. Barrett and T. L. Barrett (eds.). *Holistic Science: The Evolution of the Georgia Institute of Ecology (1940–2000).* New York: Taylor & Francis.

Swanson, F. J., R. L. Fredriksen, and F. M. McCorison. 1982. "Material Transfer in a Western Oregon Forested Watershed" (233–266). In R. L. Edmonds (ed.). *Analysis of Coniferous Forest Ecosystems in the Western United States.* Stroudsburg, PA: Hutchinson Ross.

Swift, M. J., O. W. Heal, and J. M. Anderson. 1979. *Decomposition in Terrestrial Ecosystems.* Berkeley: University of California Press. 372 p.

Symon, C., L. Arris, and O. W. Heal (eds.). 2005. *Arctic Climate Impact Assessment.* Cambridge, UK: Cambridge University Press. 1042 p.

Tansley, A. G. 1935. "The Use and Abuse of Vegetational Concepts and Terms." *Ecology* 16:284–307.

Tilman, D. 2001. "Effects of Diversity and Composition on Grassland Stability and Productivity" (183–207). In M. C. Press, N. J. Huntley, and S. Levin (eds.). *Ecology: Achievement and Challenge*. Oxford: Blackwell Science.

Tilman, D. (Chairman). 2003. *NEON: Addressing the Nation's Environmental Challenges*. Washington, DC: National Research Council, National Academy Press. 132 p.

Tinker, P. B., and J. S. I. Ingram. 1996. "The Work of Focus 3" (207–228). In B. Walker and W. Steffen (eds.). *Global Change and Terrestrial Ecosystems*. Cambridge, UK: Cambridge University Press.

Townsend, K., B. Caldwell, and K. Lajtha. 2006. "The Origin of DIRT: The Legacy of Francis D. Hole." LTER All-Scientists' meeting poster. (www.lternet.edu/asm/2006/posters/poster.php?poster_id=499).

Triska, F. J., J. R. Sedell, and S. V. Gregory. 1982. "Coniferous Forest Streams" (292–332). In R. L. Edmonds (ed.). *Analysis of Coniferous Forest Ecosystems in the Western United States*. Stroudsburg, PA: Hutchinson Ross.

Trofymow, J. A., T. R. Moore, B. Titus, C. Prescott, I. Morrison, M. Siltanen, S. Smith, J. Fyles, R. Wein, T. C. Camir, L. Duschene, L. Kozak, M. Kranabetter, and S. Visser. 2002. "Rates of Litter Decomposition over 6 years in Canadian Forests: Influence of Litter Quality and Climate." *Canadian Journal of Forest Research* 32:789–804.

Tsutsumi, T. 1971. "Accumulation and Circulation of Nutrient Elements in Forest Ecosystems" (543–552). In P. Duvigneaud (ed.). *Productivity of Forest Ecosystems*. Proceedings of the Brussels symposium. Paris: Unesco.

Ulehlova, B. 1973. "Alluvial Grassland Ecosystems: Microorganisms and Decay Processes." *Acta Scientiae Naturales Brno* 7:1–43.

U.S. National Committee for the IBP. 1971. *Report No. 4*. Washington, DC: National Academy of Sciences. 121 p.

U.S. National Committee for the IBP. 1974. *Report No. 6*. Washington, DC: National Academy of Sciences. 166 p.

Valentine, D. W., K. Kielland, F. Stuart Chapin III, A. D. McGuire, and K. Van Cleve. 2006. "Patterns of Biogeochemistry in Alaskan Boreal Forests" (241–266). In F. S. Chapin III, M. W. Oswood, K. Van Cleve, L. A. Viereck, D. L. Verbyla, and M. C. Chapin (eds.). *Alaska's Changing Boreal Forest*. New York: Oxford University Press.

Van der Drift, J. 1971. "Production and Decomposition of Organic Matter in an Oakwood in the Netherlands" (631–634). In P. Duvigneaud (ed.). *Productivity of Forest Ecosystems*. Proceedings of the Brussels symposium. Paris: Unesco.

Van Dyne, G. M. (ed.). 1969. *The Ecosystem Concept in Natural Resource Management.* New York: Academic Press. 383 p.

Van Voris, P., R. V. O'Neill, W. R. Emanuel, and H. H. Shugart Jr. 1980. "Functional Complexity and Ecosystem Stability." *Ecology* 61:1352–1360.

Vitousek, P. 2004. *Nutrient Cycling and Limitation. Hawai'i as a Model System.* Oxford: Princeton University Press. 223 p.

Vossbrinck, C. R., D. C. Coleman, and T. A. Woolley. 1979. "Abiotic and Biotic Factors in Litter Decomposition in a Semiarid Grassland." *Ecology* 60:265–271.

Walker, B. H. 1992. "Biological Diversity and Ecological Redundancy." *Conservation Biology* 6:18–23.

Walker, B. H. 1996. "Predicting a Future Terrestrial Biosphere: Challenges to GCTE Science" (595–607). In B. Walker and W. Steffen (eds.). *Global Change and Terrestrial Ecosystems.* Cambridge, UK: Cambridge University Press.

Walker, B. H., and W. Steffen (eds.). 1996. *Global Change and Terrestrial Ecosystems.* Cambridge, UK: Cambridge University Press. 619 p.

Walker, B. H., W. L. Steffen, J. Canadell, and J. S. I. Ingram (eds.). 1999. *The Terrestrial Biosphere and Global Change: Implications for Natural and Managed Ecosystems.* Synthesis Volume. IGBP Book Series No. 4. Cambridge, UK: Cambridge University Press.

Wall, D. H. (ed.). 2004. *Sustaining Biodiversity and Ecosystem Services in Soils and Sediments.* Washington, DC: Island Press. 275 p.

Wallace, J. B. 1988. "Aquatic Invertebrate Research" (257–268). In W. T. Swank and D. A. Crossley Jr. (eds.). *Forest Hydrology and Ecology at Coweeta.* Ecological Studies 66. New York: Springer-Verlag.

Wallwork, J. A. 1970. *Ecology of Soil Animals.* London: McGraw-Hill. 283 p.

Wallwork, J. A. 1982. *Desert Soil Fauna.* New York: Praeger Pub. 296 p.

Waring, R. H. (ed.). 1980. *Forests: Fresh Perspectives from Ecosystem Analysis.* Corvallis: Oregon State University Press. 199 p.

Wear, D. N., and P. Bolstad. 1998. "Land-Use Changes in Southern Appalachian Landscapes: Spatial Analysis and Forecast Evaluation." *Ecosystems* 1:575–594.

Webster, J. R., M. E. Gartz, J. J. Hains, J. L. Meyer, W. T. Swank, J. B. Waide, and J. B. Wallace. 1983. "Stability of Stream Ecosystems" (355–395). In J. R. Barnes and G. W. Minshall (eds.). *Stream Ecology.* New York: Plenum Press.

Webster, J. R., S. W. Golladay, E. F. Benfield, J. L. Meyer, W. T. Swank, and J. B. Wallace. 1992. "Catchment Disturbance and Stream Response: An Overview of Stream Research at Coweeta Hydrologic Laboratory" (231–253). In

P. Boon, G. Petts, and P. L. Calow (eds.). *River Conservation and Management.* Chichester, UK: John Wiley & Sons.

Webster, J. R., P. J. Mulholland, J. L. Tank, H. M. Valett, W. K. Dodds, B. J. Peterson, W. B. Bowden, C. N. Dahm, S. Findlay, S. V. Gregory, N. B. Grimm, S. K. Hamilton, S. L. Johnson, E. Marti, W. H. McDowell, J. L. Meyer, D. D. Morrall, S. A. Thomas, and W. M. Wollheim. 2003. "Factors Affecting Ammonium Uptake in Streams: An Inter-Biome Perspective." *Freshwater Biology* 48:1329–1352.

West, N. E., and J. J. Skujins. (eds.). 1978. *Nitrogen in Desert Ecosystems.* East Stroudsburg, PA: Dowden, Hutchinson & Ross. 307 p.

Whitford, W. G. 1988. "Effects of Harvester Ant, *Pogonomyrmex rugosus*, Nests on Soils and a Spring Annual, *Erodium texanum*." *Southwestern Naturalist* 33:482–485.

Whitford, W. G. 2000. "Keystone Arthropods as Webmasters in Desert Ecosystems" (25–41). In D. C. Coleman and P. F. Hendrix (eds.). *Invertebrates as Webmasters in Ecosystems.* Wallingford, UK: CABI Press.

Whitford, W. G. 2002. *Ecology of Desert Ecosystems.* San Diego: Academic Press. 343 p.

Whitford, W. G., D. W. Freckman, P. F. Santos, N. Z. Elkins, and L. W. Parker. 1982. "The Role of Nematodesin Decomposition in Desert Ecosystems." (98–116). In D. W. Freckman (ed.). *Nematodes in Soil Ecosystems.* Austin: University of Texas Press.

Whitman, W. B., D. C. Coleman, and W. J. Wiebe. 1998. *Perspective.* "Prokaryotes: The Unseen Majority." *Proceedings of the National Academy of Sciences of the USA* 95:6578–6583.

Whittaker, J. B. 1974. "Interactions between Fauna and Microflora at Tundra Sites" (183–196). In A. J. Holding, O. W. Heal, S. F. MacLean Jr., and P. W. Flanagan (eds.). *Soil Organisms and Decomposition in Tundra.* Stockholm: Tundra Biome Steering Committee.

Wiegert, R. G. 1965. "Energy Dynamics of the Grasshopper Populations in Old Field and Alfalfa Field Ecosystems." *Oikos* 16:161–176.

Wiegert, R. G. 1970. "Energetics of the Nest-Building Termite, *Nasutitermes costalis* (Holmgren) in a Puerto Rican Forest" (I-57–I-64). In H. T. Odum and R. F. Pigeon (eds.). *A Tropical Rain Forest: A Study of Irradiation and Ecology at El Verde, Puerto Rico.* USAEC TID-24270. Springfield, VA.

Wiegert, R. G., and F. C. Evans. 1967. "Investigations of Secondary Productivity in Grasslands" (499–518). In K. Petrusewicz (ed.). *Secondary Productivity of*

Terrestrial Ecosystems. Warsaw: Panstwowe Wydawnictwo Naukowe, Polish Academy of Sciences.

Wiegert, R. G., and P. C. Fraleigh. 1972. "Ecology of Yellowstone Thermal Effluent Systems: Net Primary Production and Species Diversity of a Successional Blue-Green Algal Mat." *Limnology and Oceanography* 17:215–228.

Wiegert, R. G., D. C. Coleman, and E. P. Odum. 1970. "Energetics of the Litter-Soil Subsystem" (93–98). In J. Phillipson (ed.), *Methods of Study in Soil Ecology*. Proc. of Symposium. Paris: IBP-UNESCO.

Wilcove, D. S., D. Rothstein, J. Dubow, A. Phillips, and E. Losos. 1998. "Quantifying Threats to Imperiled Species in the United States." *BioScience* 48:607–616.

Witkamp, M. 1971a. "Soils as Components of Ecosystems." *Annual Review of Ecology and Systematics* 2:85–110.

Witkamp, M. 1971b. "Forest Soil Microflora and Mineral Cycling" (413–424). In P. Duvigneaud (ed.). *Productivity of Forest Ecosystems*. Proceedings of the Brussels symposium. Paris: Unesco.

Witkamp, M., and D. A. Crossley Jr. 1966. "Role of Arthropods and Microflora in Breakdown of White Oak Litter." *Pedobiologia* 6:293–303.

Witkamp, M., and J. van der Drift. 1961. "Breakdown of Forest Litter in Relation to Environmental Factors." *Plant & Soil* 15:295–311.

Wolters, V., W. H. Silver, D. E. Bignell, D. C. Coleman, P. Lavelle, W. H. van der Putten, P. de Ruiter, J. Rusek, D. H. Wall, D. A. Wardle, L. Brussaard, J. M. Dangerfield, V. K. Brown, K. E. Giller, D. U. Hooper, O. Sala, J. Tiedje, and J. A. van Veen. 2000. "Effects of Global Changes on Above- and Below-Ground Biodiversity in Terrestrial Ecosystems: Implications for Ecosystem Functioning." *Bioscience* 50:1089–1098.

Woodmansee, R. G. 1978a. "Critique and Analyses of the Grassland Ecosystem Model ELM" (257–281). In G. S. Innis (ed.). *Grassland Simulation Model*. Ecological Studies 26. Heidelberg: Springer-Verlag.

Woodmansee, R. G. 1978b. "Additions and Losses of Nitrogen in Grassland Ecosystems." *BioScience* 28:448–453.

Woodwell, G. M., and D. B. Botkin. 1970. "Metabolism of Terrestrial Ecosystems by Gas Exchange Techniques: The Brookhaven Approach" (73–85). In D. E. Reichle (ed.). *Analysis of Temperate Forest Ecosystems*. Berlin: Springer-Verlag.

Woodwell, G. M., and E. V. Pecan (eds.). 1973. *Carbon and the Biosphere*. Springfield, VA: Atomic Energy Commission. 392 p.

Wookey, P. A., R. Aerts, R. D. Bardgett, F. Baptist, K. A. Brathen, J. H. C. Cornelissen, L. Gough, I. P. Hartley, D. W. Hopkins, S. Lavorel, and G. R.

Shaver. 2009. "Ecosystem Feedbacks and Cascade Processes: Understanding Their Role in the Responses of Arctic and Alpine Ecosystems to Environmental Change." *Global Change Biology* 15:1153–1172.

Woomer, P. L., and M. J. Swift 1994. (eds.). *The Biological Management of Tropical Soil Fertility*. Chichester, UK: Wiley & Sons. 243 p.

Worthington, E. B. (ed.). 1975. *The Evolution of IBP*. Cambridge, UK: Cambridge University Press. 268 p.

Yates, T. L., J. N. Mills, C. A. Parmenter, T. G. Ksiazek, R. R. Parmenter, J. R. Vande Castle, D. H. Calisher, S. T. Nichol, K. D. Abbott, J. C. Young, M. L. Morrison, B. J. Beaty, J. L. Dunnum, R. J. Baker, J. Salazar-Bravo, and C. J. Peters. 2002. "The Ecology and Evolutionary History of an Emergent Disease: Hantavirus Pulmonary Syndrome." *BioScience* 52:989–999.

Zlotin, R. I., and K. S. Khodashova. 1980. *The Role of Animals in Biological Cycling of Forest-Steppe Ecosystems*. Stroudsburg, PA: Dowden, Hutchinson & Ross, Inc. 221 p.

INDEX

Note: A "b," "f," "m," or "t" following a page number indicates a box, figure, map, or table, respectively.

215

Composition:	Publication Services
Text:	10/15 Janson
Display:	Janson
Printer and Binder:	Thomson-Shore